Beginning Silverlight 3

From Novice to Professional

Robert Lair

Beginning Silverlight 3: From Novice to Professional

ISBN-13 (pbk): 978-1-4302-2377-1

ISBN-13 (electronic): 978-1-4302-2378-8

Printed and bound in the United States of America 9 8 7 6 5 4 3 2 1

President and Publisher: Paul Manning
Lead Editor: Ewan Buckingham
Technical Reviewer: Fabio Claudio Ferracchiati
Editorial Board: Clay Andres, Steve Anglin, Mark Beckner, Ewan Buckingham, Tony Campbell, Gary Cornell, Jonathan Gennick, Michelle Lowman, Matthew Moodie, Jeffrey Pepper, Frank Pohlmann, Ben Renow-Clarke, Dominic Shakeshaft, Matt Wade, Tom Welsh
Coordinating Editor: Anita Castro
Copy Editor: Katie Stence
Compositor: Mary Sudul
Indexer: John Collin
Artist: April Milne
Cover Designer: Anna Ishchenko

Distributed to the book trade worldwide by Springer-Verlag New York, Inc., 233 Spring Street, 6th Floor, New York, NY 10013. Phone 1-800-SPRINGER, fax 201-348-4505, e-mail orders-ny@springer-sbm.com, or visit http://www.springeronline.com.

For information on translations, please e-mail info@apress.com, or visit http://www.apress.com.

Apress and friends of ED books may be purchased in bulk for academic, corporate, or promotional use. eBook versions and licenses are also available for most titles. For more information, reference our Special Bulk Sales–eBook Licensing web page at http://www.apress.com/info/bulksales.

The source code for this book is available to readers at http://www.apress.com. You will need to answer questions pertaining to this book in order to successfully download the code.

To my beautiful wife Debi, whom I love more and more each day, and to my son Max, who has made me so proud. I love you guys more than anything on this earth.

Contents at a Glance

Contents v

About the Author xii

About the Technical Reviewer xiii

Acknowledgments xiv

Chapter 1: Welcome to Silverlight 3 1

Chapter 2: Introduction to Visual Studio 2008 13

Chapter 3: Layout Management in Silverlight 3 39

Chapter 4: Silverlight 3 Controls 65

Chapter 5: Data Binding and Silverlight List Controls 105

Chapter 6: Data Access and Networking 137

Chapter 7: Navigation Framework 153

Chapter 8: Local Storage in Silverlight 183

Chapter 9: Introduction to Expression Blend 213

Chapter 10: Styling in Silverlight 235

Chapter 11: Transformations and Animation 267

Chapter 12: Custom Controls 289

Chapter 13: Deployment 311

Index 323

Contents

Contents at a Glance...iv

About the Author xii

About the Technical Reviewer xiii

Acknowledgments xiv

■ Chapter 1: Welcome to Silverlight 3..1

The Evolution of the User Interface...1

Rich Internet Application Solutions..3

What Is Silverlight?..3

Benefits of Silverlight 4

  Cross-Platform/Cross-Browser Support 5

  Cross-Platform Version of the .NET Framework 5

  XAML, a Text-Based Markup Language 5

  Use of Familiar Technologies 6

  Small Runtime and Simple Deployment 6

The Silverlight Development Environment...8

New Features in Silverlight 3...10

  Improved Performance 11

Summary 11

■ Chapter 2: Introduction to Visual Studio 2008 13

What Is Visual Studio? 13

What's New in Visual Studio 2008? 14

    JavaScript IntelliSense and Debugging 14

    Multi-Targeting Support 28

    Transparent IntelliSense Mode 30

Building Your First Silverlight Application in Visual Studio 31

    Try It Out: Hello World in Silverlight 3 31

    Hosting Your Silverlight Application: Web Site or Web Application? 36

Summary 37

■ **Chapter 3: Layout Management in Silverlight 3** **39**

Layout Management 39

The Canvas Panel 40

    Try It Out: Using the Canvas Panel 41

    Filling the Entire Browser Window with Your Application 44

The StackPanel Control 45

    Try It Out: Using the StackPanel Control..45

    Try It Out: Nesting StackPanel Controls...47

The Grid Control 49

    Try It Out: Using the Grid Control 49

    Try It Out: Nesting a Grid and Spanning a Column 52

The WrapPanel Control 56

    Try It Out: Using the WrapPanel Control 56

The DockPanel Control 59

    Try It Out: Using the DockPanel Control...60

Summary 63

■ **Chapter 4: Silverlight 3 Controls** **65**

Setting Control Properties...65

    Attribute Syntax...65

    Element Syntax..66

Type-Converter-Enabled Attributes 66

Attached Properties 66

Nesting Controls Within Controls 67

Handling Events in Silverlight 68

Try It Out: Declaring an Event in XAML 68

Try It Out: Declaring an Event Handler in Managed Code 72

The Border Control 76

User Input Controls 80

Try It Out: Working with the TextBox Control 80

Try It Out: Working with the RadioButton and CheckBox Controls 84

Extended Controls 87

Adding an Extended Control 87

Try It Out: Using the GridSplitter 88

AutoCompleteBox 90

ViewBox 92

Modal Windows 93

Try It Out: Using the Modal Child Window 95

Summary 103

Chapter 5: Data Binding and Silverlight List Controls 105

Data Binding 105

The Binding Class 106

Try It Out: Simple Data Binding in Silverlight 106

Element to Element Binding 114

Try It Out: Element to Element Binding 114

The DataGrid Control 116

Try It Out: Building a Simple DataGrid 117

The Columns Collection 122

Try It Out: Building a DataGrid with Custom Columns 124

The ListBox Control 130

   Default and Custom ListBox Items 131

   Try It Out: Building a ListBox with Custom Content 133

Summary 135

■Chapter 6: Data Access and Networking 137

Data Access in Silverlight Applications 137

Accessing Data Through Web Services 138

   Try It Out: Accessing Data Through a WCF Service 138

Accessing Services from Other Domains 149

Accessing Data Through Sockets 150

Summary 152

■Chapter 7: Navigation Framework 153

Frame and Page Object 153

   Try It Out: Creating a Silverlight Navigation Application 153

Benefits of the Navigation Framework 164

   Deep Linking 164

The NavigationService Object 165

   Try it Out: Using the NavigationService Object 166

Passing Data to Navigation Pages 168

   Try it Out: Passing Data to Navigation Pages 169

Uri Mapping 172

   Try it Out: Uri Mapping and the Navigation Framework 173

Silverlight Navigation Application Template 175

   Try it Out: Using the Silverlight Navigation Application Template 175

Using Multiple Frames 179

   Try it Out: Using Multiple Frames 180

Summary 182

■**Chapter 8: Local Storage in Silverlight**..**183**

Working with Isolated Storage..183

Using the Isolated Storage API 183

Try It Out: Creating a File Explorer for Isolated Storage 186

Managing Isolated Storage 207

Viewing and Clearing Isolated Storage.. 207

Try It Out: Increasing the Isolated Storage Quota 209

Summary 212

■**Chapter 9: Introduction to Expression Blend**..**213**

Key Features in Expression Blend 213

Visual XAML Editor 214

Visual Studio 2008 Integration 214

Split-View Mode 214

Visual State Manager and Template Editing Support 215

World-Class Timeline.. 215

Try It Out: Working with Projects in Expression Blend 216

Exploring the Workspace 221

Toolbox.. 221

Project Panel 223

Properties Panel 223

Objects and Timeline Panel 225

Laying Out an Application with Expression Blend 225

Working with the Grid Control in Expression Blend.. 225

Try It Out: Editing a Layout Grid with Expression Blend 225

Summary 233

■**Chapter 10: Styling in Silverlight** **235**

Inline Properties..235

Try It Out: Setting Inline Properties with Visual Studio 235

Try It Out: Setting Inline Properties with Expression Blend 243

Silverlight Styles 251

    Try It Out: Using Styles As Static Resources 253

    Defining Styles at the Application Level 259

    Merged Resource Dictionaries 261

    Silverlight Style Hierarchy 262

    Inheriting Styles Using BasedOn 264

Summary 265

Chapter 11: Transformations and Animation **267**

Introduction to Silverlight Animation 267

    Silverlight Storyboards 268

    Types of Animation in Silverlight 269

Programmatically Controlling Animations 271

Using Expression Blend to Create Animations 273

    Viewing a Storyboard in the Expression Blend Timeline 273

    Try It Out: Creating an Animation with Expression Blend 274

Creating Transformations in Silverlight 282

    Transformation Types 283

    Try It Out: Using Expression Blend to Transform Silverlight Objects 285

Summary 288

Chapter 12: Custom Controls **289**

When to Write Custom Controls 289

Silverlight Control Toolkit 290

Silverlight Control Model 291

    Parts and States Model 291

    Dependency Properties 292

Creating Custom Controls in Silverlight 293

    Implementing Custom Functionality 293

Try It Out: Building a Custom Control 294

Summary 309

■**Chapter 13: Deployment** **311**

Deploying Silverlight Applications 311

XAP Files 311

Hosting Silverlight Content 311

Assembly Caching 312

Try It Out: Exploring Assembly Caching 313

Out of Browser Support 317

Customizing the Install Application Dialog 319

Out of Browser API 320

Removing Installed Applications 322

Summary 322

Index 323

About the Author

 **Robert Lair** has been working with .NET technologies since prior to its alpha and built the original IBuySpy E-Commerce and Portal applications that were used by Microsoft to introduce ASP.NET to the development community. He is a published author of many books and magazine articles including Beginning Silverlight 2. Robert has also been a speaker at a number of .NET technical conferences. Technologies in which Robert specializes include: Silverlight, mainframe modernization to .NET, ASP.NET custom application development, Sharepoint development and integration, and many related technologies. Today Robert works for T3 Technologies (http://www.t3t.com), a company that offers mainframe alternatives on the Windows platform. Follow Robert on twitter at http://www.twitter.com/robertlair and on the web at http://www.robertlair.net.

About the Technical Reviewer

■ **Fabio Claudio Ferracchiati** is a prolific writer on cutting-edge technologies. Fabio has contributed to more than a dozen books on .NET, C#, Visual Basic, and ASP.NET. He is a .NET Microsoft Certified Solution Developer (MCSD) and lives in Rome, Italy. You can read his blog at http://www.ferracchiati.com.

Acknowledgments

There are a number of people to whom I would like to express my appreciation, people who have helped me in many ways. This book proved to be a great challenge, with the short development cycles of Silverlight 3. Without these people this book would never have been possible.

I would also like to thank my family for being patient and forgiving for the time this book took away from our times together. A special thanks goes out to my wife Debi, who has always supported me, even when it requires a sacrifice for her. Your support has gotten me through so many of life's challenges. I never could have done it without you.

I would like to thank the many people at Apress that made this book happen. I would especially like to thank Anita Castro, Ewan Buckingham, Katie Stence, Dominic Shakeshaft and Fabio Claudio Ferracchiati. Without all of your hard work, this book would never have happened, thank you all.

Finally, I would like to thank my neighbors on Lexington Court for being such great friends. Their friendship means so much to me and they helped me get through rough times. I am very lucky to have such a great group of neighbors that I can call close friends.

CHAPTER 1

Welcome to Silverlight 3

This chapter introduces Silverlight, a Microsoft cross-browser, cross-platform plug-in that allows you to create rich interactive (or Internet) applications (RIAs) for the Web. It begins with a brief look at the evolution of user interfaces, and then provides an overview of Silverlight. You'll learn how Silverlight fits into RIA solutions, the benefits it brings to developers, and the tools involved in developing Silverlight-enabled applications.

The Evolution of the User Interface

Software user interfaces are constantly evolving and improving. I remember back when I was still working with an early version of Windows and looking at Mac OS with envy. Then, I remember seeing Linux systems with radical new desktop interfaces. More recently, I found myself looking again at the Mac OS X Dock (see Figure 1-1) and wanting that for my Windows XP machine—to the point where I purchased a product that mimicked it. I was dedicated to Windows through it all, but I was envious of some of the user experiences the different environments offered.

Figure 1-1. *The Mac OS Dock feature*

The evolution of the user interface continues in the Windows Vista operating system. One example is the interface for switching between applications. In past versions of Windows, when you pressed Alt+Tab to switch from one program to another, you would see a rather ugly interface offering nothing but icons. Today, when you press Alt+Tab in Vista, you get a much more user-friendly interface, presenting a clipping of the content of each window as you tab through your choices, as shown in Figure 1-2.

Figure 1-2. *Windows Vista Alt+Tab user interface*

In addition, Vista offers an even cooler way to switch between applications using the Desktop Window Manager. When you press the Windows key along with Tab, Vista displays all open windows in a cascading shuffle effect, which allows you to see a large-scale version of each window (see Figure 1-3). If there is animated content in any of the windows, it actually shows up in the view! This means if you have a video or a game playing in one of the windows, you will see that in action as you shuffle through the windows.

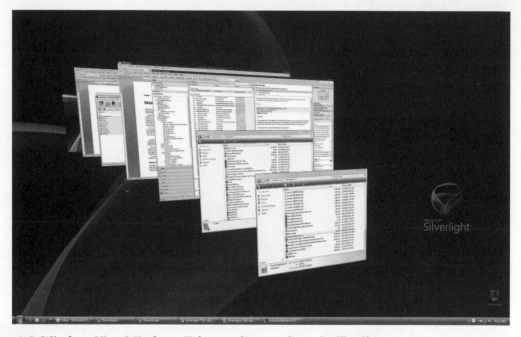

Figure 1-3. *Windows Vista Windows+Tab cascading windows shuffle effect*

These features reflect how developers have built standard desktop applications, which are meant to be installed and executed on individual client machines. Desktop applications allow for very rich and responsive user interfaces and additional features, such as offline support. Performance of the application depends on the machine on which it is installed. A challenge for desktop applications is deployment. The application needs to have a code base for each target platform, and every machine needs to have the application installed and maintained.

In contrast, we have web applications, which are HTML-focused programs designed to run within a browser and across platforms. For the Microsoft-based developer, this has recently meant developing with ASP.NET and building web services to offer services over the Internet. The focus of most of the logic and code has been placed on the server for the benefit of application performance. The price has been a poor user interface.

With recent technologies, the line between the desktop and web approaches for developing applications has started to blur. As a result, a third approach has surfaced. This new approach is termed RIA, which is defined as a web application that has the features and functionality found in traditional desktop applications.

Rich Internet Application Solutions

The concept of RIA has been around for quite some time, but the term rich Internet application was first used in 2002 in a Macromedia white paper. Before then, the terms remote scripting and X Internet were used to describe the concept.

Today, many different solutions fit the description of RIAs, but there is one consistent characteristic: all RIA solutions involve a runtime that runs on the client machine and architecturally sits between the user and the server.

In recent years, the technology that is most commonly used in RIAs is Flash. When Flash was introduced, it brought to the Web rich user experiences never seen before. However, due to the lack of tools allowing Microsoft .NET developers to integrate Flash into their applications, to those developers Flash just seemed like a tool for adding some pretty effects to a web page, but nothing functional.

Then a wonderful thing happened when Adobe purchased Macromedia. All of the sudden, Flash was married to some of the development tools offered by Adobe. Microsoft retaliated by announcing Silverlight, formerly known as Windows Presentation Foundation Everywhere (WPF/E). Silverlight is the technology that many .NET developers have been waiting for.

What exactly is Silverlight? And, what impact does Silverlight actually have on us as .NET developers? Well, I'm glad you asked.

What Is Silverlight?

As I explained in the previous section, all RIAs have one characteristic in common: a client runtime that sits between the user and the server. In the case of Microsoft's RIA solution, Silverlight is this client runtime. Specifically, Silverlight is a cross-platform, cross-browser plug-in that renders user interfaces and graphical assets on a canvas that can be inserted into an HTML page.

The markup used to define a Silverlight canvas is called Extensible Application Markup Language (XAML, pronounced "zammel"). XAML is an XML-based language that is similar to HTML in some ways. Like HTML, XAML defines which elements appear, as well as the layout of those elements. However, unlike HTML, XAML goes far beyond simple element definition and layout. Using XAML, you can also specify timelines, transformations, animations, and events.

The following is an example of a Silverlight canvas defined in XAML:

```
<Canvas
    xmlns="http://schemas.microsoft.com/client/2007"
    xmlns:x="http://schemas.microsoft.com/winfx/2006/xaml"
    Width="640" Height="480"
    Background="White"
    x:Name="Page">
    <Rectangle
        RenderTransformOrigin="0.5,0.5"
        x:Name="rectangle"
        Width="292"
        Height="86"
        Fill="#FFFF0000"
        Stroke-"#ΓΓ000000"
        StrokeThickness="3"
        Canvas.Left="115"
        Canvas.Top="70">
    </Rectangle>
</Canvas>
```

Figure 1-4 shows this canvas in Microsoft Expression Blend, the design tool used to edit and create XAML for Silverlight applications. You can see that this XAML simply defines a rectangle on a canvas, as well as the properties associated with that rectangle, including its name, location, size, color, and border.

This simple example is just intended to give you an idea of what XAML looks like. You'll learn more about XAML in upcoming chapters. For now, let's continue by looking at the benefits of Silverlight.

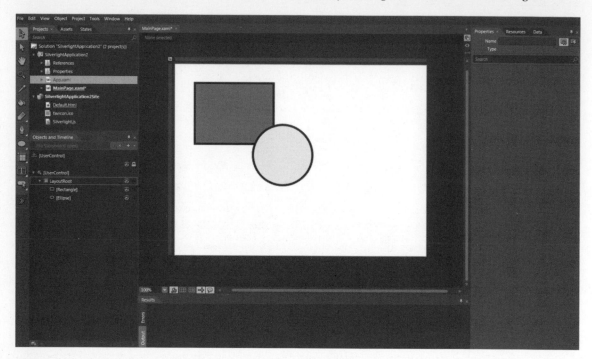

Figure 1-4. A basic XAML canvas in Microsoft Expression Blend

Benefits of Silverlight

Naturally, Silverlight offers all of the same benefits of RIAs, but there are a few features that set it apart from other RIA solutions, including the following:

- It offers cross-platform/cross-browser support.
    - It provides a cross-platform version of the .NET Framework.
    - XAML is a text-based markup language.
    - Silverlight uses familiar technologies.
- It's easy to deploy the Silverlight runtime to clients.

Let's take a closer look at each of these benefits.

Cross-Platform/Cross-Browser Support

When ASP.NET was released a number of years ago, one of the benefits touted was cross-browser support. Developers would need to have only one code base, and that code base would work in all modern browsers. For the most part, this is true. No matter which browser you are using, the application will function. However, in order to receive all of the bells and whistles offered by the ASP.NET controls, you must use the latest version of Internet Explorer. If you are using any other browser, you actually get a downgraded version of the web site, which contains fewer features.

Validation controls are a prime example. If you are using a browser that ASP.NET recognizes as an "upscale" browser, you can take advantage of client-side validation. If you are using any other browser, the validation controls still function, but require a postback to the server to do the validation. So, although ASP.NET is cross-browser, users can get different experiences, depending on which browser they are using.

With Silverlight, this changes. Microsoft is once again pulling out the term cross-browser, and also adding cross-platform, and this time they mean it. As a developer, you can create a Silverlight application and rest assured that it will run exactly the same on all supported platforms and browsers.

Currently, two platforms are supported. Naturally, the first is Windows-based platforms, and the second is Mac OS platforms. As for browser support, Internet Explorer and Firefox are currently covered. Microsoft has committed support for Safari as well, so it may be on the list by the time you're reading this book.

This leaves one large platform unsupported: Linux. Although Microsoft does not have plans to support Linux, others do. The Mono project, which is sponsored by Novell, is an open source initiative to develop and run .NET client and server applications on Linux, Solaris, Mac OS X, Windows, and Unix. The Mono team has indicated that it will soon have a Silverlight implementation, currently called the Moonlight runtime. With this addition, developers will be able to develop Silverlight applications for Windows, Macintosh, and Linux systems with one code base. Furthermore, the user experience will be identical, no matter which platform you are using.

Cross-Platform Version of the .NET Framework

Silverlight 1.0 was released by Microsoft in the summer of 2007, but this version supported only Ecma languages that are interpreted in the client. Although Silverlight 1.0 works well for developers who are already familiar with client-side scripting, many developers have their eyes on the second release of Silverlight, version 2. Silverlight 1.0 is more or less in direct competition with Flash—some have called it Microsoft's "Flash killer." However, things really get exciting with Silverlight 2.

Silverlight 2 and beyond contains its own cross-platform version of the .NET Framework, which means it has its own version of the common language runtime (CLR), the full type system, and a .NET Framework programming library that you can use in Visual Studio 2008 to build rich user experiences in the browser.

XAML, a Text-Based Markup Language

Another advantage to Silverlight is that its foundation is based on a text-based markup language. For other RIA solutions such as Flash, the base is a compiled file. This is not nearly as friendly to developers as a text-based format, for obvious reasons.

XAML is very easy to write and modify. As an example, let's say you want to change the opacity of an object. If you were using Flash to do this, you would need to open the Flash project file, find the right layer and object, and then make the adjustment there. You then would need to recompile and republish the file. In contrast, with Silverlight, you simply open the XAML file, change the opacity property of the object, and save the file.

Another advantage of XAML is that it can be created dynamically at runtime. If you think about it, the implications of this are huge. Consider the similarities between HTML and XAML. Both are text-based markup languages that have a decent similarity to XML. HTML is the base foundation of files published on the Internet. Since HTML was introduced, a number of technologies have been built on top of it. In the Microsoft camp, for example, Active Server Pages (ASP) was first introduced to allow developers to dynamically modify HTML at runtime. Today, we have ASP.NET. XAML has the same potential, since it is a text-based markup language on which developers can expand.

Use of Familiar Technologies

Microsoft is very good at creating tools that make application development easy. The Visual Studio integrated development environment (IDE) has been around for quite some time, and although new features are continually added to the tool, the environment itself has remained remarkably consistent.

Silverlight development is no different. At the core of developing Silverlightapplications is Visual Studio 2008, the latest version in Visual Studio's long history. This gives Silverlight a distinct advantage, as developers do not need to learn how to use a new development environment.

In addition to Visual Studio, Microsoft has released a suite of tools called Expression Studio. Included in this suite is Microsoft Expression Blend, which is used to edit and create XAML for Silverlight applications. While Expression Blend looks completely different, it still has many of the same elements as Visual Studio. In addition, Expression Blend works off of the same project as Visual Studio. This means that as you make changes in each of the editors—opening a project in Visual Studio, and then opening the same project in Expression Blend to edit the XAML—the edited files will request to be refreshed when opened again in the other tool.

Small Runtime and Simple Deployment

Since Silverlight requires that a client runtime be installed on the client machine, it is vital that this runtime has a small footprint and downloads quickly. Microsoft worked very hard to get the installation size as small as possible. The developers clearly succeeded with Silverlight 1.0, as the download size is a tiny 1MB. For Silverlight 2, however, they had a harder chore ahead of them, since Silverlight 2 contains its own .NET Framework and object library. Microsoft went to each .NET Framework team and allocated it a size to fit its portion. The end result is astonishing—Silverlight 2 is approximately 4MB in size. In Silverlight 3, even with the large amount of new features that have been added to the Silverlight runtime, the file size is still under 5MB.

As for pushing the Silverlight runtime out to clients, Microsoft has provided a very easy detection mechanism. If the client does not have the proper Silverlight runtime installed, it will display a logo, as shown in Figure 1-5.

Figure 1-5. *Silverlight runtime required logo*

When users click the icon in the logo, they are taken to a web page that walks them through the process of installing the Silverlight runtime. Once the runtime is finished installing, the Silverlight application is immediately available to the user, as shown in the example in Figure 1-6.

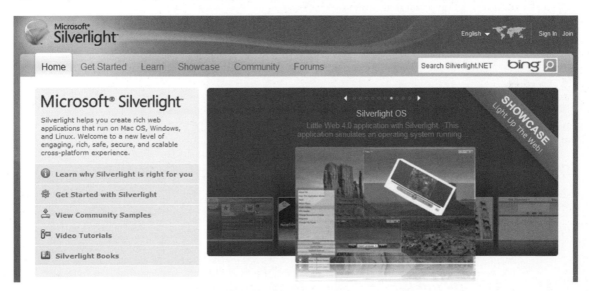

Figure 1-6. *Silverlight application after installation of runtime*

The Silverlight Development Environment

In the past, setting up an environment to work with Microsoft's latest and greatest has been relatively straightforward, typically involving only the setup of the latest version of Visual Studio and the appropriate software development kit. However, with Silverlight, the situation is quite a bit different due to the introduction of many new tools. Let's look at the tools involved in setting up a Silverlight 3 development environment.

1. *Visual Studio 2008 and SP1*: As noted, this is the latest version of Microsoft's IDE, the successor to Visual Studio 2005 (see Figure 1-7). For your Silverlight environment you should install Visual Studio 2008 along with Service Pack 1. Installing Visual Studio 2008 automatically installs Microsoft .NET Framework 3.5. Chapter 2 covers Visual Studio 2008 in more depth.

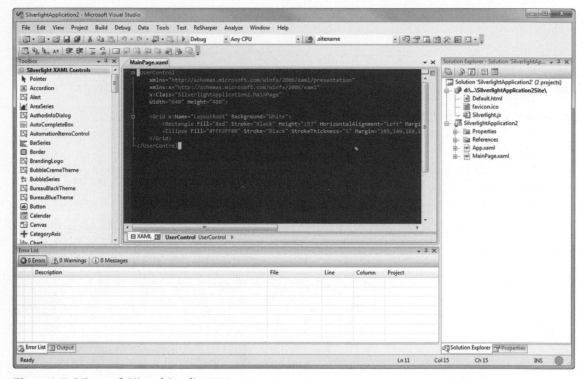

Figure 1-7. *Microsoft Visual Studio 2008*

2. *Silverlight Tools for Visual Studio 2008*: This is basically a package that adds the necessary items to Visual Studio to teach it how to handle Silverlight projects. The packages includes a number of items, some of which are listed below:

    •   *Silverlight 3 Runtime*: Required on every computer that wishes to view a Silverlight-enabled web application.

- • *Silverlight 3 Software Development Kit*: This SDK is a collection of samples, Silverlight QuickStarts, documentation, and controls that are used to develop Silverlight applications.

- • *Silverlight Project Templates for Visual Studio 2008*: This adds the Silverlight templates in Visual Studio. As an example, it will add the template that enable you to create a Silverlight project from the "Add New Project" in Visual Studio.

3. *Expression Blend 3*: The next thing to install for your Silverlight development environment is Expression Blend (see Figure 1-8). Expression Blend a design tool for building XAML based interfaces including Windows Presentation Foundation (WPF) and Silverlight. Expression Blend is not required for creating Silverlight solutions, but is the only designer that provides design-mode WYSIWYG functionality until Visual Studio 2010 is released (currently expected to hit mid-2010). Expression Blend 3 is covered in detail in Chapter 11.

Figure 1-8. Microsoft Expression Blend 2

4. **Silverlight 3 Toolkit**. The Silverlight Toolkit is an open source CodePlex project whose goal is to develop additional controls for Silverlight applications. Controls within the toolkit are assigned a status that describes their maturity as controls and the controls are supported by the open source community. You can download the toolkit for Silverlight 3 at http://www.codeplex.com/silverlight.

New Features in Silverlight 3

Silverlight continues to evolve and Microsoft continues to add new features to Silverlight in each version. There are many new features introduced in Silverlight 3. This section will go over some of those new features and will indicate where those features are discussed in this book.

- *Navigation* Framework: The Navigation Framework provides developers with a way to build Silverlight applications that have multiple page views that integrate with browser history and provide support for deep linking allowing users to enter a URL that will take them to a specific state in the Silverlight application. The Navigation Framework is discussed in Chapter 8.

- *New Controls*: With each new version of Silverlight, more and more controls are added. This is no different with Silverlight 3, which has added a number of new controls such as the WrapPanel, DockPanel, TreeView, Label, ViewBox and AutoCompleteBox. These controls are discussed in Chapters 3 to 5.

- *Modal Window Support*: Anyone that has developed applications for windows desktop is familiar with the modal popup window. This is a window that pops up and disables the rest of the application until it is closed. Using modal window support is discussed in Chapter 4.

- *Element to Element Binding*: When binding target UI elements are bound to a source. In previous versions of Silverlight the only options for the source was data. In Silverlight 3, elements can be bound to other elements allowing for the property of a control to be bound to another controls property. Element to Element binding is discussed in Chapter 5.

- *Data Validation*: Silverlight 3 contains some new data validation features that help developers handle validation exceptions in their applications. In previous versions of Silverlight, the validation exceptions were more or less swallowed up by the framework and therefore there was no way to easily report these errors to the user interface.

- *Local Networking*: In some scenarios you may need to have multiple Silverlight applications contained within an HTML or ASP.NET screen. Perhaps you need to have some HTML content between the two Silverlight applications and you didn't want to include that content within a single Silverlight application. This is easily accomplished, but if you need those two Silverlight applications to be able to communicate with each other, you will need a way to send messages back and forth. Silverlight 3 introduces a new API called LocalConnection that allows you to add local networking between your Silverlight applications. You can have one application send a message that is then received from the second application.

- *Perspective 3D*: Silverlight 3 adds the ability to simulate an object in 3D space with perspective 3D.

- *New Features in Transformation and Animation*: A number of new transformation and animation features have been added with Silverlight 3. Some of these include adding blur and drop shadow effects as well as animation easing for smoother and more realistic animations such as bounce and elastic effects.

- *Assembly Caching*: Silverlight 3 now has the ability to cache assemblies locally on a client machine. This means that you can create a Silverlight package without including all the Silverlight assemblies and utilize them from the client machine. If the desired assembly is not present on the client machine, it is simply downloaded from Microsoft's web site and cached for future use. Assembly Caching is discussed in Chapter 13.

- *Out of Browser Support*: A very commonly requested feature of Silverlight 2 was to add the ability for Silverlight applications to be run outside the browser. This feature is now present in Silverlight 3, and allows for users to install Silverlight applications directly to their machine and run them without a browser. Out of Browser support is discussed in Chapter 13.

Improved Performance

In addition to these new features, there has also been an improvement in the performance of Silverlight 3 applications. First of all, the Silverlight application packages (XAP Files, refer to Chapter 13) have improved compression. This means that your Silverlight application's output filesize will be smaller. Smaller file size means faster downloads and less of a wait for users wanting to run your application. In addition to improved compression, Silverlight 3 introduces Assembly Caching, which allows your applications to utilize assemblies cached on a user's end machine. This means that your applications will be even smaller in size since the packages do not require you to include these assemblies. In addition to the Silverlight packages themselves, a number of performance improvements have been made throughout Silverlight features, such as improved font animations and support for additional http bindings for WCF web services including Binary message encoding.

Summary

In this chapter, you looked at the evolution of user interfaces in applications, as well as the history of RIAs. I then introduced Silverlight, talked about the benefits it brings to developers today, and how it fits into RIA solutions. Finally, you learned about the tools involved in developing Silverlight-enabled applications.

Now it is time to get your hands dirty and start building some Silverlight applications! In the next chapter, I will provide an introduction to Microsoft Visual Studio 2008, one of the primary tools used to build Silverlight applications.

CHAPTER 2

■ ■ ■

Introduction to Visual Studio 2008

The previous chapter mentioned the tools required to develop RIAs that utilize the Silverlight technology. At the core of all of these tools is Microsoft's flagship development product, Visual Studio. This chapter provides an introduction to Visual Studio 2008, the latest version. You will learn about some of the new features that are particularly helpful for developers building RIAs with Silverlight, and then work through an exercise to try out Visual Studio 2008's enhanced JavaScript IntelliSense and debugging support. Finally, you will have an opportunity to create your first Silverlight application using Visual Studio 2008. Let's get started with a brief introduction to the Visual Studio IDE.

What Is Visual Studio?

Any developer who has developed applications using technologies related to Microsoft's Visual Basic, ASP, or .NET has used some version of Visual Studio on a regular basis. This is because Visual Studio is Microsoft's primary development product. Whether you are developing desktop applications, web applications, mobile applications, web services, or just about any other .NET solution, Visual Studio is the environment you will be using.

Visual Studio is an IDE that allows .NET developers to implement a variety of .NET solutions within the confines of one editor. An IDE is a software application that contains comprehensive facilities to aid developers in building applications. Visual Studio fits this description for a number of reasons. First, Visual Studio offers a very rich code-editing solution. It includes features such as source code color-coding and code completion. Second, it offers an integrated debugger, which allows you to place breakpoints in your source code to stop execution at any given point, as well as step through the source line by line, analyzing the state of objects and fields at any given point in the execution. Add to these features rich support for application deployment, installation, and integration with database services, and you can understand how Visual Studio is an extremely valuable tool for developers.

■ **Note** This book assumes a basic understanding of Visual Studio. If you're new to Visual Studio, I recommend that you get started with a book devoted to the subject, such as *Beginning C# 2008, Second Edition* by Christian Gross (Apress, 2008).

The History of Visual Studio

Visual Studio has quite a history. The first version was called Visual Studio 97, which was most commonly known for Visual Basic 5.0. In 1998, Microsoft released Visual Studio 6.0. That version included Visual Basic 6.0, as well as Microsoft's first web-based development tool, Visual InterDev 1.0, which was used to develop ASP applications.

Next came the introduction of Microsoft .NET and ASP.NET 1.0, prompting Visual Studio.NET. As Microsoft was enhancing and releasing new versions of Microsoft .NET and ASP.NET, it also continued enhancing Visual Studio by releasing Visual Studio 2003 and then Visual Studio 2005. In addition, Microsoft has introduced a line of free development tools known as the Visual Studio Express tools, as well as the Visual Studio Team System, which can be used by large programming teams to build enterprise-level systems.

This brings us to the latest version of Visual Studio, which Microsoft developed under the code name Orcas and has now dubbed Visual Studio 2008.

What's New in Visual Studio 2008?

Microsoft has introduced a variety of new features in Visual Studio 2008, many of which are geared toward helping developers build RIAs with Silverlight and related Microsoft technologies, such as the Windows Communication Foundation (WCF), ADO.NET Data Services, and Ajax. Let's look at some of the new features in Visual Studio 2008 that are particularly helpful to Silverlight application developers.

JavaScript IntelliSense and Debugging

Client-side scripting is a major component of developing RIAs. With the adoption of technologies like Ajax and Silverlight, developers can integrate client-side scripting into applications to enhance the user experience.

In response to the growing necessity for integrating client-side scripting into ASP.NET applications, Microsoft has implemented an extensive upgrade to Visual Studio's JavaScript IntelliSense and debugging support. Here, you'll look at the IntelliSense and debugging improvements, and then try a test run to see them in action.

IntelliSense Improvements

The first major improvement of JavaScript IntelliSense in Visual Studio 2008 is type inference. Since JavaScript is a dynamic language, a variable can be one of many different types, depending on its current state. For example, in the following code snippet, the variable x represents a different type each time it is assigned.

```
function TypeInference()
{
    var x;
    x = document.getElementById("fieldName");
    // x is now an HTML element
    alert(x.tagName);
    x = 10;
```

```
// x is now an integer
alert(x.toFixed());
x = new Date();
// x is now a date
alert(x.getDay());
}
```

In this example, the variable x represents three different types during the execution of the function:

- First, it represents an HTML element. When the user types x followed by a period, the code-completion choices will be specific to an HTML element, as shown in Figure 2-1.

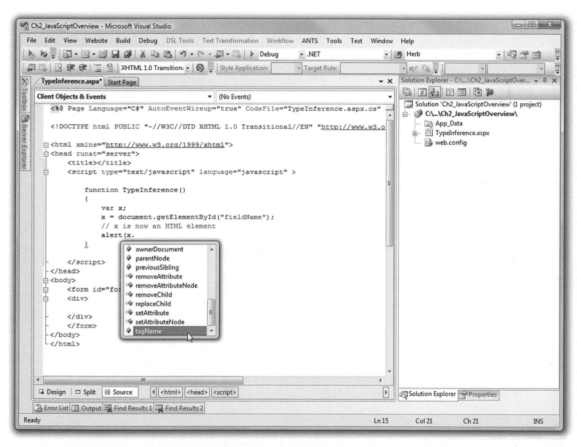

Figure 2-1. Code completion with type inference for an HTML element

- In the next line, x is assigned to the value 10. At this point, x has become an integer, and the code-completion choices that appear are specific to an integer, as shown in Figure 2-2.

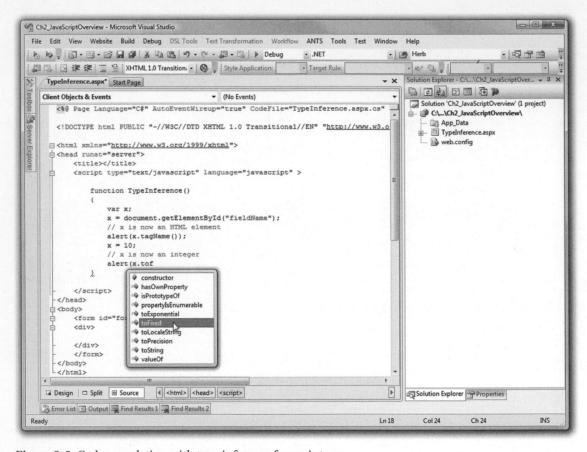

Figure 2-2. *Code completion with type inference for an integer*

- Finally, x is assigned to a date type. At this point, x represents a date type, and the code-completion choices include date-specific properties and methods.

The second notable enhancement to JavaScript IntelliSense in Visual Studio 2008 is the support for IntelliSense in external script files. In fact, there are many levels to this enhancement. First, developers will have IntelliSense while they are editing the external script files. Second, by adding a reference to other external script files, developers can get IntelliSense for functions and fields from other script files. Finally, developers will receive IntelliSense in the actual pages that reference the external script files.

Another new feature of JavaScript IntelliSense is the ability to add XML comments to your code, which will provide additional information in the IntelliSense display. These are similar to standard C# XML comments, which have been available in C# since it was initially released. The following example shows some XML comments added to a JavaScript function.

```
function HelloWorld(FirstName, LastName)
{
    /// <summary>Returns a hello message to the given name</summary>
```

```
/// <param name="FirstName">Person's First Name</param>
/// <param name="LastName">Person's Last Name</param>
/// <returns>string</return>
return ("Hello " + FirstName + " " + LastName);
}
```

This is a function called `HelloWorld`, which simply accepts a first and last name and returns a hello message customized for that person. This function is located in a file called JScripts.js. Notice the four XML comments added to the start of the function. These provide a summary of the function, give a description of the function's parameters, and indicate the value returned by the function. With these extra lines in place, when you add the function in your code, IntelliSense will now display this additional information. First, when you start typing `HelloWorld`, Visual Studio's JavaScript IntelliSense will help you complete the method call. After you have typed `HelloWorld` and the opening parenthesis, it will display the two parameters and their descriptions, as shown in Figure 2-3.

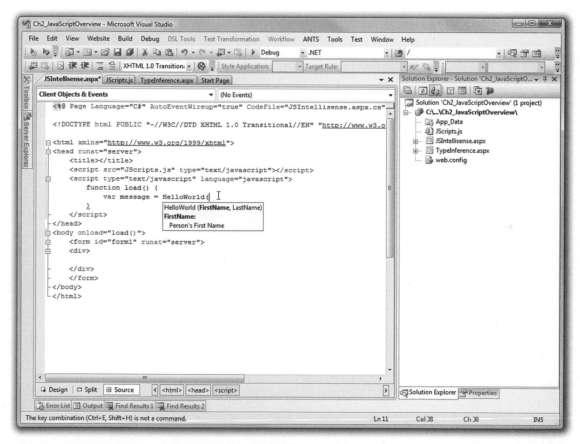

Figure 2-3. IntelliSense for a JavaScript function with parameter tags

Now that you have reviewed the JavaScript IntelliSense features added to Visual Studio 2008, let's take a look at the new JavaScript debugging features, which are equally as useful and long-awaited.

New Debugging Features

In previous versions of Visual Studio, ASP.NET developers were severely limited in the debugging they could do in client-side scripting. Some of the more industrious developers would find a third-party JavaScript debugging tool to assist them. However, the majority of developers would simply use hacks, such as adding alerts throughout their client-side scripting. When an alert was not hit, they could identify where the error had occurred and at least determine the basic location where attention was required.

In Visual Studio 2008, JavaScript debugging is now integrated directly into the IDE, and believe it or not, it actually works!

Figure 2-4 shows an example where a breakpoint was placed on a line of code in a local script section of an ASP.NET page. At this point, you are in Visual Studio's JavaScript debugger, and you can step through the code one line at a time. If a line of code references a function in an external script file (as in the example), that script file will be opened, and you will be able to debug that script file as well. In addition, you can hover the mouse over code and see the current value of the objects while you are debugging your application.

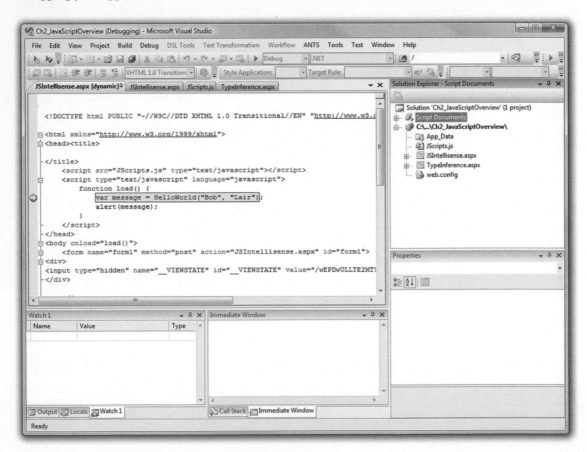

Figure 2-4. *JavaScript debugging in Visual Studio 2008*

As if that were not enough, Visual Studio's JavaScript debugging also allows you to use the Immediate window to enter JavaScript code directly while you are debugging. This is extremely powerful, because it allows you to evaluate a line of code at any point in the process—your entries will be processed immediately.

To get started debugging JavaScript in Visual Studio, there is only one setting that you need to confirm within your browser to make certain that client-side debugging is enabled. In Internet Explorer, choose View ~TRA Internet Options. This will display the Internet Options dialog box. Select the Advanced tab and find the two entries "Disable script debugging (Internet Explorer)" and "Disable script debugging (Other)." Make certain both of these options are *unchecked*, as shown in Figure 2-5, and click the OK button to close the dialog box.

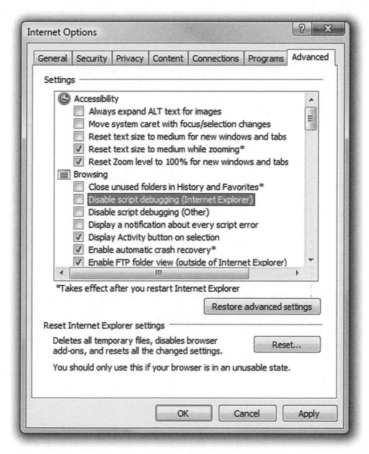

Figure 2-5. Uncheck the "Disable script debugging" boxes in the Internet Explorer Internet Options dialog box.

Try It Out: JavaScript IntelliSense and Debugging

Now that we have looked at some of the new JavaScript IntelliSense and debugging features in Visual Studio 2008, let's take them for a test drive.

1. Start Visual Studio 2008 and select File ~TRA New ~TRA Project from the main menu, as shown in Figure 2-6.

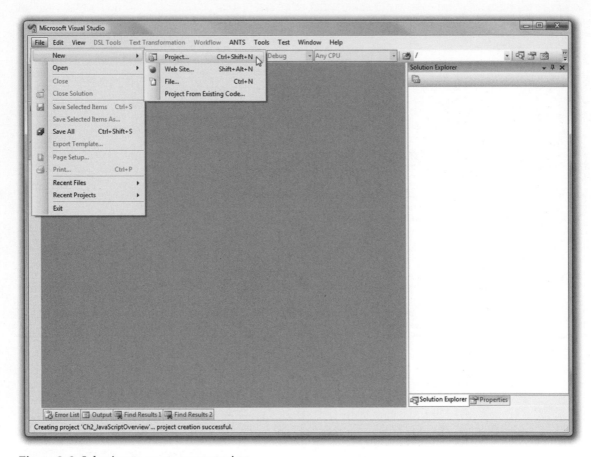

Figure 2-6. *Selecting to create a new project*

2. In the New Project dialog box, select Visual C# as the project type and ASP.NET Web Application as the template. Name the project Ch2_JavaScriptOverview, as shown in Figure 2-7.

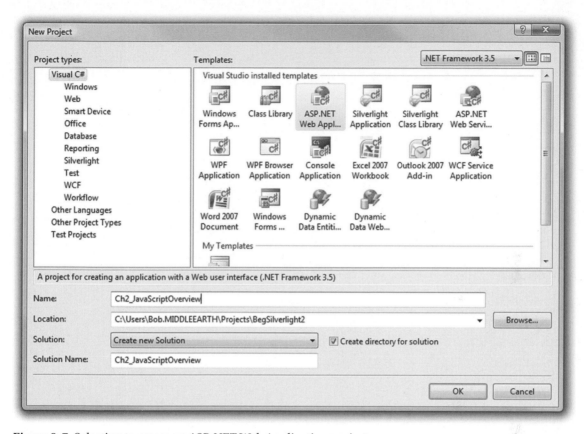

Figure 2-7. Selecting to create an ASP.NET Web Application project

3. A new Web Application project will now be created for you, with the Default.aspx file open. Select Project ~TRA Add New Item from the main menu.

4. In the Add New Item dialog box, make sure that the Visual C# category is selected on the left and select JScript File in the Templates pane. Name the file HelloWorld.js, as shown in Figure 2-8. Then click the Add button.

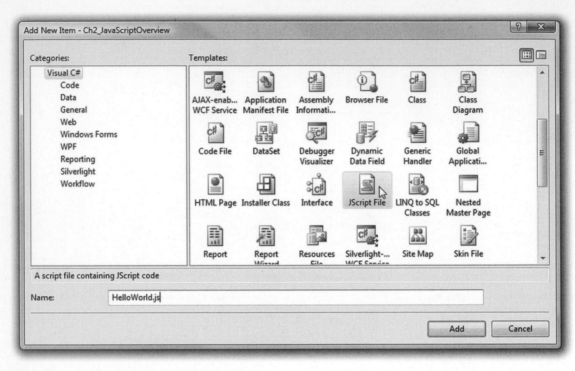

Figure 2-8. *Adding a JavaScript file to a project*

5. The JavaScript file will be added to the project and opened by default. In this file, add a new function called `HelloWorld()`, as follows:

```
function HelloWorld(FirstName, LastName)
{
    return ("Hello " + FirstName + " " + LastName);
}
```

6. As you typed the function, you got some IntelliSense assistance. Also notice the color-coding of the JavaScript.

7. Now insert some XML comments to display some additional IntelliSense information when the function is used. Add the following comments (shown in bold):

```
function HelloWorld(FirstName, LastName)
{
    /// <summary>Returns a hello message to the given name</summary>
    /// <param name="FirstName">Person's First Name</param>
    /// <param name="LastName">Person's Last Name</param>
    /// <returns>string</return>
    return ("Hello " + FirstName + " " + LastName);
}
```

8. Once again, select Project ~TRA Add New Item. This time, select Web Form as the template and name the file JSIntellisense.aspx.

9. In this new file, add a script reference to your HelloWorld.js script file. You can either drag the script file to the page header or simply edit the HTML of the form manually so that it appears as follows:

```
<html xmlns="http://www.w3.org/1999/xhtml" >
<head runat="server">
    <title></title>
    <script src="HelloWorld.js" type="text/javascript"></script>
</head>
<body>
    <form id="form1" runat="server">
    <div>

    </div>
    </form>
</body>
</html>
```

10. Next, add a local function that will run when the page loads. To do this, add a new <SCRIPT> section and call the function in the page body's onload event so that the method is called when the page is loaded, as follows:

```
<html xmlns="http://www.w3.org/1999/xhtml" >
<head runat="server">
    <title>Untitled Page</title>
    <script src="HelloWorld.js" type="text/javascript"></script>
    <script type="text/javascript" language="javascript">
        function load()
        {

        }
    </script>
</head>
<body onload="load()">
    <form id="form1" runat="server">
    <div>

    </div>
    </form>
</body>
</html>
```

11. Now call the HelloWorld() method. Go ahead and start typing the boldfaced line of code in the load function:

```
<html xmlns="http://www.w3.org/1999/xhtml" >
<head runat="server">
    <title>Untitled Page</title>
    <script src="HelloWorld.js" type="text/javascript"></script>
    <script type="text/javascript" language="javascript">
        function load()
```

```
        {
            var message = HelloWorld("Bob", "Lair");
            alert(message);
        }
    </script>
</head>
<body onload="load()">
    <form id="form1" runat="server">
    <div>

    </div>
    </form>
</body>
</html>
```

12. You will see that Visual Studio's IntelliSense tries to help you, as shown in
    Figure 2-9. With HelloWorld selected in the IntelliSense box, you can simply
    press the Tab key, and Visual Studio will automatically finish the function
    name. As you continue typing, you will also notice that the XML comments
    you added for the function appear (see Figure 2-3).

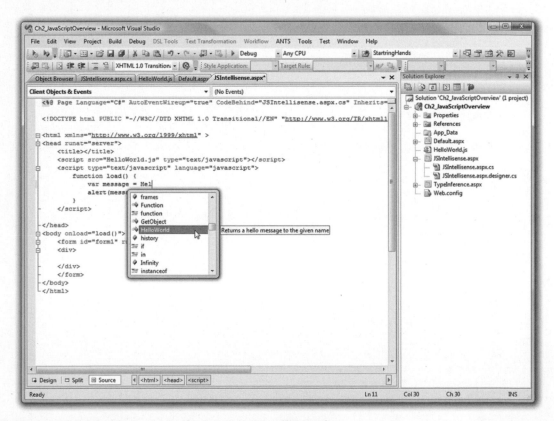

Figure 2-9. HelloWorld appears in the JavaScript IntelliSense box.

13. When you are finished, press F5 to start the project. If you are prompted with a Debugging Not Enabled dialog box, choose "Modify the Web.config file to enable debugging," as shown in Figure 2-10, and then click OK to continue.

Figure 2-10. *VisualStudio will display this dialog box if debugging is not enabled.*

14. When the page is loaded, you will see an alert box appear with your message, as shown in Figure 2-11. Click OK to close the alert box.

Figure 2-11. *Customized hello message*

15. Next, let's give JavaScript debugging a try. Stop the project and return to your Visual Studio project.

16. In the JSIntellisense.aspx file, add a breakpoint by clicking in the gray area to the left of the line calling the HelloWorld() function. In design mode, the breakpoint will show up as a red dot with a white diamond, as shown in Figure 2-12.

17. Press F5 to restart the project. Visual Studio will appear in debug mode, with execution stopped on your line with the breakpoint. The breakpoint will show up as a red dot with a yellow arrow, indicating the application process has been halted at the breakpoint, as shown in Figure 2-13.

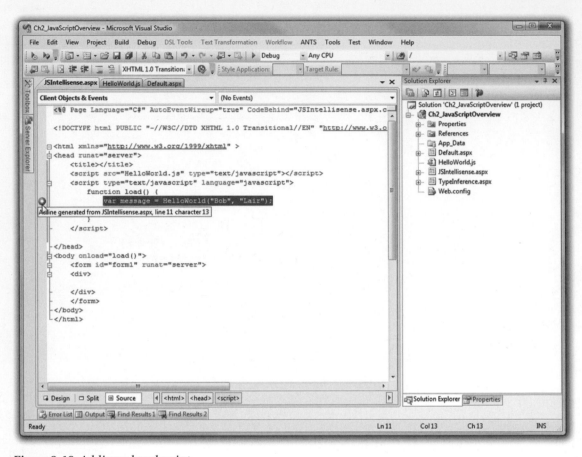

Figure 2-12. Adding a breakpoint

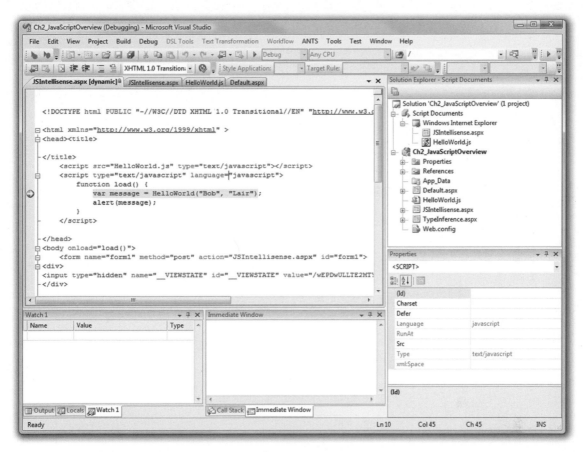

Figure 2-13. *Debugging stopped at the inserted breakpoint.*

18. Press F10 to step to the next line. If you hover your mouse over the variable message, you will see its value is currently set to "Hello Bob Lair". You can also see the value of message in the Locals window.

19. Let's change the value of message. In the Immediate window, type in the following line of code and press Enter to execute it.

```
message = HelloWorld("Robert", "Lair")
```

20. The Immediate window will change the value of message to the output of the new call to the HelloWorld method, as shown in Figure 2-14.

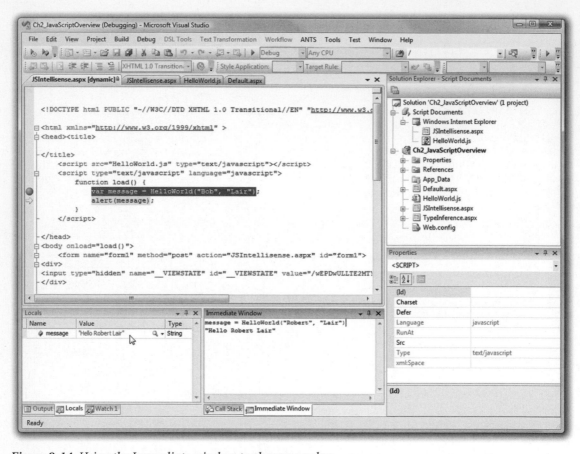

Figure 2-14. *Using the Immediate window to change a value*

This example gave you an idea of the new JavaScript IntelliSense and debugging features in Visual Studio 2008, which are far more advanced than anything ASP.NET developers have had with previous versions. These should prove to be very valuable tools in your client-side scripting tool belt.

Now, let's continue looking at other new features in the latest version of Visual Studio.

Multi-Targeting Support

My company builds ASP.NET solutions for clients, and each time a new version of the .NET Framework is released, we face a maintenance problem. Naturally, we would like to take advantage of the new features of Visual Studio and the latest .NET Framework in our new projects, but we must also be able to support the existing client base.

In the past versions of Visual Studio, projects were tied to a specific version of the .NET Framework. For example, applications written in ASP.NET 1.0 needed to be upgraded to ASP.NET 1.1 in order to take advantage of Visual Studio 2005.

An associated problem is how to handle existing systems that you only want to maintain, and have no intention of upgrading to a newer .NET Framework. For developers to support such systems, while still taking advantage of newer Visual Studio features for other projects, they would need to run different versions of Visual Studio side by side. From a personal perspective, my worst situation was when I had Visual Studio 6.0, Visual Studio .NET (2002), Visual Studio 2003, and Visual Studio 2005 installed on my laptop at the same time. What a pain!

Microsoft has helped alleviate this problem by adding *multi-targeting support* to Visual Studio 2008. This allows you to use Visual Studio 2008 for a specific targeted version of the .NET Framework. Therefore, your Visual Studio 2005 projects that are using .NET 2.0 or .NET 3.0 can be edited with Visual Studio 2008, without being forced to upgrade to .NET 3.5. In addition, you can create new projects for a targeted platform. When you create a new project in Visual Studio, you will notice a new drop-down menu at the top-right corner of the New Project dialog box. As shown in Figure 2-15, this lists the different .NET Frameworks. If you change the selection here, the new project will be targeted to that version of the .NET Framework.

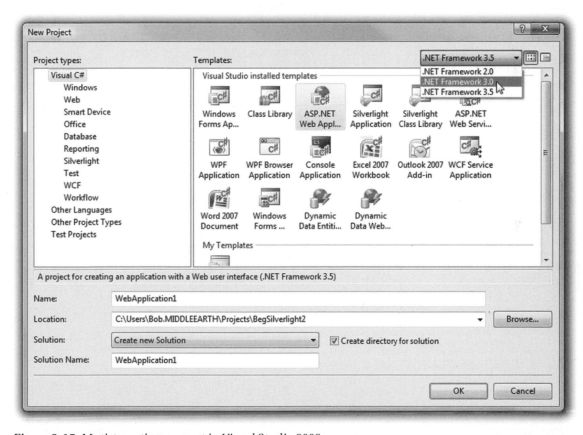

Figure 2-15. *Muti-targeting support in Visual Studio 2008*

If you open a Visual Studio 2005 project in Visual Studio 2008, you will be prompted to upgrade the project by default. If you choose not to upgrade the project, the project will be opened as a Visual Studio 2005 project within Visual Studio 2008.

■ **Note** If you open a project using a version of the .NET Framework prior to 2.0, you will be forced to upgrade. There is no support for these earlier versions in Visual Studio's 2008's multi-targeting feature. That said, Microsoft is committed to keeping this feature working for future versions of Visual Studio. Consequently, it seems safe to say that developers will need only the latest version of Visual Studio installed from this point forward.

Transparent IntelliSense Mode

One of the problems with IntelliSense in past versions of Visual Studio was that the pop-up window hid the source code. You would need to close the pop-up window to see the source code beneath it, and then start typing again.

A new feature in Visual Studio 2008 is the semitransparent IntelliSense pop-up window. When the IntelliSense window appears, you can press the Ctrl key to make the pop-up window semitransparent, allowing you to see the source code under the window. Figures 2-16 and 2-17 illustrate this feature.

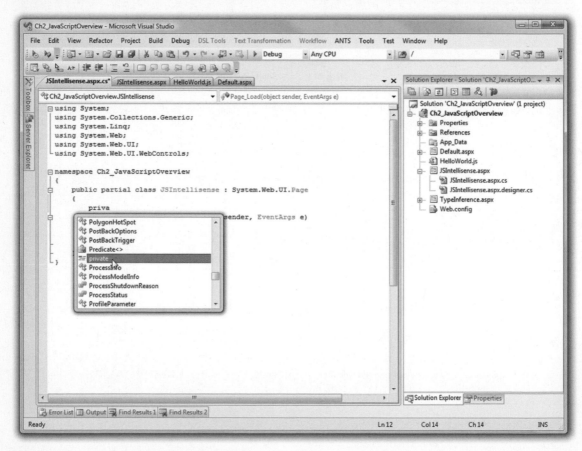

Figure 2-16. *Default IntelliSense pop-up window*

This feature works in all languages across Visual Studio, including the JavaScript IntelliSense covered earlier in this chapter.

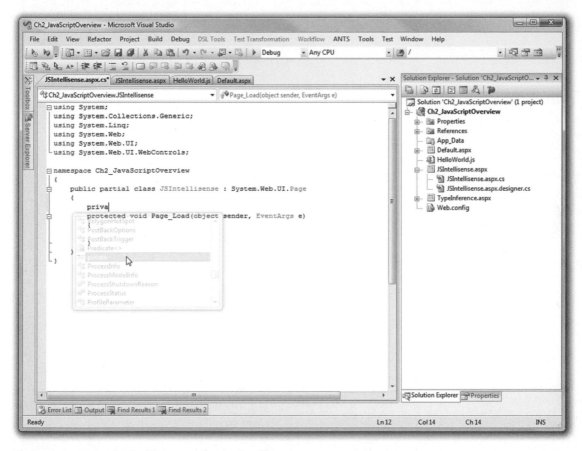

Figure 2-17. *Press the Ctrl key to make the IntelliSense pop-up window transparent.*

Building Your First Silverlight Application in Visual Studio

The best way to explore the Visual Studio IDE is to get your hands dirty and play around with it. Let's build a Silverlight application.

Try It Out: Hello World in Silverlight 3

In this exercise, you'll build the Hello World Silverlight 3 application. I personally hate the Hello World sample, but it is used often because it is so simple and provides a good introduction. Who am I to break with tradition? Let's get started.

1. Start Visual Studio 2008 and Select File ~TRA New ~TRA Project from the main menu.

31

2. In the New Project dialog box, select Visual C# as the project type, and in the list under that type, choose Silverlight. Select Silverlight Application as the template and name the project Ch2_HelloWorld, as shown in Figure 2-18. Then click OK.

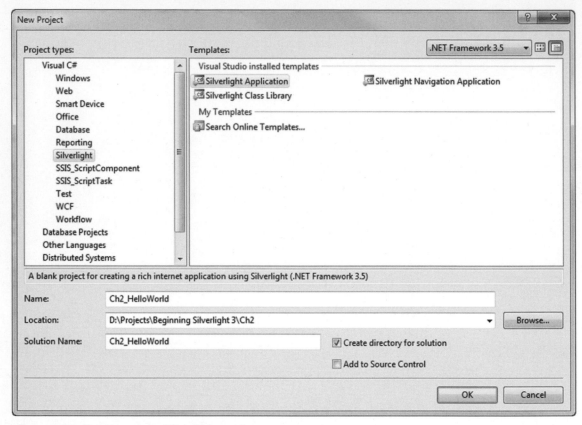

Figure 2-18. Creating a new Silverlight project

3. Visual Studio will display the Add Silverlight Application dialog box, informing you that your Silverlight application needs to be hosted in an HTML web page. It offers the choices of hosting the Silverlight application in a web site or within a project. For this exercise, select Web Application Project and stick with the default name of Ch2_HelloWorld.Web, as shown in Figure 2-19. Then click OK. See the next section for more information about choosing whether to use a Web Site or Web Application project for your own Silverlight applications.

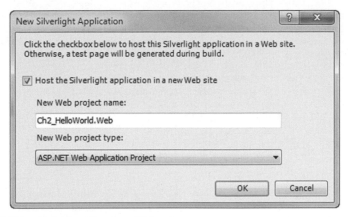

Figure 2-19. The Add Silverlight Application dialog box

4.   Visual Studio will now create the base project for you. Notice that there are two projects created within your solution: one called Ch2_HelloWorld.Web and one called Ch2_HelloWorld, as shown in Figure 2-20.

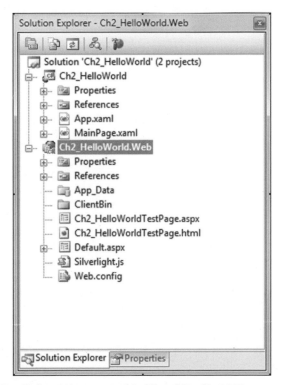

Figure 2-20. The default Silverlight project created in Visual Studio 2008

5. Visual Studio has already opened the MainPage.xaml file, which is where you will start working. Let's begin by adding a TextBlock control, which will display our "Hello World!" message. Add the TextBlock within your Canvas object, as follows:

```
<UserControl x:Class="Ch2_HelloWorld.MainPage"
    xmlns="http://schemas.microsoft.com/winfx/2006/xaml/presentation"
    xmlns:x="http://schemas.microsoft.com/winfx/2006/xaml"
    Width="400" Height="300">
    <Grid x:Name="LayoutRoot" Background="White">
      <TextBlock x:Name="HelloMessage" Text="Hello World!" FontSize="30" />
    </Grid>
</UserControl>
```

6. Save the project and run it by pressing F5. If you see the Debugging Not Enabled dialog box (as shown in Figure 2-10), select "Modify the Web.config to enable debugging" and click OK. The result should be as shown in Figure 2-21.

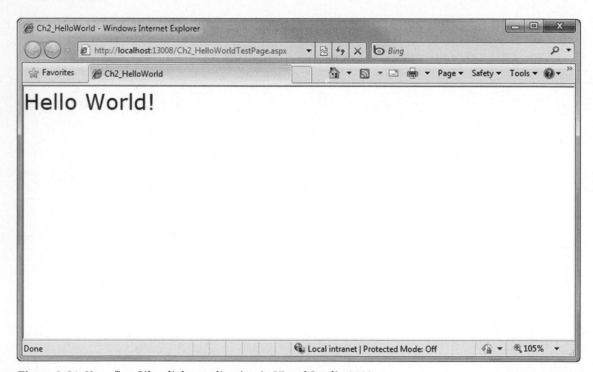

Figure 2-21. Your first Silverlight application in Visual Studio 2008

7. I know this isn't very interesting, so let's change things up a bit by setting the display message in the MainPage.xaml.cs code behind. In the code behind, you will notice a constructor for your Page class, which contains one method called InitializeComponent(). Under that method, change the Text property of your TextBlock as follows (the line shown in bold):

```
namespace Ch2_HelloWorld
{
    public partial class Page : UserControl
    {
        public Page()
        {
            InitializeComponent();
            this.HelloMessage.Text = "Hello Universe!";
        }
    }
}
```

8. Rebuild the application and run it again. Your result should look like Figure 2-22.

Figure 2-22. *The final result from our first Silverlight Application in Visual Studio 2008*

9. Close the application.

There you go! You have built your first Silverlight application. Of course, this application is extremely simple, but you did get an idea of how things work in Visual Studio 2008.

Hosting Your Silverlight Application: Web Site or Web Application?

In Visual Studio 2008, should you use a Web Site project or a Web Application project to host your Silverlight application? The main difference between a Web Site and a Web Application project is how the files are compiled and deployed. Each has its advantages and disadvantages. In the end, the choice pretty much comes down to user preference. Let's take a quick look at each approach.

Using a Visual Studio Web Site

A Visual Studio web site is nothing more than a group of files and folders in a folder. There is no project file. Instead, the site simply contains all the files under the specific folder, including all text files, images, and other file types.

A Visual Studio wsite is compiled dynamically at runtime. An assembly will not be created, and you won't have a bin directory.

The following are some advantages of using a Visual Studio web site:

- You don't need a project file or virtual directory for the site.

- The site can easily be deployed or shared by simply copying the folder containing the site.

The following are some disadvantages of this approach:

- There is no project file that you can double-click to open the site in Visual Studio. Rather, you must browse to the folder after opening Visual Studio.

- By default, all files within the site's directory are included in the Web Site project. If there are files within the site's directory that you do not wish to be a part of the web site, you must rename the file, adding the extension .exclude.

Using a Visual Studio Web Application Project

A Visual Studio Web Application project is the more traditional type of web project used prior to Visual Studio 2005. When Microsoft developers introduced the "Web Site" concept, they did not take into account the many developers who were comfortable with the project- based solution approach. To accommodate those developers, Microsoft announced the Visual Studio 2005 Web Application project as an add-on to Visual Studio 2005. In Visual Studio 2008, this project type is once again a part of Visual Studio.

The following are some of the advantages of using a Web Application project:

- All of the code files are compiled into a single assembly, placed in the bin directory.

- You can easily exclude files from a project, since all files within the project are defined within the project file.

- It's easier to migrate from older versions of Visual Studio.

A disadvantage is that it can be more difficult to share your solution with others, if that is your intent.

In the end, both approaches have their pros and cons. You need to determine which one is more suitable for your application, depending on your specific purpose and goals. For more information about these project types, refer to the MSDN documentation.

Summary

This chapter introduced Visual Studio 2008 and some of the new features offered in this version, including the new JavaScript IntelliSense features, additional JavaScript debugging support, and multi-targeting support. In addition, you built your very first Silverlight application.

In the next chapter, you are going to start to dive into some of the Silverlight controls, beginning with the layout management controls. These controls enable you to lay out your Silverlight applications.

CHAPTER 3

■ ■ ■

Layout Management in Silverlight 3

The previous chapter provided an overview of Visual Studio 2008, one of the primary tools used in developing Silverlight applications. In this chapter, you are going to start to dive into some Silverlight 3 development by looking at the layout management controls.

As you have learned, Silverlight applications consist of a number of Silverlight objects that are defined by XAML. Layout management involves describing the way that these objects are arranged in your application. Silverlight 3 includes five layout management controls: Canvas, StackPanel, Grid, WrapPanel, and DockPanel. You will take a look at each of these in-depth. By the end of this chapter, you should have a good understanding of when to use which layout control.

Layout Management

Silverlight provides a very flexible layout management system that lets you specify how controls will appear in your Silverlight application. You can use a static layout as well as a liquid layout that allows your layout to automatically adjust as your Silverlight application is resized in the browser.

Each of the five layout controls provided in Silverlight 3 has its advantages and disadvantages, as summarized in Table 3-1.

Let's begin by looking at the most basic layout control: the Canvas panel.

Table 3-1. *Layout Control Pros and Cons*

Control	Description	Pros	Cons
Canvas	Based on absolute position of controls.	Very simple layout.	Requires that every control have a Canvas.Top and Canvas.Left property attached to define its position on the canvas.
StackPanel	Based on horizontal or vertical "stacks" of controls.	Allows for a quick dynamic layout. Nesting StackPanel controls can provide some interesting layouts.	The layout is limited to stacks of items. Spacing is limited to adding margins to the individual controls and to adjusting the alignment (with the VerticalAlignment and HorizontalAlignment properties).

Grid	Mimics using table elements in HTML to lay out controls.	The most flexible and powerful layout control. You can define just about any type of layout using the Grid control.	Grid definitions can get somewhat complex at times. Nesting Grid components can be confusing.
WrapPanel	Based on horizontal or vertical "stacks" of controls wrapping to a second row or column when width or height is reached.	Very similar to the StackPanel, except the WrapPanel automatically wraps items to a second row or column so it is ideal for layouts containing an unknown number of items.	Limited control of layout as wrapping is automatic when items reach maximum width or height.
DockPanel	Layout is based on "docked" horizontal or vertical panels.	Provides an easy way to create basic layout, consuming the entire application space in vertical or horizontal panels.	Layout is limited to horizontal or vertical "fill" panels, often used in conjunction with other nested layout controls.

The Canvas Panel

The Canvas panel is a basic layout control that allows you to position Silverlight objects using explicit coordinates relative to the canvas location. You can position an object within the Canvas panel by using two XAML attached properties: Canvas.Left and Canvas.Top. Figure 3-1 shows how the object's position is affected by these properties.

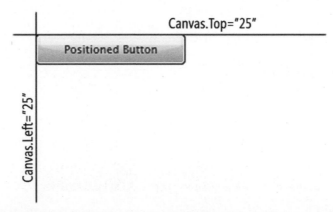

Figure 3-1. The XML attached properties Canvas.Top and Canvas.Left allow you to position the Canvas.

The objects within a Canvas panel have no layout policies placed on them by the layout control and will not resize automatically when your application is resized within the browser.

Try It Out: Using the Canvas Panel

Let's try out a quick example of using the Canvas panel.

1. Open Visual Studio 2008 and create a new Silverlight application called Ch3_CanvasPanel. Allow Visual Studio to create a Web Site project to host the application.

2. When the project is created, you should be looking at the MainPage.xaml file. If you do not see the XAML source, switch to that view so you can edit the XAML. Within the main Grid element, add a Canvas element. Assign it a Width property of 300 and a Height property of 300. In order to see the Canvas panel in the application, also set the background color to green. The following XAML adds this Canvas:

```
<UserControl x:Class="Ch3_CanvasPanel.MainPage"
    xmlns="http://schemas.microsoft.com/winfx/2006/xaml/presentation"
    xmlns:x="http://schemas.microsoft.com/winfx/2006/xaml"
    Width="400" Height="300">
    <Grid x:Name="LayoutRoot" Background="White">

        <Canvas Background="Green" Width="300" Height="200">
        </Canvas>

    </Grid>
</UserControl>
```

3. At this point, your Silverlight application doesn't look that exciting. It contains only a single green rectangle positioned at the very center of your application, as shown in Figure 3-2.

Figure 3-2. Default Canvas with an empty background

4. Let's add a button to this Canvas panel. Add the following code to place the button, which has the label Button1, a Width property of 100, and a Height property of 30. (The Button control is covered in detail in Chapter 4.)

```
<UserControl x:Class="Ch3_CanvasPanel.MainPage"
    xmlns="http://schemas.microsoft.com/winfx/2006/xaml/presentation"
    xmlns:x="http://schemas.microsoft.com/winfx/2006/xaml"
    Width="400" Height="300">
    <Grid x:Name="LayoutRoot" Background="White">

        <Canvas Background="Green" Width="300" Height="200">
            <Button Width="100" Height="30" Content="Button 1" />
        </Canvas>

    </Grid>
</UserControl>
```

5. Figure 3-3 shows the button within the canvas.

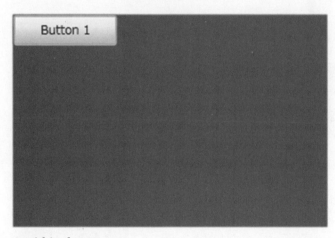

Figure 3-3. *Single button within the canvas*

6. Let's add another button to the Canvas, but this time position it below and a bit to the right of the first button by setting its Canvas.Top and Canvas.Left as attached properties. Give this button the label Button 2, as follows:

```
<Grid x:Name="LayoutRoot" Background="White">

    <Canvas Background="Green" Width="300" Height="200">
        <Button Width="100" Height="30" Content="Button 1" />
        <Button Width="100" Height="30" Content="Button 2"
            Canvas.Left="10" Canvas.Top="40" />
    </Canvas>

</Grid>
```

7. At this point, you now have two buttons within the canvas, but at different locations, as shown in Figure 3-4. This is still not very exciting, but this is about as cool as it gets with the Canvas.

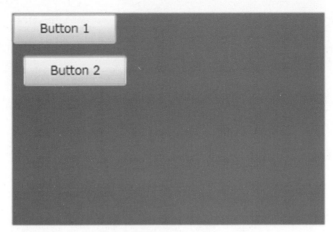

Figure 3-4. *Two buttons positioned relative to the canvas*

8. Go ahead and run the solution to see the end result as it will appear in the browser. The output is shown in Figure 3-5.

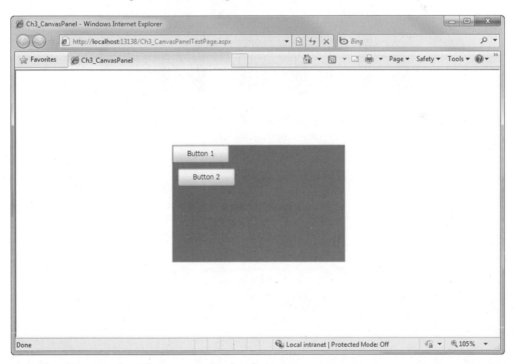

Figure 3-5. *The canvas and two buttons as seen in a browser*

Filling the Entire Browser Window with Your Application

By default, in a new Silverlight project, the root UserControl object is set to a width of 400 and a height of 300. In some cases, you may wish to set the width and height of your Silverlight application within the browser. At other times, however, you will want your Silverlight application to take up the entire window of your browser, and to resize as the browser is resized. This is done very easily within Silverlight. When you wish for the width and height to be set to 100%, simply omit the element's Height and Width attributes.

As an example, the following source has been adjusted for the Canvas panel and the Silverlight application to take up the entire browser:

```
<UserControl x:Class="Ch3_CanvasPanel.MainPage"
    xmlns="http://schemas.microsoft.com/winfx/2006/xaml/presentation"
    xmlns:x="http://schemas.microsoft.com/winfx/2006/xaml">
    <Grid x:Name="LayoutRoot" Background="White">

        <Canvas Background="Green">
        </Canvas>

    </Grid>
</UserControl>
```

With the omission of the Height and Width declarations for UserControl and Canvas, when you run the Silverlight application, you will see that the canvas takes up 100% of the browser window, as shown in Figure 3-6. It will resize as the browser resizes.

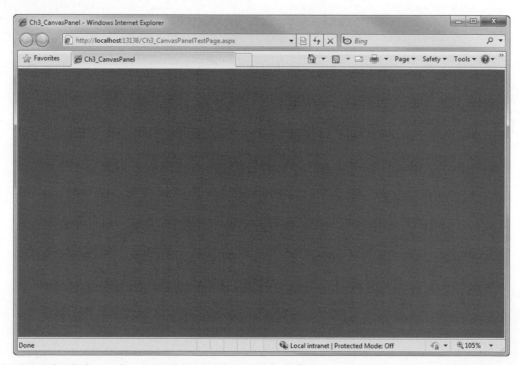

Figure 3-6. *Silverlight application taking up the entire browser*

As you've seen, the Canvas panel is a simple layout control. It can be used very effectively in a fixed layout. However, in most cases, you will want to use a static layout for your applications. The StackPanel control provides a more fluid layout control.

The StackPanel Control

The StackPanel provides developers with a quick layout option for positioning objects. The StackPanel control allows you to position Silverlight objects in more of a flow layout, stacking objects either horizontally or vertically. Figure 3-7 shows the basic concept of this layout control.

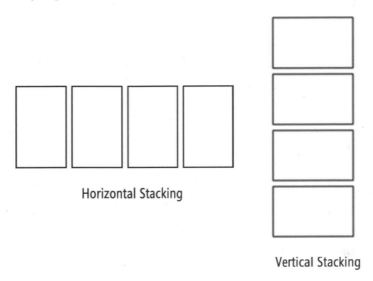

Figure 3-7. The StackPanel control orientations

Try It Out: Using the StackPanel Control

To better understand the StackPanel control, let's run through an exercise.

1. In Visual Studio 2008, create a new Silverlight application named *Ch3_StackPanel* and allow Visual Studio to create a Web Site project to host the application.

2. When the project is created you should be looking at the MainPage.xaml file. If you do not see the XAML source, switch so that you can edit the XAML. Within the main Grid element, add a StackPanel control and also three buttons with the labels Button 1, Button 2, and Button 3. Give all three buttons a width of 100 and a height of 30. The following XAML adds the StackPanel control and buttons (the new code is highlighted in bold in all the exercises):

```
<UserControl x:Class="Ch3_StackPanel.MainPage"
    xmlns="http://schemas.microsoft.com/winfx/2006/xaml/presentation"
    xmlns:x="http://schemas.microsoft.com/winfx/2006/xaml"
    Width="400" Height="300">
```

```
        <Grid x:Name="LayoutRoot" Background="White">
            <StackPanel>
                <Button Width="100" Height="30" Content="Button 1"></Button>
                <Button Width="100" Height="30" Content="Button 2"></Button>
                <Button Width="100" Height="30" Content="Button 3"></Button>
            </StackPanel>
        </Grid>
</UserControl>
```

3. At this point, your application should appear as shown in Figure 3-8. Notice that the buttons are stacked vertically. This is because the default stacking orientation for the StackPanel control is vertical.

Figure 3-8. *The StackPanel control with its default orientation*

4. Change the orientation of the StackPanel control to be horizontal by setting the Orientation property to Horizontal, as follows:

```
<Grid x:Name="LayoutRoot" Background="White">
    <StackPanel Orientation="Horizontal" >
        <Button Width="100" Height="30" Content="Button 1"></Button>
        <Button Width="100" Height="30" Content="Button 2"></Button>
        <Button Width="100" Height="30" Content="Button 3"></Button>
    </StackPanel>
</Grid>
```

5. With this simple change, the buttons are now stacked horizontally, as shown in Figure 3-9.

Figure 3-9. *The StackPanel control with horizontal orientation*

6. Notice that all the buttons are touching each other, which is unattractive. You can easily space them out by using their Margin property. In addition, you can center the buttons by setting the StackPanel control's HorizontalAlignment property to Center. Other options for HorizontalAlignment include Left, Right, and Stretch (which stretches the content to the left and right). Make the following changes to adjust the buttons:

```
<Grid x:Name="LayoutRoot" Background="White">
    <StackPanel Orientation="Horizontal" HorizontalAlignment="Center">
        <Button Width="100" Height="30" Content="Button 1" Margin="5"></Button>
```

```
        <Button Width="100" Height="30" Content="Button 2" Margin="5"></Button>
        <Button Width="100" Height="30" Content="Button 3" Margin="5"></Button>
    </StackPanel>
</Grid>
```

7. After you have made these changes, your buttons are spaced out nicely in the center of the application, as shown in Figure 3-10.

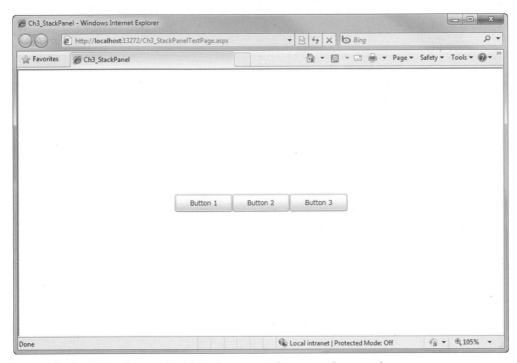

Figure 3-10. *The StackPanel control with buttons spaced apart and centered*

Try It Out: Nesting StackPanel Controls

Microsoft designed the control framework so that any object can be contained within another object. One way you can enhance your layout is by nesting a layout control within another layout control. In this example, you will nest a StackPanel control within another StackPanel control, but realize that you can nest any layout control within any other layout control to get the exact layout functionality you are seeking.

1. In Visual Studio 2008, create a new Silverlight application named Ch3_NestedStackPanel and allow Visual Studio to create a Web Site project to host the application.

2. In the MainPage.xaml file, add the following items:

47

- A StackPanel control to the root Grid with its Orientation property set to Horizontal and the HorizontalAlignment property set to Center.

- Within that StackPanel, add two buttons with the labels Button Left and Button Right.

- In between the two buttons, add another StackPanel with Orientation set to Vertical and VerticalAlignment set to Center.

- Within that nested StackPanel, include three buttons with the labels Button Middle 1, Button Middle 2, and Button Middle 3.

- All buttons should have a Margin property set to 5, and should have Height set to 30 and Width set to 100.

3. Here is what the updated source looks like:

```
<Grid x:Name="LayoutRoot" Background="White">
    <StackPanel Orientation="Horizontal" HorizontalAlignment="Center">
        <Button Width="100" Height="30" Content="Button Left" Margin="5" />
        <StackPanel VerticalAlignment="Center">
            <Button Width="100" Height="30" Content="Button Middle 1"
                    Margin="5"></Button>
            <Button Width="100" Height="30" Content="Button Middle 2"
                    Margin="5"></Button>
            <Button Width="100" Height="30" Content="Button Middle 3"
                    Margin="5"></Button>
        </StackPanel>
        <Button Width="100" Height="30" Content="Button Right"
Margin="5"></Button>
    </StackPanel>
</Grid>
```

4. The cool result of this code is shown in Figure 3-11.

Figure 3-11. *Nested StackPanel controls*

5. Run the application to see the results.

As you can see from these two exercises, the StackPanel control is a very useful layout option, and you will probably use it often in your Silverlight applications. By nesting Silverlight controls, you have a lot of flexibility when designing your applications. However, in the event that you want more control of the positioning of items in your application, without needing to resort to the absolute positioning used by the Canvas control, the Grid control may be just the layout option you need.

The Grid Control

The Grid control provides more fine-tuned layout in Silverlight applications. As a comparison, you can think of using the Grid layout control as similar to using table elements to position items in HTML, only more flexible. With the Grid control, you can define rows and columns, thus creating grid cells, and then add objects to individual cells in the grid or to multiple cells, by using spanning.

To specify in which cell to place an object, you use the Grid.Column and Grid.Row attached properties. Note that these properties are *base zero*, so the top-left cell it is row 0 and column 0. Figure 3-12 illustrates the row and column locations for the grid.

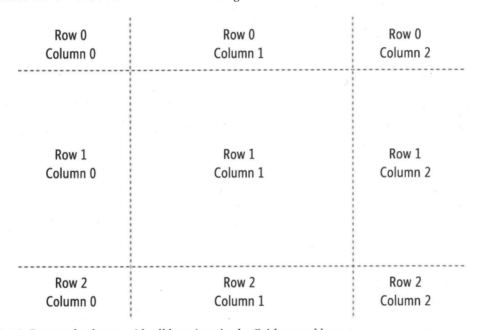

Figure 3-12. *Row and column grid cell locations in the Grid control layout*

For most developers, the Grid control will most likely be the layout option of choice, due to its flexibility. At the same time, the Grid control is significantly more complex than the others, as you'll see in the following exercises.

Try It Out: Using the Grid Control

Let's try out a simple Grid panel with four buttons.

1. In Visual Studio 2008, create a new Silverlight application named Ch3_GridPanel and allow Visual Studio to create a Web Site project to host the application.

2. For this example, you are going to need a bit more space in which to work. In the MainPage.xaml file, start out by changing the UserControl's Width to 600 and Height to 400, as follows:

```
<UserControl x:Class="Ch3_GridPanel.MainPage"
    xmlns="http://schemas.microsoft.com/winfx/2006/xaml/presentation"
    xmlns:x="http://schemas.microsoft.com/winfx/2006/xaml"
    Width="600" Height="400">
    <Grid x:Name="LayoutRoot" Background="White">

    </Grid>
</UserControl>
```

3.   Add a new Grid control to the Silverlight application. In order to better see
     what is going on, turn on the display of grid lines by setting the ShowGridLines
     property to true. The following code shows these additions. Keep in mind that
     since you have not designated a size for the grid, it will automatically take up
     the entire size of the parent, and in this case, the entire Silverlight application.

```
<UserControl x:Class="Ch3_GridPanel.MainPage"
    xmlns="http://schemas.microsoft.com/winfx/2006/xaml/presentation"
    xmlns:x="http://schemas.microsoft.com/winfx/2006/xaml"
    Width="600" Height="400">
    <Grid x:Name="LayoutRoot" Background="White">
        <Grid ShowGridLines="True">

        </Grid>
    </Grid>
</UserControl>
```

4.   Next, define the rows and columns in the Grid control. You do this using the
     XAML property elements Grid.RowDefinitions and Grid.ColumnDefinitions.
     Add the following XAML to your new grid:

```
<Grid x:Name="LayoutRoot" Background="White">
    <Grid ShowGridLines="True">

        <Grid.RowDefinitions>
            <RowDefinition Height="70" />
            <RowDefinition Height="*" />
            <RowDefinition Height="70" />
        </Grid.RowDefinitions>

        <Grid.ColumnDefinitions>
            <ColumnDefinition Width="150" />
            <ColumnDefinition Width="*" />
            <ColumnDefinition Width="150" />
        </Grid.ColumnDefinitions>

    </Grid>
</Grid>
```

5.   Notice that for the center row and column, you are setting the Height and
     Width properties to "*". The asterisk tells the row and column to take up all
     available space. As the Grid control is resized with the browser window, those
     columns will be resized to take up all the space not consumed by the fixed-
     sized columns. After you have added these row and column definitions, your
     canvas should appear as shown in Figure 3-13.

Figure 3-13. *Grid with columns and rows*

6. You can now add objects to the different grid cells. Place a button in each of the four corner cells, giving the buttons the corresponding labels Top Left, Top Right, Bottom Left, and Bottom Right. To place the buttons, add the following code:

```
<Grid x:Name="LayoutRoot" Background="White">
    <Grid ShowGridLines="True">

        <Grid.RowDefinitions>
            <RowDefinition Height="70" />
            <RowDefinition Height="*" />
            <RowDefinition Height="70" />
        </Grid.RowDefinitions>

        <Grid.ColumnDefinitions>
            <ColumnDefinition Width="150" />
            <ColumnDefinition Width="*" />
            <ColumnDefinition Width="150" />
        </Grid.ColumnDefinitions>

        <Button Width="100" Height="30" Content="Top Left"
                Margin="5" Grid.Row="0" Grid.Column="0"></Button>
        <Button Width="100" Height="30" Content="Top Right"
                Margin="5" Grid.Row="0" Grid.Column="2"></Button>
        <Button Width="100" Height="30" Content="Bottom Left"
                Margin="5" Grid.Row="2" Grid.Column="0"></Button>
```

51

```
    <Button Width="100" Height="30" Content="Bottom Right"
            Margin="5" Grid.Row="2" Grid.Column="2"></Button>

  </Grid>
</Grid>
```

After the buttons are added, your application should look like Figure 3-14.

Figure 3-14. The grid with buttons in the four corners

Try It Out: Nesting a Grid and Spanning a Column

Next, you will nest another Grid control in the center cell of the Grid control you just added. This will make the application layout somewhat complex, but it will also serve to show how Grid panels are defined using XAML.

1. In the MainPage.xaml within the Ch3_GridPanel project, add the following items:

   • A Grid control positioned at Grid.Column=1 and Grid.Row=1

   • Three RowDefinition and two ColumnDefinition elements

   • Buttons in the four corners of the new Grid control, as you just did in the outer Grid panel

2. The source code should look like the following:

```
<Grid x:Name="LayoutRoot" Background="White">
```

```xml
<Grid ShowGridLines="True">

    <Grid.RowDefinitions>
        <RowDefinition Height="70" />
        <RowDefinition Height="*" />
        <RowDefinition Height="70" />
    </Grid.RowDefinitions>

    <Grid.ColumnDefinitions>
        <ColumnDefinition Width="150" />
        <ColumnDefinition Width="*" />
        <ColumnDefinition Width="150" />
    </Grid.ColumnDefinitions>

    <Button Width="100" Height="30" Content="Top Left"
            Margin="5" Grid.Row="0" Grid.Column="0"></Button>
    <Button Width="100" Height="30" Content="Top Right"
            Margin="5" Grid.Row="0" Grid.Column="2"></Button>
    <Button Width="100" Height="30" Content="Bottom Left"
            Margin="5" Grid.Row="2" Grid.Column="0"></Button>
    <Button Width="100" Height="30" Content="Bottom Right"
            Margin="5" Grid.Row="2" Grid.Column="2"></Button>

    <Grid Grid.Column="1" Grid.Row="1"  ShowGridLines="True">

        <Grid.RowDefinitions>
            <RowDefinition Height="*" />
            <RowDefinition Height="*" />
            <RowDefinition Height="*" />
        </Grid.RowDefinitions>

        <Grid.ColumnDefinitions>
            <ColumnDefinition Width="*" />
            <ColumnDefinition Width="*" />
        </Grid.ColumnDefinitions>

        <Button Width="100" Height="30" Content="Nested Top Left"
            Margin="5" Grid.Row="0" Grid.Column="0"></Button>
        <Button Width="100" Height="30" Content="Nested Top Right"
            Margin="5" Grid.Row="0" Grid.Column="2"></Button>
        <Button Width="100" Height="30" Content="Nested B. Left"
            Margin="5" Grid.Row="2" Grid.Column="0"></Button>
        <Button Width="100" Height="30" Content="Nested B. Right"
            Margin="5" Grid.Row="2" Grid.Column="2"></Button>

    </Grid>

</Grid>
</Grid>
```

3. At this point, your application should look like Figure 3-15. Now, this is a pretty cool layout.

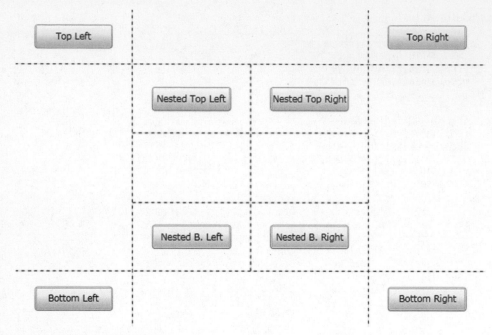

Figure 3-15. *Nested grid with buttons*

4. Notice that you have not placed anything in the two columns in the middle row of the new grid. Here, you're going to add a button that spans these two columns, so the button will appear in the center of the row. In order to do this, add the new button to the Grid control with the Grid.ColumnSpan attached property set to 2. The source changes to the innermost Grid control are as follows:

```
<Grid Grid.Column="1" Grid.Row="1"  ShowGridLines="True">

    <Grid.RowDefinitions>
        <RowDefinition Height="*" />
        <RowDefinition Height="*" />
        <RowDefinition Height="*" />
    </Grid.RowDefinitions>

    <Grid.ColumnDefinitions>
        <ColumnDefinition Width="*" />
        <ColumnDefinition Width="*" />
    </Grid.ColumnDefinitions>

    <Button Width="100" Height="30" Content="Nested Top Left"
        Margin="5" Grid.Row="0" Grid.Column="0"></Button>
    <Button Width="100" Height="30" Content="Nested Top Right"
        Margin="5" Grid.Row="0" Grid.Column="2"></Button>
    <Button Width="100" Height="30" Content="Nested B. Left"
        Margin="5" Grid.Row="2" Grid.Column="0"></Button>
```

```
<Button Width="100" Height="30" Content="Nested B. Right"
    Margin="5" Grid.Row="2" Grid.Column="2"></Button>

<Button Width="100" Height="30" Content="Nested Center"
    Margin="5" Grid.Row="1" Grid.Column="0"
    Grid.ColumnSpan="2"></Button>

</Grid>
```

5. Now that you have added the button to the center column, your application should look like Figure 3-16. Notice how the button spans the two columns and appears in the center. For experienced HTML developers who are used to laying out their forms with tables, this approach should be very comfortable, as it closely mimics using the colspan attribute for a <TD> tag.

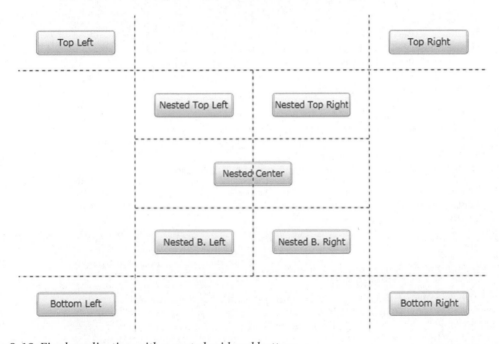

Figure 3-16. *Final application with a nested grid and buttons*

In this example, you saw how to create a relatively complex layout using the Grid control. As you can see, this is a very powerful and flexible layout tool for your Silverlight applications.

The WrapPanel Control

The WrapPanel control is a new control in Silverlight 3 that was previously available through the Silverlight Toolkit. It is very similar to the StackPanel control with one major difference: when items in a WrapPanel will not fit within the width or height of the control, they automatically wrap to a new row (if horizontal orientation) or column (if vertical orientation). This makes the WrapPanel ideal for laying out an unknown number of items as they will automatically wrap to take up the entire space of the control.

As an example, if you look at Figure 3-17 you will see how the WrapPanel will handle placing six items when set to horizontal and vertical orientation. Horizontally, the WrapPanel will place the items one after the other to the right, until no other items can fit within the width of the control. At that time, it will start to place the items in a new row directly below the first row. The same is true for vertical orientation except the items are stacked below the previous item until new items cannot fit within the height of the control, at which time they will be place directly to the right of the previous row.

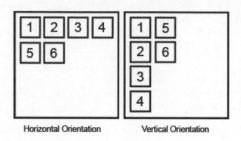

Horizontal Orientation   Vertical Orientation

Figure 3-17. *The WrapPanel control orientations*

Try It Out: Using the WrapPanel Control

In this exercise, we will explore the WrapPanel control and how it can be used to display an unknown number of items in stacks vertically and horizontally. Let's get started.

1. Open Visual Studio 2008 and create a new Silverlight application called Ch3_WrapPanel. Allow Visual Studio to create a web application to host the application.

2. When the project is created, the file MainPage.xaml will be automatically created and will be opened in the XAML designer. We are going to add two rows to the root Grid control and then we will place a WrapPanel in the first row and a button with the label Add New Item in the second row.

    In order to get the proper XML namespace added for the WrapPanel, add it by double-clicking on the control from the Toolbox in Visual Studio. That way Visual Studio will automatically add the Xml namespace to the page. Once the panel has been added, you can then modify the tag however you would like.

    When you are finished adding the controls, your XAML should look like the following code:

```
<UserControl
    x:Class="Ch3_WrapPanel.MainPage"
    xmlns:controls="clr-namespace:System.Windows.Controls;assembly=System.Windows.Controls"
    xmlns="http://schemas.microsoft.com/winfx/2006/xaml/presentation"
    xmlns:x="http://schemas.microsoft.com/winfx/2006/xaml"
    Width="400" Height="300">
    <Grid x:Name="LayoutRoot" Background="White">

        <Grid.RowDefinitions>
```

```
        <RowDefinition />
        <RowDefinition Height="50" />
    </Grid.RowDefinitions>

    <controls:WrapPanel x:Name="wrapPanel" />

    <Button x:Name="addItem"
            Click="addItem_Click"
            Content="Add New Item"
            Grid.Row="1" />

    </Grid>
</UserControl>
```

3. Now we need to add the code behind the button click event. Right click on addItem_Click in the XAML and choose "Navigate to Event Handler." This will take you to the code behind of MainPage.xaml. Add the following code within the addItem_Click event handler.

```
private void addItem_Click(object sender, RoutedEventArgs e)
{
    Rectangle newRect = new Rectangle();
    newRect.Width = 50;
    newRect.Height = 50;
    newRect.Margin = new Thickness(5);
    newRect.Fill = new SolidColorBrush(Color.FromArgb(255, 0, 0, 0));

    wrapPanel.Children.Add(newRect);
}
```

4. We can now test the application. Once the application appears, start pressing the Add New Item button and watch the items appear horizontally as well as wrap to a new row when a new item cannot fit within the width of the control (see Figure 3-18).

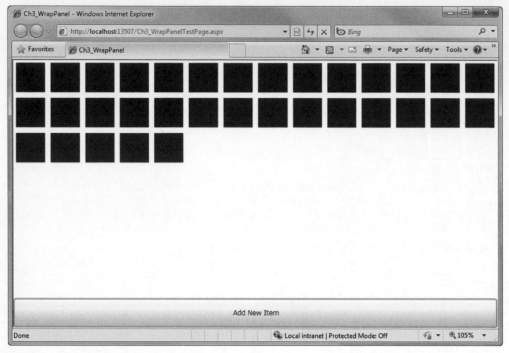

Figure 3-18. *Completed Horizontal WrapPanel*

5. At this point, you can then go into the XAML designer for `MainPage.xaml`, add the property `Orientation="Vertical"` to the `WrapPanel`, and test the application once again. This time you will notice that the items appear vertically and wrap to new columns once they reach the maximum height, as shown in Figure 3-19.

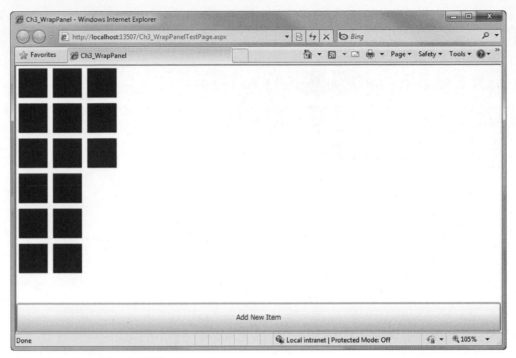

Figure 3-19. Completed Vertical WrapPanel

The DockPanel Control

The DockPanel control is also a new control in Silverlight 3 that was previously available through the Silverlight Toolkit. It provides the ability to dock controls in all four directions: top, bottom, right, and left. Consider Figure 3-20, which is a possible layout with the DockPanel control involving five controls. The first two controls are docked in the left panel; the third control is docked in the top-center panel; the fourth control is docked in the bottom-center panel; and the fifth control is docked in the right panel.

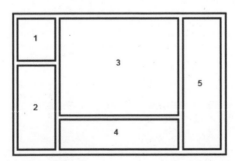

Figure 3-20. Possible layout with the DockPanel

To achieve this layout without the DockPanel would involve nested layout controls or a fairly complex Grid control. The point is that the for certain situations the DockPanel can definitely be a very effective control.

Try It Out: Using the DockPanel Control

In this exercise, we will explore the DockPanel control and how it can be used to layout controls docked in different directions.

1. Open Visual Studio 2008 and create a new Silverlight application called Ch3_DockPanel. Allow Visual Studio to create a web application to host the application.

2. When the project is created, the file MainPage.xaml will be automatically created and will be opened in the XAML designer. We will add a DockPanel to the root Grid and then add buttons that are docked in different positions.

   In order to get the proper XML namespace added for the DockPanel, add it by double-clicking on the control from the Toolbox in Visual Studio. That way Visual Studio will automatically add the Xml namespace and assembly reference to the page. Once the panel has been added, you can then modify the tag how you would like.

   The default dock behavior is to dock the control left. However, if you want to change that you can use the Dock extended property to change this behavior. As an example to dock a control to the right, you would add the property controls:DockPanel.Dock="Right" to the control. (Note that we included the xmlns, attribute, which is required.)

   When you are finished adding the controls, your XAML should look like the following:

```xml
<UserControl
    x:Class="Ch3_DockPanel.MainPage"
    xmlns:controls="clr-namespace:System.Windows.Controls;assembly=System.Windows.Controls"
    xmlns="http://schemas.microsoft.com/winfx/2006/xaml/presentation"
    xmlns:x="http://schemas.microsoft.com/winfx/2006/xaml"
    Width="400" Height="300">
    <Grid x:Name="LayoutRoot" Background="White">
        <controls:DockPanel>
            <Button Content="Left Button" controls:DockPanel.Dock="Left" />
            <Button Content="Right Button" controls:DockPanel.Dock="Right" />
            <Button Content="Bottom Button" controls:DockPanel.Dock="Bottom" />
        </controls:DockPanel>
    </Grid>
</UserControl>
```

3. The result of this code should appear as shown in Figure 3-21.

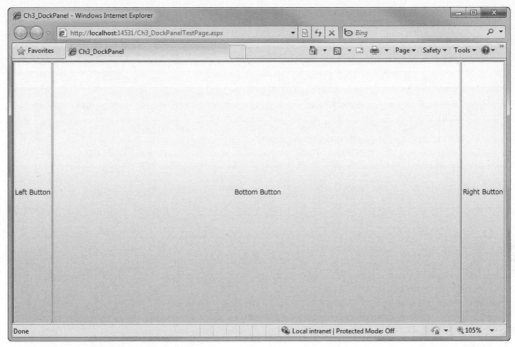

Figure 3-21. *Buttons placed in the DockPanel*

4. Notice that the last button placed in the DockPanel automatically fills the remaining space. This is the default behavior of the DockPanel. However, if you do not want the DockPanel to do this, simply add the LastChildFill property set to False to the DockPanel.

```
<Grid x:Name="LayoutRoot" Background="White">
    <controls:DockPanel LastChildFill="False">
        <Button Content="Left Button" controls:DockPanel.Dock="Left" />
        <Button Content="Right Button" controls:DockPanel.Dock="Right" />
        <Button Content="Bottom Button" controls:DockPanel.Dock="Bottom" />
    </controls:DockPanel>
</Grid>
```

Once you have added this property, the result should appear as shown in Figure 3-22.

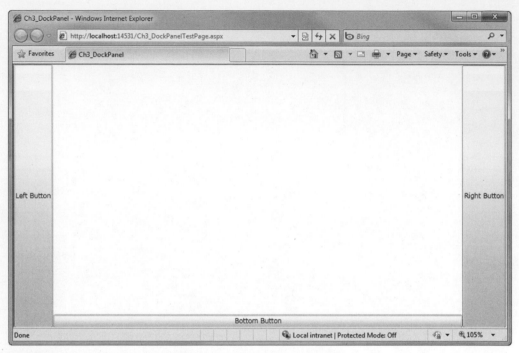

Figure 3-22. Buttons placed in the DockPanel Without LastChildFill

5. The order in which you place the controls in the DockPanel determines how they are docked with the other controls. For example, notice that button labeled Bottom Button is docked around the left and right button, because they were added earlier in the DockPanel. However, if we add another button to the first button in the DockPanel and dock it to the top it will occupy the entire width of the control.

```
<Grid x:Name="LayoutRoot" Background="White">
    <controls:DockPanel LastChildFill="False">
        <Button Content="Top Button" controls:DockPanel.Dock="Top" />
        <Button Content="Left Button" controls:DockPanel.Dock="Left" />
        <Button Content="Right Button" controls:DockPanel.Dock="Right" />
        <Button Content="Bottom Button" controls:DockPanel.Dock="Bottom" />
    </controls:DockPanel>
</Grid>
```

Once you have added this control, the result should appear as shown in Figure 3-23.

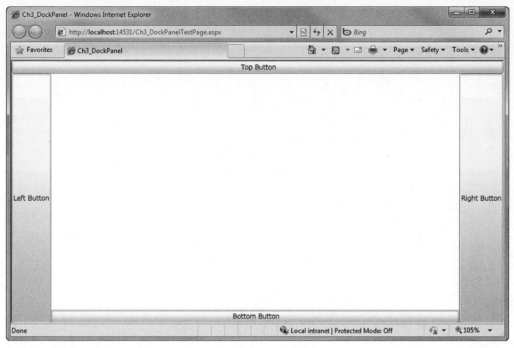

Figure 3-23. Buttons placed in the DockPanel with Top Dock

Summary

In this chapter, we explored the three layout controls that are available out of the box in Silverlight 3. We looked at the Canvas, StackPanel, and Grid, WrapPanel, and DockPanel controls. In the next chapter, we will take an in-depth look at the form controls that come bundled with Silverlight 3.

CHAPTER 4

■■■

Silverlight 3 Controls

For those who have worked with Silverlight 1.0, one of the first observations you most likely made was the lack of common controls such as the Button, TextBox, and ListBox. In fact, Silverlight 1.0 provided only two basic controls: Rectangle and TextBlock. From these, the developers were expected to implement all of the rich controls they needed. As you can imagine, it was quite a bit of work to create all of the form controls using just these two base controls.

Since then, Microsoft's vision of Silverlight has gone beyond basic animations to spark up your applications and into the realm of feature-rich user interfaces (UIs). To this end, Silverlight 3 includes a strong base of controls that you can use within your Silverlight applications.

In this chapter, you will first look at the Silverlight controls in general by examining control properties and events. You will then take a brief tour of some of the more common form controls included in Silverlight 3. This chapter is meant to provide a high-level introduction to these common Silverlight controls. You will continue to work with the controls throughout the remainder of the book, so you will see more specific usage scenarios.

Setting Control Properties

The most straightforward and simple way to set a property is by using attribute syntax. However, in some cases, you will use element syntax.

Attribute Syntax

Most properties that can be represented as a simple string can be set using attribute syntax. Setting an attribute in XAML is just like setting an attribute in XML. An XML element contains a node and attributes. Silverlight controls are defined in the same way, where the control name is the node, and the properties are defined as attributes.

As an example, you can easily use attribute syntax to set the Width, Height, and Content properties of a Button control, as follows:

```
<Button Width="100" Height="30" Content="Click Me!"></Button>
```

Element Syntax

Element syntax is most commonly used when a property cannot be set using attribute syntax because the property value cannot be represented as a simple string. Again, this is very similar to using elements in XML. The following is an example of setting the background color of a button:

```
<Button Width="100" Height="30" Content="Click Me!">
    <Button.Background>
        <SolidColorBrush Color="Blue"/>
    </Button.Background>
    <Button.Foreground>
        <SolidColorBrush Color="Red"/>
    </Button.Foreground>
</Button>
```

Type-Converter-Enabled Attributes

Sometimes when defining a property via an attribute, the value cannot be represented as a simple string—rather, it is converted to a more complex type. A common usage of a type- converter-enabled attribute is Margin. The Margin property can be set as a simple string, such as in the following:

```
<Button Width="100" Content="Click Me!" Margin="15"></Button>
```

When you set the Margin property in this fashion, the left, right, top, and bottom margins are all set to 15 pixels. What if you want to set the top margin to 15 pixels, but you want the other three margins to be 0? In order to do that, you would set the Margin property as follows:

```
<Button Width="100" Content="Click Me!" Margin="0,15,0,0"></Button>
```

In this case, Silverlight takes the string "0,15,0,0" and converts it into a more complex type. The string is converted to four values: left margin = 0, top margin = 15, right margin = 0, and bottom margin = 0.

This type-conversion concept is not new to Silverlight. For those of you familiar with Cascading Style Sheets (CSS), the same sort of structure exists. As an example, when you are defining a border style, within the simple string value for a border, you are actually setting the thickness, color, and line style. The following border assignment in CSS will set the border thickness to 1 pixel, the line style to be solid, and the color to #333333 (dark gray):

```
border: 1px solid #333333;
```

Attached Properties

In Chapter 3, you learned how to set a control's position within a Canvas panel by using attached properties. An *attached property* is a property that is attached to parent control. In the Chapter 3's example, you specified the Button control's position within the Canvas object by setting two attached properties: Canvas.Top and Canvas.Left. These two properties reference the Button control's parent, which is the Canvas.

```
<Canvas>
    <Button Width="100" Content="Click Me!"
            Canvas.Top="10" Canvas.Left="13" />
</Canvas>
```

Nesting Controls Within Controls

When you first look at the controls included in Silverlight 2, you will probably feel pretty comfortable, as they seem what would be expected. However, when you dig a bit deeper into the control features, you will find that the controls are much more flexible and powerful than they first appear.

One of the key features of controls in Silverlight 2 is the ability to put just about anything within a control. A Button control can contain a StackPanel, which can contain an Ellipse control and a TextBlock control. There really are few limitations as to what the contents of a control can be. Figure 4-1 shows an example of a standard Silverlight 2 Button control containing a StackPanel, a nested StackPanel, an Ellipse, a TextBlock, and a ListBox.

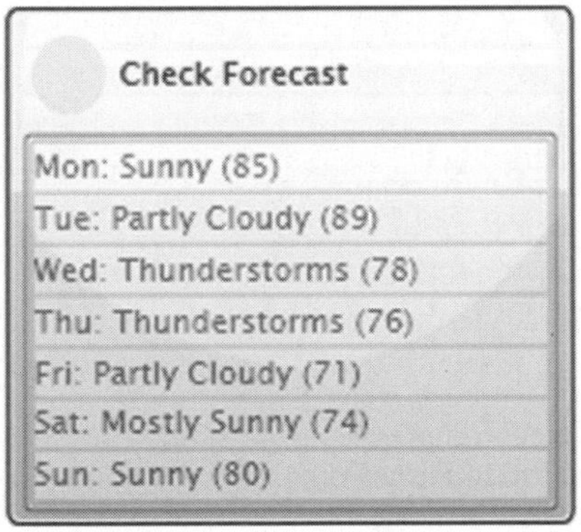

Figure 4-1. A Button control with nested controls

The following code was used to produce the control in Figure 4-1:

```
<Button Height="180" Width="200">
    <StackPanel Orientation="Vertical">
        <StackPanel Margin="5"
            VerticalAlignment="Center"
            Orientation="Horizontal">

            <Ellipse Fill="Yellow" Width="25" />
            <TextBlock VerticalAlignment="Center"
                Margin="5" Text="Check Forecast" />

        </StackPanel>
        <ListBox FontSize="11" Opacity="0.5"
            Margin="2" x:Name="lstForecastGlance">
            <ListBoxItem>
                <TextBlock VerticalAlignment="Center"
                    Text="Mon: Sunny (85)" />
            </ListBoxItem>
            <ListBoxItem>
                <TextBlock VerticalAlignment="Center"
                    Text="Tue: Partly Cloudy (89)" />
            </ListBoxItem>
```

```
        <ListBoxItem>
            <TextBlock VerticalAlignment="Center"
                Text="Wed: Thunderstorms (78)" />
        </ListBoxItem>
        <ListBoxItem>
            <TextBlock VerticalAlignment="Center"
                Text="Thu: Thunderstorms (76)" />
        </ListBoxItem>
        <ListBoxItem>
            <TextBlock VerticalAlignment="Center"
                Text="Fri: Partly Cloudy (71)" />
        </ListBoxItem>
        <ListBoxItem>
            <TextBlock VerticalAlignment="Center"
                Text="Sat: Mostly Sunny (74)" />
        </ListBoxItem>
        <ListBoxItem>
            <TextBlock VerticalAlignment="Center"
                Text="Sun: Sunny (80)" />
        </ListBoxItem>
    </ListBox>
  </StackPanel>
</Button>
```

As the code shows, the example simply nests additional content within the Button control. As you can imagine, this can be a very powerful feature.

Handling Events in Silverlight

As with other Microsoft programming frameworks, Silverlight provides an event mechanism to track actions that take place within Silverlight 3 applications. Two types of actions are tracked within Silverlight:

- Actions that are triggered based on some input from the user. Input actions are handled and "bubbled" up from the browser to the Silverlight object model.

- Actions that are triggered based on a change of state of a particular object, including the object's state in the application. These actions are handled directly from the Silverlight object model.

Event handlers are methods that are executed when a given event is triggered. You can define event handlers either in the XAML markup itself or in managed code. The following exercises will demonstrate how to define event handlers in both ways.

Try It Out: Declaring an Event in XAML

Let's get started by defining event handlers within the XAML markup.

1. Open Visual Studio 2008 and create a new Silverlight project called Ch4_EventHandlers. Allow Visual Studio to create a Web Site project to host the application.

2. When the project is created, you should be looking at the MainPage.xaml file. If you do not see the XAML source, switch to that view so that you can edit the XAML. Within the root Grid of the Silverlight page, add grid row and column definitions (as explained in Chapter 3) to define four rows and two columns, as follows:

```
<Grid x:Name="LayoutRoot" Background="White" ShowGridLines="True">

    <Grid.RowDefinitions>
        <RowDefinition Height="70" />
        <RowDefinition Height="70" />
        <RowDefinition Height="70" />
        <RowDefinition Height="*" />
    </Grid.RowDefinitions>

    <Grid.ColumnDefinitions>
        <ColumnDefinition Width="150" />
        <ColumnDefinition Width="*" />
    </Grid.ColumnDefinitions>
</Grid>
```

3. Next, add a Button control to the upper-left grid cell and a TextBlock control in the upper-right cell.

```
<Grid x:Name="LayoutRoot" Background="White" ShowGridLines="True">

    <Grid.RowDefinitions>
        <RowDefinition Height="70" />
        <RowDefinition Height="70" />
        <RowDefinition Height="70" />
        <RowDefinition Height="*" />
    </Grid.RowDefinitions>

    <Grid.ColumnDefinitions>
        <ColumnDefinition Width="150" />
        <ColumnDefinition Width="*" />
    </Grid.ColumnDefinitions>

    <Button Width="125" Height="35" Content="XAML Event"></Button>
    <TextBlock Text="Click the XAML Event!" Grid.Column="1"
        VerticalAlignment="Center" HorizontalAlignment="Center" />
</Grid>
```

4. Add the Click property to the button. When you type Click=, Visual Studio 2008 will prompt you with the option of automatically creating a new event handler, as shown in Figure 4-2. When the <New Event Handler> option is displayed, simply press Enter, and Visual Studio will complete the Click property, as follows:

```
<Button Width="125" Height="35"
    Content="XAML Event" Click="Button_Click" />
```

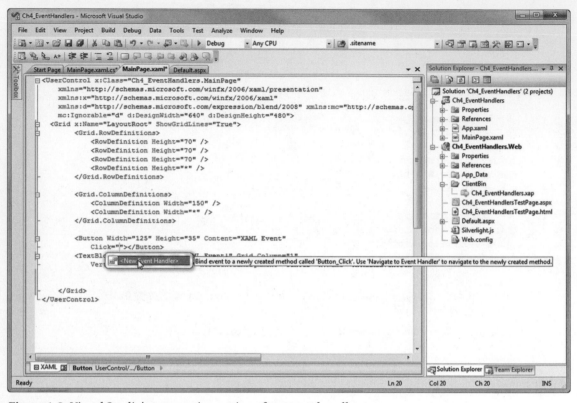

Figure 4-2. Visual Studio's automatic creation of an event handler

In addition, Visual Studio automatically adds an event handler called Button_Click to the code-behind class for the Silverlight application, as follows:

```
public partial class Page : UserControl
{
    public Page()
    {
        InitializeComponent();
    }

    private void Button_Click(object sender, RoutedEventArgs e)
    {

    }
}
```

5. For this example, you will change the Text property within the TextBlock. In order to do this, you first need to give the TextBlock a name so you can access it from the code behind. Add the following code.

```
<TextBlock Text="Click the XAML Event!" Grid.Column="1"
      VerticalAlignment="Center" HorizontalAlignment="Center"
      x:Name="txtXAMLEventText" />
```

6. Now change the Text property of the TextBlock within the Button_Click event, as follows:

```
private void Button_Click(object sender, RoutedEventArgs e)
{
    txtXAMLEventText.Text = "Thank you for clicking!";
}
```

7. Run the application and click the XAML Event button. The text to the right of the button will change to "Thank you for clicking." Figures 4-3 and 4-4 show the application before and after clicking the XAML Event button.

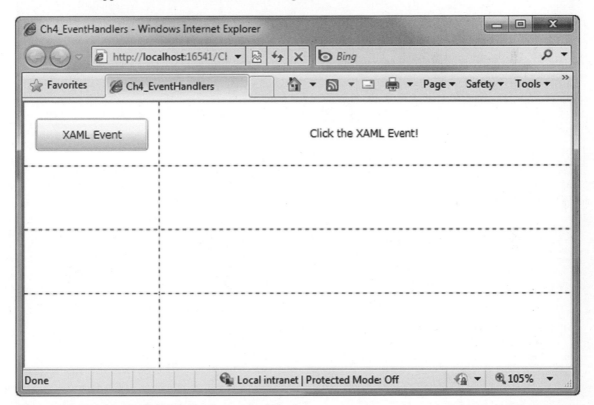

Figure 4-3. The TextBlock before the button is clicked

Now that you have seen how to define an event handler in the XAML markup, in the next exercise, you will continue by adding another event handler using managed code.

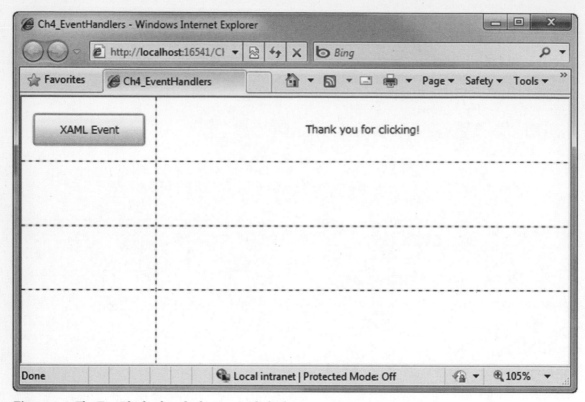

Figure 4-4. *The TextBlock after the button is clicked*

Try It Out: Declaring an Event Handler in Managed Code

Let's continue with the project named Ch4_EventHandlers from the previous exercise. You'll add another button and wire up its event handler using managed code.

1. Add another button and TextBlock in the second row of the Grid, as follows:

```
<Grid x:Name="LayoutRoot" Background="White" ShowGridLines="True">

    <Grid.RowDefinitions>
        <RowDefinition Height="70" />
        <RowDefinition Height="70" />
        <RowDefinition Height="70" />
        <RowDefinition Height="*" />
    </Grid.RowDefinitions>

    <Grid.ColumnDefinitions>
        <ColumnDefinition Width="150" />
        <ColumnDefinition Width="*" />
    </Grid.ColumnDefinitions>
```

```
<Button Width="125" Height="35" Content="XAML Event"
    Click="Button_Click"></Button>
<TextBlock Text="Click the XAML Event!" Grid.Column="1"
    VerticalAlignment="Center" HorizontalAlignment="Center"
    x:Name="txtXAMLEventText" />

<Button Width="125" Height="35" Content="Managed Event"
    Grid.Row="1" ></Button>
<TextBlock Text="Click the Managed Event!" Grid.Column="1"
    VerticalAlignment="Center" HorizontalAlignment="Center"
    Grid.Row="1" />
```
`</Grid>`

2. In order to reference the new `Button` control in managed code, you must give it and the `TextBlock` control a name, as shown in the following snippet:

```
<Button Width="125" Height="35" Content="Managed Event"
    Grid.Row="1" x:Name="btnManaged" ></Button>
<TextBlock Text="Click the Managed Event!" Grid.Column="1"
    VerticalAlignment="Center" HorizontalAlignment="Center"
    Grid.Row="1" x:Name="txtManagedEventText" />
```

Your page should now appear as shown in Figure 4-5.

Figure 4-5. *The updated Silverlight page*

Next, you need to add the event handler. Right-click the Silverlight page and select View Code. This will switch to the code behind of the page.

From here, you will use the standard CLR language-specific syntax for adding event handlers. Since you are using C#, the syntax is to use the += operator and assign it to a new `EventHandler`. Visual Studio 2008 will help you with this.

3. After the InitializeComponent() method call in the Page constructor, start typing "this.btnManaged.Click +=". At this point, Visual Studio will display the message "new RoutedEventHandler(bntManaged_Click); (Press TAB to insert)," as shown in Figure 4-6. Press Tab to complete the event handler definition.

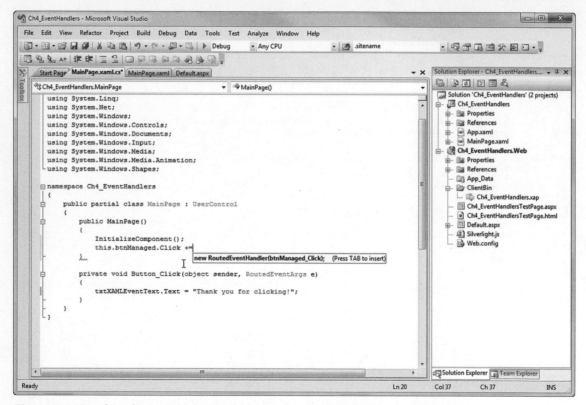

Figure 4-6. *Visual Studio assisting with wiring up an event handler in managed code*

4. Visual Studio will once again prompt you for the name of the event handler. Go ahead and press Tab again to accept the default name. At this point, your source should look like this:

```
namespace Ch4_EventHandlers
{
    public partial class MainPage : UserControl
    {
        public MainPage()
        {
            InitializeComponent();
            this.btnManaged.Click += new RoutedEventHandler(btnManaged_Click);
        }

        void btnManaged_Click(object sender, RoutedEventArgs e)
```

```
    {
        throw new NotImplementedException();
    }

    private void Button_Click(object sender, RoutedEventArgs e)
    {
        txtXAMLEventText.Text = "Thank you for clicking!";
    }
    }
}
```

5. Now the only thing left to do is add the code to the event handler. You will notice that, by default, Visual Studio added code to automatically throw a NotImplementedException. Remove that line and replace it with the following line to change the TextBlock control's text.

```
void btnManaged_Click(object sender, RoutedEventArgs e)
{
    txtManagedEventText.Text = "Thank you for clicking";
}
```

6. Run the application and click the Managed Event button. You will see the text for the second TextBlock is updated to say "Thank you for clicking," as shown in Figure 4-7.

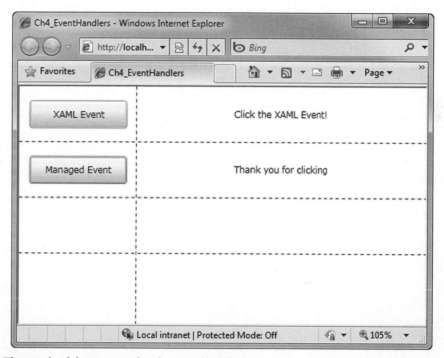

Figure 4-7. The result of the managed code event handler

This exercise demonstrated how to wire up an event handler using C# and managed code.

In the remainder of the chapter, we will take a tour of the more commonly used form controls in Silverlight 2. Let's start off by looking at the Border control.

The Border Control

The Border control provides a way to add a border and background to any one control in Silverlight. Even though a border is applied to only one control, you can always place a border around a StackPanel or Grid, and as a result include many controls within a border.

The syntax to add a Border control to your Silverlight project is very simple, as you can see from the following example:

```
<UserControl x:Class="Ch4_BorderControl.Page"
    xmlns="http://schemas.microsoft.com/winfx/2006/xaml/presentation"
    xmlns:x="http://schemas.microsoft.com/winfx/2006/xaml"
    Width="400" Height="300">
    <Grid x:Name="LayoutRoot" Background="White">
        <Border BorderThickness="2" BorderBrush="Black" Margin="10">
            <StackPanel Margin="10">
                <Button Content="Sample Button" Margin="5" />
                <TextBlock Text="Sample TextBlock" Margin="5" />
                <ListBox Margin="5">
                    <ListBoxItem>
                        <TextBlock Text="ListItem 1" />
                    </ListBoxItem>
                    <ListBoxItem>
                        <TextBlock Text="ListItem 2" />
                    </ListBoxItem>
                    <ListBoxItem>
                        <TextBlock Text="ListItem 3" />
                    </ListBoxItem>
                    <ListBoxItem>
                        <TextBlock Text="ListItem 4" />
                    </ListBoxItem>
                </ListBox>
            </StackPanel>
        </Border>
    </Grid>
</UserControl>
```

Figure 4-8 shows the results.

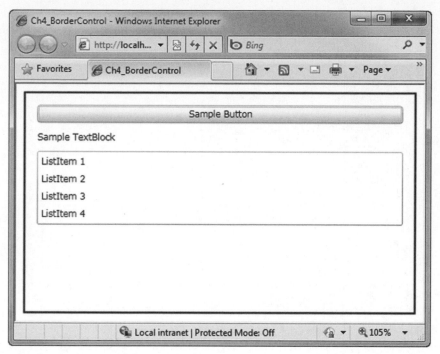

Figure 4-8. *Using the Border control*

Another feature of the Border control is the ability to round the corners of the border using the CornerRadius property. Here is how the preceding example could be modified to provide a Border control with a CornerRadius property of 10.

```
<Border BorderThickness="2" BorderBrush="Black" Margin="10" CornerRadius="10">
 . . .
</Border>
```

The border with rounded corners is shown in Figure 4-9.

You can declare a background color for your border using the Background property. Like the BorderBrush property, the Background property can be set to either a color or a brush type. Here is an example of setting a border with a background color of silver:

```
<Border BorderThickness="2" BorderBrush="Black" Margin="10" CornerRadius="10"
    Background="Silver">
 . . .
</Border>
```

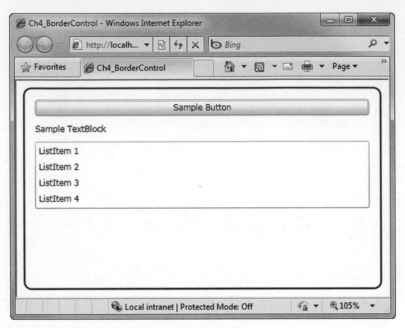

Figure 4-9. *Border control with a CornerRadius property of 10*

Figure 4-10 shows the result of adding the background color.

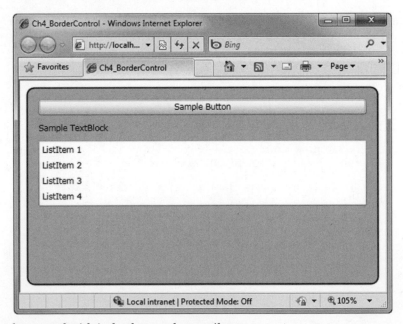

Figure 4-10. *Border control with its background set to silver*

The following is an example of a more complex Border control that contains a gradient for the border and background, by using a Brush object.

```
<Border BorderThickness="2" Margin="10" CornerRadius="10">
    <Border.Background>
        <LinearGradientBrush>
            <LinearGradientBrush.GradientStops>
                <GradientStop Color="Green" Offset="0" />
                <GradientStop Color="White" Offset="1" />
            </LinearGradientBrush.GradientStops>
        </LinearGradientBrush>
    </Border.Background>
    <Border.BorderBrush>
        <LinearGradientBrush>
            <LinearGradientBrush.GradientStops>
                <GradientStop Color="Black" Offset="0" />
                <GradientStop Color="White" Offset="1" />
            </LinearGradientBrush.GradientStops>
        </LinearGradientBrush>
    </Border.BorderBrush>

    <StackPanel Margin="10">
        <Button Content="Sample Button" Margin="5" />
        <TextBlock Text="Sample TextBlock" Margin="5" />
        <ListBox Margin="5">
            <ListBoxItem>
                <TextBlock Text="ListItem 1" />
            </ListBoxItem>
            <ListBoxItem>
                <TextBlock Text="ListItem 2" />
            </ListBoxItem>
            <ListBoxItem>
                <TextBlock Text="ListItem 3" />
            </ListBoxItem>
            <ListBoxItem>
                <TextBlock Text="ListItem 4" />
            </ListBoxItem>
        </ListBox>
    </StackPanel>
</Border>
```

Figure 4-11 shows the border with the gradient applied.

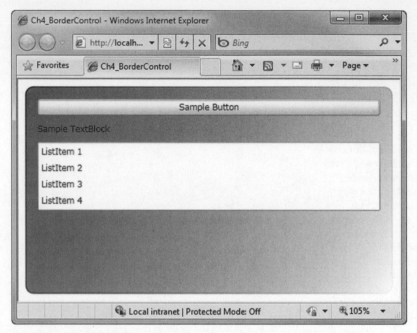

Figure 4-11. Border control with gradient brushes for the border and background

User Input Controls

One of the most common controls in applications is a text box, which is the standard control for collecting basic string input from the user. Also ubiquitous are check boxes and radio buttons, which allow users to select from a list of choices—more than one choice in the case of check boxes, and a single choice in the case of radio buttons. Silverlight 2 provides the TextBox, CheckBox, and RadioButton for these standard controls. The following exercises will also give you a chance to work with the Ellipse and Rectangle controls.

Try It Out: Working with the TextBox Control

This exercise demonstrates the use of the TextBox control in Silverlight 2 by creating a simple application that will request the red, green, and blue values to fill an ellipse with a given color. The resulting application will appear as shown in Figure 4-12.

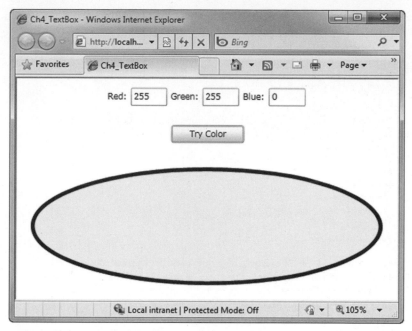

Figure 4-12. Sample application using TextBox controls

1. In Visual Studio 2008, create a new Silverlight application named
   Ch4_TextBox. Allow Visual Studio to create a Web Application project to host
   your application.

2. In the MainPage.xaml file, within the root Grid element, add three
   RowDefinition items, as follows:

```
<UserControl x:Class="Ch4_TextBox.MainPage"
    xmlns="http://schemas.microsoft.com/winfx/2006/xaml/presentation"
    xmlns:x="http://schemas.microsoft.com/winfx/2006/xaml"
    Width="400" Height="300">
    <Grid x:Name="LayoutRoot" Background="White" >

        <Grid.RowDefinitions>
            <RowDefinition Height="50" />
            <RowDefinition Height="50" />
            <RowDefinition />
        </Grid.RowDefinitions>

    </Grid>
</UserControl>
```

Add three TextBox and TextArea controls contained in a horizontal-oriented StackPanel to the first row, a Button control to the second row, and an Ellipse control to the third row. In addition, place a TextBlock in the third row to stack on top of the Ellipse control for error-reporting purposes. Name each of the TextBox controls, as well as the Button control and the TextBlock. These additions are shown in the following code:

```xml
<UserControl x:Class="Ch4_TextBox.MainPage"
    xmlns="http://schemas.microsoft.com/winfx/2006/xaml/presentation"
    xmlns:x="http://schemas.microsoft.com/winfx/2006/xaml"
    Width="400" Height="300">
    <Grid x:Name="LayoutRoot" Background="White" >

        <Grid.RowDefinitions>
            <RowDefinition Height="50" />
            <RowDefinition Height="50" />
            <RowDefinition />
        </Grid.RowDefinitions>

        <StackPanel Orientation="Horizontal" HorizontalAlignment="Center">
            <TextBlock VerticalAlignment="Center" Text="Red:" />
            <TextBox x:Name="txtRed"
                Height="24" Width="50" Margin="5" />
            <TextBlock VerticalAlignment="Center" Text="Green:" />
            <TextBox x:Name="txtGreen"
                Height="24" Width="50" Margin="5" />
            <TextBlock VerticalAlignment="Center" Text="Blue:" />
            <TextBox x:Name="txtBlue"
                Height="24" Width="50" Margin="5" />
        </StackPanel>

        <Button x:Name="btnTry" Content="Try Color"
            Grid.Row="1" Width="100" Height="24" />
        <Ellipse x:Name="ellipse" Grid.Row="2"
            Stroke="Black" StrokeThickness="5" Margin="20" />
        <TextBlock x:Name="lblColor" Grid.Row="2"
            HorizontalAlignment="Center" VerticalAlignment="Center"
            FontSize="20" FontFamily="Arial" FontWeight="Bold"  />

    </Grid>
</UserControl>
```

Now add the Click event to the Button control. Do this in the code behind, as explained earlier in try it out section "Declaring an Event in XAML."

```csharp
namespace Ch4_TextBox
{
    public partial class MainPage : UserControl
    {
        public MainPage()
        {
            InitializeComponent();
```

```
            this.btnTry.Click += new RoutedEventHandler(btnTry_Click);
        }

        void btnTry_Click(object sender, RoutedEventArgs e)
        {

        }
    }
}
```

3. When the button is clicked, the application will change the Fill property of the Ellipse control, which expects a SolidColorBrush. You can create the SolidColorBrush using the Colors.FromArgb() method, which accepts four arguments: one for opacity, and one byte each for the red, green, and blue values. You will get the red, green, and blue values from the TextBox controls using the Text property.

```
void btnTry_Click(object sender, RoutedEventArgs e)
{
        this.ellipse.Fill = new SolidColorBrush(
            Color.FromArgb(
                255,
                byte.Parse(this.txtRed.Text),
                byte.Parse(this.txtGreen.Text),
                byte.Parse(this.txtBlue.Text)
            )
        );
}
```

Since the values for red, green, and blue must be an integer from 0 to 255, you can either validate them using Silverlight validation (refer to Chapter 7) or take the easy way out and just wrap your code in a try/catch block, and then report the error using the TextBlock. You'll go with the latter approach here. To keep things clean, you will make sure the error message is cleared if all works correctly. Here is the updated code:

```
void btnTry_Click(object sender, RoutedEventArgs e)
{
    try
    {
        this.ellipse.Fill = new SolidColorBrush(
            Color.FromArgb(
                255,
                byte.Parse(this.txtRed.Text),
                byte.Parse(this.txtGreen.Text),
                byte.Parse(this.txtBlue.Text)
            )
        );

        this.lblColor.Text = "";
    }
    catch
```

```
    {
        this.lblColor.Text = "Error with R,G,B Values";
    }
}
```

4. Build and run the application to see what you get. Type **255**, **0**, and **0** in the Red, Green, and Blue text boxes, respectively, and then click the Try Color button. You should see the ellipse turn red. Just for the fun of it, if you leave one of the values blank or enter a value other than 0 through 255, you will see the error message.

Now that we have taken a quick look at the TextBox control, let's turn our attention to two other common controls: CheckBox and RadioButton.

Try It Out: Working with the RadioButton and CheckBox Controls

The following exercise will give you a first look at the RadioButton and CheckBox controls. You will build a simple survey, as shown in Figure 4-13.

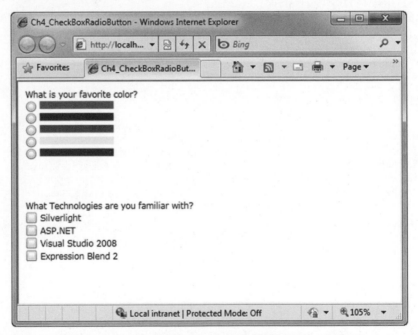

Figure 4-13. Sample application using the RadioButton and CheckBox controls

1. Create a new Silverlight application in Visual Studio 2008 and call it Ch4_CheckBoxRadioButton. Allow Visual Studio to create a Web Site project to host the application.

2. In the MainPage.xaml file, divide the root Grid into two rows. In each row, place a StackPanel with vertical orientation and a Margin property set to 10.

```xml
<UserControl x:Class="Ch4_CheckBoxRadioButton.MainPage"
    xmlns="http://schemas.microsoft.com/winfx/2006/xaml/presentation"
    xmlns:x="http://schemas.microsoft.com/winfx/2006/xaml"
    Width="400" Height="300">

    <Grid x:Name="LayoutRoot" Background="White">

        <Grid.RowDefinitions>
            <RowDefinition />
            <RowDefinition />
        </Grid.RowDefinitions>

        <StackPanel Orientation="Vertical" Grid.Row="0" Margin="10">
        </StackPanel>

        <StackPanel Orientation="Vertical" Grid.Row="1" Margin="10">
        </StackPanel>

    </Grid>

</UserControl>
```

The top row will be used to demonstrate the use of the RadioButton control, and the bottom row will feature the CheckBox control. Let's begin with the RadioButton.

The RadioButton control allows users to select only one selection out of a number of RadioButton controls that share the same group name. This is set using the RadioButton's Grouping property.

Although you could simply type in each of the color choices for the radio buttons as text using the Content property, I thought it would be less boring to use colored rectangles instead. As we discussed earlier in the section "Nesting Controls Within Controls", one of the benefits of Silverlight 2 controls is that you can nest just about anything within the different controls. This is just another example of that flexibility.

3. Place five RadioButton controls in the first StackPanel, each with a Rectangle control of a different color. For the group name, use FavoriteColor. To make the content of the RadioButton controls display as left-justified, set the HorizontalAlignment property to Left for each one. Here is the code:

```xml
<StackPanel Orientation="Vertical" Grid.Row="0" Margin="10">

    <TextBlock Text="What is your favorite color?" />
    <RadioButton HorizontalAlignment="Left" GroupName="FavoriteColor">
        <Rectangle Width="100" Height="10" Fill="Red" />
    </RadioButton>
    <RadioButton HorizontalAlignment="Left" GroupName="FavoriteColor">
        <Rectangle Width="100" Height="10" Fill="Blue" />
    </RadioButton>
    <RadioButton HorizontalAlignment="Left" GroupName="FavoriteColor">
        <Rectangle Width="100" Height="10" Fill="Green" />
    </RadioButton>
    <RadioButton HorizontalAlignment="Left" GroupName="FavoriteColor">
```

```
        <Rectangle Width="100" Height="10" Fill="Yellow" />
    </RadioButton>
    <RadioButton HorizontalAlignment="Left" GroupName="FavoriteColor">
        <Rectangle Width="100" Height="10" Fill="Purple" />
    </RadioButton>
```

```
</StackPanel>
```

Next, do the same for the CheckBox controls in the bottom row, except here, just go the boring route and supply the choices as text. In addition, CheckBox controls are left-justified by default, and they do not need to be grouped. Here is the code for the CheckBox portion:

```
<StackPanel Orientation="Vertical" Grid.Row="1" Margin="10">

    <TextBlock Text="What Technologies are you familiar with?" />
    <CheckBox Content="Silverlight" />
    <CheckBox Content="ASP.NET" />
    <CheckBox Content="Visual Studio 2008" />
    <CheckBox Content="Expression Blend 2" />

</StackPanel>
```

4. Go ahead and run the solution to see the end result as it will appear in the browser. The output is shown in Figure 4-14. Notice that, as you would expect, you are able to select only one radio button at a time, but you can click as many check boxes as you wish.

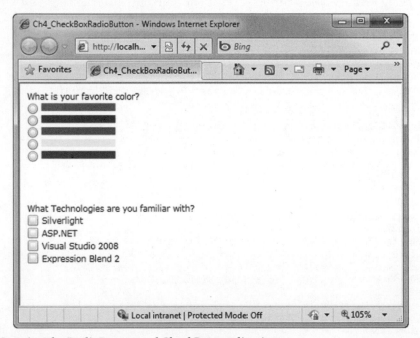

Figure 4-14. Creating the RadioButton and CheckBox application

Extended Controls

When a Silverlight application is deployed, it goes into an .xap file. This file will need to be downloaded by every client that accesses the Silverlight application.

A big benefit of Silverlight is that the size of this .xap file is kept very small. One reason this file can be small is that the most commonly used controls are included in the Silverlight Runtime, which is already present on every machine with Silverlight installed.

However, Silverlight provides a number of controls beyond this commonly used set of controls. These controls are included in two separate assemblies: System.Windows.Controls.dll and System.Windows.Controls.Data.dll. These dynamic link libraries (DLLs) will be included in the application .xap file only if the developer used a control from one of these extended control sets in that application.

Adding an Extended Control

When a developer uses a control from one of the other control libraries, an additional xmlns declaration will be added in the UserControl definition. This xmlns will have a prefix associated with it that will then be used to reference the individual controls.

For example, if you add a DataGrid to your Silverlight application in Visual Studio, your source will appear as follows:

```
<UserControl
    xmlns:data=
     "clr-namespace:System.Windows.Controls;assembly=System.Windows.Controls.Data"
    x:Class="SilverlightApplication1.Page"
    xmlns="http://schemas.microsoft.com/winfx/2006/xaml/presentation"
    xmlns:x="http://schemas.microsoft.com/winfx/2006/xaml"
    Width="400" Height="300">
    <Grid x:Name="LayoutRoot" Background="White">
        <data:DataGrid></data:DataGrid>
    </Grid>
</UserControl>
```

Notice the additional xmlns declaration pointing to the System.Windows.Controls namespace within the System.Windows.Controls.Data assembly.

■ **Tip** To view which controls belong to which assemblies, first create a new Silverlight application and add a DataGrid and GridSplitter to the root Grid. Then select View ~TRA Object Browser from the Visual Studio 2008 main menu. From the Object Browser's Browse drop-down list (in the top-left corner), select My Solution and browse the listing for three assemblies: System.Windows, System.Windows.Controls.Data, and System.Windows.Controls. Within each of those assemblies, drill down to the System.Windows.Controls namespace in order to see all of the controls that reside in that assembly.

Now we will work through an exercise using one of the controls in the System.Windows.Controls assembly.

Try It Out: Using the GridSplitter

One of the controls that resides in the System.Windows.Controls assembly is the GridSplitter. This control provides the ability for a user to change the width of a column or row in an application. If used properly, the GridSplitter can greatly improve the appearance of your application, as well as the user experience. In the following exercise, you will implement a simple GridSplitter.

1. Create a new Silverlight application in Visual Studio 2008 called Ch4_GridSplitter. Allow Visual Studio to create a Web Site project to host the application.

2. In the MainPage.xaml file, divide the root Grid into two columns. The first column should be 150 pixels in width, and the second should take up the remainder of the application. To be able to see what is going on in the grid, set ShowGridLines to True. Also add two TextBlock controls to the application: one in the first column and one in the second column. Your source should appear as follows:

```
<UserControl x:Class="Ch4_GridSplitter.Page"
    xmlns="http://schemas.microsoft.com/winfx/2006/xaml/presentation"
    xmlns:x="http://schemas.microsoft.com/winfx/2006/xaml"
    Width="400" Height="300">
    <Grid x:Name="LayoutRoot" Background="White" ShowGridLines="True">
        <Grid.ColumnDefinitions>
            <ColumnDefinition Width="150" />
            <ColumnDefinition />
        </Grid.ColumnDefinitions>

        <TextBlock Text="Apress, Inc." />
        <TextBlock Grid.Column="1"
            Text="Beginning Silverlight 2 by Robert Lair" />
    </Grid>
</UserControl>
```

At this point, your Silverlight application should look like Figure 4-15.

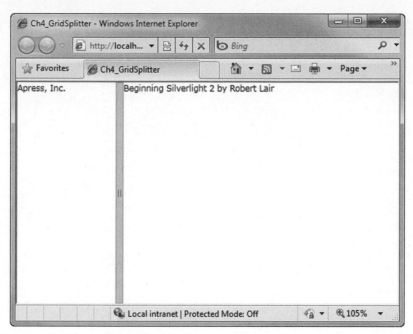

Figure 4-15. The setup for the GridSplitter example

Notice that you cannot see all of the text in the second column. Let's add a GridSplitter control to the application so users can resize the two columns to be able to view all the text in both columns.

3. Within the XAML, place the cursor just below the TextBlock definitions you added. Then, in the Visual Studio Toolbox, double-click the GridSplitter control. This will add the xmlns to the System.Windows.Controls assembly, and it will also add the GridSplitter to the application. Then set the Background property of the GridSplitter to LightGray. The source appears as follows:

```
<Grid x:Name="LayoutRoot" Background="White" ShowGridLines="True">
    <Grid.ColumnDefinitions>
        <ColumnDefinition Width="150" />
        <ColumnDefinition />
    </Grid.ColumnDefinitions>

    <TextBlock Text="Apress, Inc." />
    <TextBlock Grid.Column="1"
        Text="Beginning Silverlight 2 by Robert Lair" />

    <basics:GridSplitter Background="LightGray"></basics:GridSplitter>

</Grid>
```

You no longer need to see the grid lines, so remove the ShowGridLines property.

89

4. Run the application. It should look similar to Figure 4-16. Notice that you can now click and drag the GridSplitter to resize the two Grid columns.

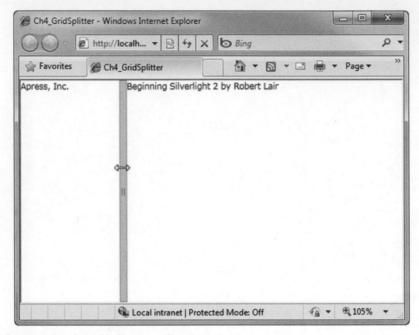

Figure 4-16. *The completed GridSplitter application*

As you can see, it's quite easy to gain the rich functionality of a grid splitter in your application with the Silverlight GridSplitter control.

AutoCompleteBox

The AutoCompleteBox is a new control available in Silverlight 3 that was previously included in the Silverlight Toolkit. Its functionality is nothing new to users, as the auto-complete textboxes have been around for many years. As you start typing in a textbox, a number of items that fit what you are typing are displayed below it. You can then pick an item from list instead of having to finish typing it yourself. The AutoCompleteBox in Silverlight is contained in the Silverlight.Windows.Controls namespace and located in the Silverlight.Windows.Controls.Input assembly. This means in order to use the control, you must add an xmlns entry, as we discussed in the previous section.

```
xmlns:input="clr-namespace:System.Windows.Controls;assembly=System.Windows.Controls.Input"
```

To define an AutoCompleteBox in XAML is no different than defining other controls, such as the Button.

```
<input:AutoCompleteBox  x:Name="Color" />
```

In the code behind, you can then easily add the items that are displayed when the user types by binding a collection to the ItemsSource property. As an example we can bind to a simple string array containing colors.

```
public MainPage()
{
    InitializeComponent();
    this.Color.ItemsSource = new string[]
    {
        "aqua", "azure", "beige", "black", "blue", "brown", "cyan",
        "gold", "gray", "ivory", "lime", "magenta", "maroon", "navy",
        "olive", "orange", "pink", "purple", "red", "tan", "teal",
        "violet", "wheat", "white", "yellow"
    };
}
```

When this control is displayed and a user starts to type in the textbox, you will see that the colors matching the typed text are displayed below in a list, as shown in Figure 4-17.

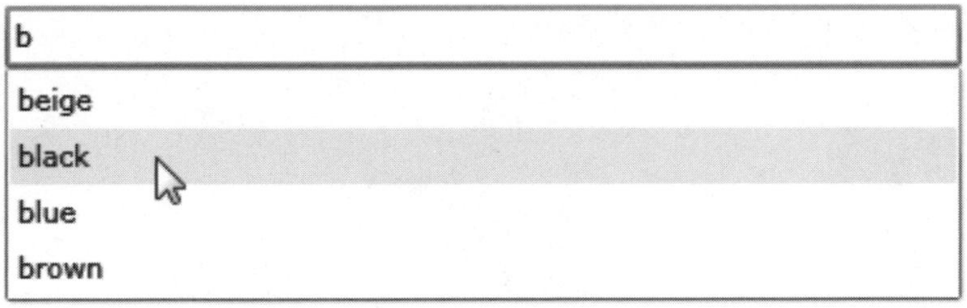

Figure 4-17. *The AutoCompleteBox*

Another thing you may have noticed is that many times when you see an autocomplete textbox, it will automatically complete the text for you as you type. This is controlled by the property IsTextCompletionEnabled, which by default is set to False.

```
<input:AutoCompleteBox x:Name="Color"
    IsTextCompletionEnabled="True"  />
```

Once this property has been set, you will see that the text will automatically complete as you type, as shown in Figure 4-18.

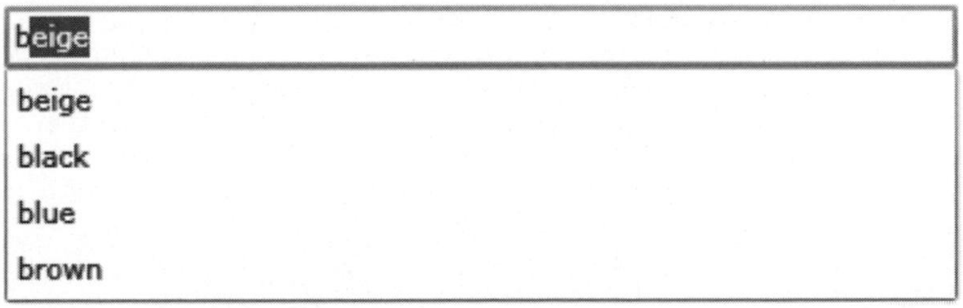

Figure 4-18. *The AutoCompleteBox with IsTextCompletionEnabled set to true*

ViewBox

The ViewBox is another new control available in Silverlight 3 that was previously included in the Silverlight Toolkit. Any content placed within the ViewBox are automatically sized to fill the entire ViewBox. This can be ideal if you want to automatically position things the way you want within the ViewBox. When you need items to change size, instead of changing each item individually, you can simply change the size of the ViewBox and all items are automatically resized to fit. As a quick example of using the ViewBox, consider a simple scenario of an icon and text under the icon, as shown in Figure 4-19.

```
<StackPanel>
    <Image Source="/bookmark.png" />
    <TextBlock Text="Star" FontSize="30"
            HorizontalAlignment="Center" />
</StackPanel>
```

Figure 4-19. *Default icon and text label*

If you want to resize these two items without a ViewBox, you would need to change the size of each item. However, by placing the two items within a ViewBox, all you need to do is resize the ViewBox itself. To demonstrate this, you place the same source for the icon and text in three different sized ViewBox controls.

```
<StackPanel Orientation="Horizontal" HorizontalAlignment="Center">
    <controls:Viewbox Width="40" Margin="5">
        <StackPanel>
            <Image Source="/bookmark.png" />
            <TextBlock Text="Star" FontSize="30"
                    HorizontalAlignment="Center" />
        </StackPanel>
    </controls:Viewbox>
    <controls:Viewbox Width="100" Margin="5">
        <StackPanel>
            <Image Source="/bookmark.png" />
            <TextBlock Text="Star" FontSize="30"
                    HorizontalAlignment="Center" />
        </StackPanel>
    </controls:Viewbox>
    <controls:Viewbox Width="200" Margin="5">
        <StackPanel>
```

```
            <Image Source="/bookmark.png" />
            <TextBlock Text="Star" FontSize="30"
                        HorizontalAlignment="Center" />
        </StackPanel>
    </controls:Viewbox>
</StackPanel>
```

The result of this code is shown in Figure 4-20. As you can see, the icon and text are resized to fit each ViewBox and the proportion and positioning is maintained.

Figure 4-20. *Icon and Text Label within three ViewBox controls*

Modal Windows

A new feature added in Silverlight 3 is the Modal Child Window. This provides functionality to pop up a window that disables the rest of the application until the window is closed, something that is very common in Windows desktop development.The Silverlight Modal window's visual appearance and content is defined by XAML just like everything else in Silverlight, which gives the developer a lot of control.

REFACTORING THE CHILD WINDOW

■ **Note** Out of the box, the Child Window can only operate as a modal dialog, which means that it has to disable the content of the application while it is open. However, some of you may prefer to have the option to allow the child window to behave more like a standard window. Good news! The Child Window was developed out of the Silverlight Toolkit project on CodePlex, and as a result, you have access to the entire source code under MsPL license. You can download the source from http://www.codeplex.com/silverlight and make any modifications you would like, including refactoring the Child Window to not only operate as a modal dialog, but also as a standard floating and draggable window.

To show a modal dialog, you will create an instance of the window and call its Show() method. The Show() method is an asynchronous call, and it returns immediately. Therefore, you will not be able to get the result from the dialog using this method. Instead, you need to handle the Closed event from the window and check the DialogResult there.

```
Confirm confirmDlg = new Confirm();
confirmDlg.Closed += new EventHandler(confirmDlg_Closed);
confirmDlg.Show();

void confirmDlg_Closed(object sender, EventArgs e)
{
    Confirm confirmDlg = (Confirm)sender;
    if (confirmDlg.DialogResult == true)
    {
        // User Clicked OK
    }
    else if (confirmDlg.DialogResult = false)
    {
        // User Clicked Cancel
    }
}
```

Note that the DialogResult is not a standard Boolean type, it is a nullable Boolean. Therefore, there are three possible values: true, false, and null. In C#, a nullable Boolean is specified with the syntax bool?.

```
void confirmDlg_Closed(object sender, EventArgs e)
{
    Confirm confirmDlg = (Confirm)sender;
    bool? Result = confirmDlg.DialogResult;
}
```

In addition to simply getting a true/false/null response from the Child Window, you can implement your own properties that can be passed from the dialog. To retrieve these property values, in the Closed() event handler you cast the sender object to your Child Window's type and simply access the property.

```
void confirmDlg_Closed(object sender, EventArgs e)
{
    Confirm confirmDlg = (Confirm)sender;
    string myPropValue = confirmDlg.MyProperty;
}
```

Let's run through a quick exercise to show how to create a modal popup window in Silverlight.

Try It Out: Using the Modal Child Window

In this exercise, you will create a simple registration form that accepts a first and last name. When the user presses on the button to register button, a modal window will appear with a terms and conditions notice that users must agree to before proceeding. You will not fully code the registration form, but rather you will just send a result to a TextBlock so you can see what is going on. Let's get started.

1. Create a new Silverlight application in Visual Studio 2008 called Ch4_ModalWindow. Allow Visual Studio to create a Web Application project to host the application.

2. In the MainPage.xaml file, divide the root Grid into five rows and two columns. The first four rows should be 40 pixels in height, and the fifth row should take up the remainder of the application. The first column should be 150 pixels in width, and the second should take up the remainder of the application.

```xml
<Grid x:Name="LayoutRoot" Background="White">
    <Grid.RowDefinitions>
        <RowDefinition Height="40" />
        <RowDefinition Height="40" />
        <RowDefinition Height="40" />
        <RowDefinition Height="40" />
        <RowDefinition />
    </Grid.RowDefinitions>

    <Grid.ColumnDefinitions>
        <ColumnDefinition Width="150" />
        <ColumnDefinition />
    </Grid.ColumnDefinitions>
</Grid>
```

3. In the first row, add a TextBlock for a header with the Text "Register for a new Account" that spans both columns. In the second row, add a TextBlock in the first column with the Text "First Name", and add a TextBox in the second column. Add some Margin and Padding to improve the appearance.

```xml
<Grid x:Name="LayoutRoot" Background="White">
    …

    <TextBlock Text="Register for a New Account"
            FontSize="20"
            FontWeight="Bold"
            Margin="5"
            Grid.ColumnSpan="2" />

    <TextBlock Padding="5"
            Margin="5"
            Text="First Name"
            FontSize="12"
            Grid.Row="1" />

    <TextBox Padding="5"
            Margin="5"
```

```
            FontSize="12"
            Grid.Column="1"
            Grid.Row="1" />
```

```
</Grid>
```

4. In the third row, add another TextBlock in the first column with the Text "Last Name", and add a TextBox in the second column. Add some Margin and Padding to improve the appearance. In the fourth row, add a Button to the second column with the Text "Register". Finally, in the fifth row, add a TextBlock to the second column with the Text blank. Name the TextBlock "Result." Your XAML should now appear like the following code, as shown in Figure 4-21.

```
<Grid x:Name="LayoutRoot" Background="White">

    <Grid.RowDefinitions>
        ...
    </Grid.RowDefinitions>

    <Grid.ColumnDefinitions>
        ...
    </Grid.ColumnDefinitions>

    <TextBlock Text="Register for a New Account"
                FontSize="20"
                FontWeight="Bold"
                Margin="5"
                Grid.ColumnSpan="2" />

    <TextBlock Padding="5"
                Margin="5"
                Text="First Name"
                FontSize="12"
                Grid.Row="1" />

    <TextBox Padding="5"
                Margin="5"
                FontSize="12"
                Grid.Column="1"
                Grid.Row="1" />

    <TextBlock Padding="5"
                Margin="5"
                Text="Last Name"
                FontSize="12"
                Grid.Row="2" />

    <TextBox Padding="5"
                Margin="5"
                FontSize="12"
                Grid.Column="1"
                Grid.Row="2" />
```

```xaml
<Button Content="Register"
        Padding="5"
        Margin="5"
        FontSize="12"
        Grid.Column="1"
        Grid.Row="3"
        Click="Button_Click" />

<TextBlock Text=""
           FontSize="14"
           FontWeight="Bold"
           Grid.Column="1"
           Grid.Row="4"
           Margin="5"
           x:Name="Result" />
```

```xaml
</Grid>
```

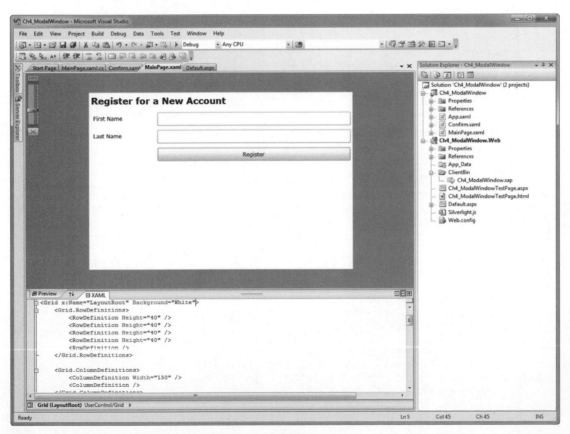

Figure 4-21. *Modal window example with finished XAML layout*

5. Now that you have the main form laid out, you will now turn your attention to the Child Window. To add a Child Window to the project, right click on the Silverlight project (Ch4_ModalWindow) and select Add New Item. From the Add New Item dialog, select Silverlight Child Window and name the window Confirm.xaml, as shown in Figure 4-22.

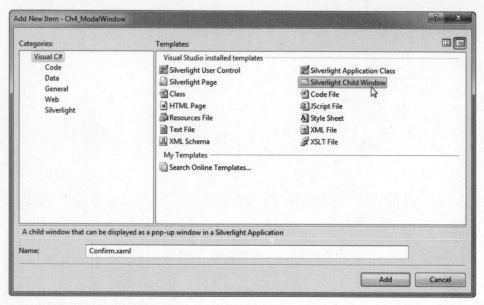

Figure 4-22. Adding a Silverlight Child Window

6. When the Child Window has been added to the project, it will contain the following XAML by default.

```
<controls:ChildWindow x:Class="Ch4_ModalWindow.Confirm"
    …
    Width="400" Height="300"
    Title="Confirm">

  <Grid x:Name="LayoutRoot" Margin="2">

     <Grid.RowDefinitions>
        <RowDefinition />
        <RowDefinition Height="Auto" />
     </Grid.RowDefinitions>

     <Button x:Name="CancelButton"
             Content="Cancel" Click="CancelButton_Click"
             Width="75" Height="23" HorizontalAlignment="Right"
             Margin="0,12,0,0" Grid.Row="1" />

     <Button x:Name="OKButton"
             Content="OK" Click="OKButton_Click"
```

```
                    Width="75" Height="23" HorizontalAlignment="Right"
                    Margin="0,12,79,0" Grid.Row="1" />

    </Grid>

</controls:ChildWindow>
```

Notice that there are already two buttons added for you, one for Cancel and one for OK. If you look at the code behind for the window, you will also see that some code is already present.

```
namespace Ch4_ModalWindow
{
    public partial class Confirm : ChildWindow
    {
        public Confirm()
        {
            InitializeComponent();
        }

        private void OKButton_Click(object sender, RoutedEventArgs e)
        {
            this.DialogResult = true;
        }

        private void CancelButton_Click(object sender, RoutedEventArgs e)
        {
            this.DialogResult = false;
        }
    }
}
```

Two event handlers, one for each button, have been wired up, however you will notice that the only code is simply setting the DialogResult property on the window. In the property setter, it will automatically set the response and will execute the dialog's Close() method, so that is all the code you need.

7. For now, you will leave the Child Window as-is, but you need to call it from the Silverlight application. Open the MainPage.xaml.cs code behind file. Add the Button_Click event as well the code to create an instance of the Child Window and execute the Show() method.

```
private void Button_Click(object sender, RoutedEventArgs e)
{
    Confirm confirmDlg = new Confirm();
    confirmDlg.Show();
}
```

Go ahead and run the application and press the Register button. You will see that the Child Window appears, as shown in Figure 4-23. You can drag the window, but notice that the main user interface for your application is inaccessible. Click OK or Cancel and you will notice that the Child Window closes and the application's user interface is once again functioning.

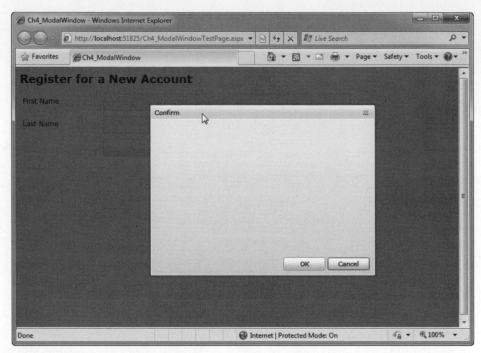

Figure 4-23. *The default Child Window*

8. Very cool, but let's not stop there. You can now modify the Child Window to show that its content can be customized however you like by editing the window's XAML. To do this, open the Confirm.xaml file in XAML design mode. Change the Title of the window to "Terms and Conditions." Let's also change the size of the Window to be 200 pixels in height. In addition, you will change the Text of the two button to read "I Accept" and "I Do Not Accept." Because you are changing the text, you must also adjust the width of the buttons and the margins. (Note that you can just as easily put these two buttons in a Horizontal StackPanel instead of spacing them using Margins.) Finally, you will add two TextBlock controls to the first row of the root Grid for the header, and one below it for the terms and conditions text. Your updated XAML should now appear similar to the following.

```
<Grid x:Name="LayoutRoot" Margin="2">

    <Grid.RowDefinitions>
        <RowDefinition />
        <RowDefinition Height="Auto" />
    </Grid.RowDefinitions>

    <StackPanel>

        <TextBlock Text="Please Accept the Terms and Conditions to Continue"
                FontWeight="Bold" FontSize="12" />
```

```
    <TextBlock Text="These are the terms and conditions..." />

</StackPanel>

<Button x:Name="CancelButton"
        Content="I Do Not Accept" Click="CancelButton_Click"
        Width="125"
        Height="23" HorizontalAlignment="Right"
        Margin="0,12,0,0" Grid.Row="1" />

<Button x:Name="OKButton"
        Content="I Accept" Click="OKButton_Click"
        Width="100"
        Height="23" HorizontalAlignment="Right"
        Margin="0,12,134,0" Grid.Row="1" />

</Grid>
```

9. Go ahead and run the application again and press the Register button to open the Child Window. Notice that the content changes are reflected, as shown in Figure 4-24. Keep in mind that the content of these window controls are completely customizable with XAML. You can add whatever controls you wish with any layout you wish.

Figure 4-24. The modified Child Window

101

10. Now let's add code to retrieve results from the dialog. Open the MainPage.xaml.cs file and within the Button_Click event handler, wire up another event handler for the Child Window's Closed() event. In this new event handler, you need to get the Child Window's instance, which is sent to the handler in the sender object. Once you have the window's instance, you can retrieve the DialogResult property, which will contain either true, false, or null.

```
private void Button_Click(object sender, RoutedEventArgs e)
{
    Confirm confirmDlg = new Confirm();
    confirmDlg.Closed += new EventHandler(confirmDlg_Closed);
    confirmDlg.Show();
}

void confirmDlg_Closed(object sender, EventArgs e)
{
    Confirm confirmDlg = (Confirm)sender;

    if (confirmDlg.DialogResult == true)
    {
        this.Result.Text = "Terms and Conditions Accepted";
    }
    else if (confirmDlg.DialogResult == false)
    {
        this.Result.Text = "Terms and Conditions Not Accepted";
    }
}
```

11. Run the application. Press the Register button to display the Child Window. Press the I Accept button from the Child Window. You will see that the Result TextBlock is updated to read "Terms and Conditions Accepted," as shown in Figure 4-25.

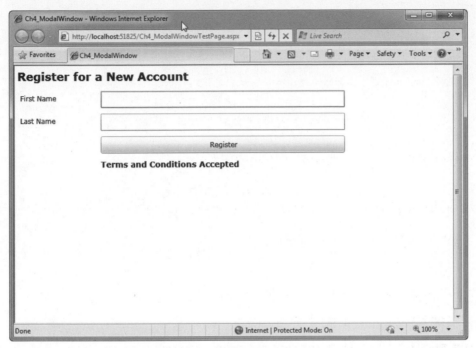

Figure 4-25. *Retrieving the DialogResult from a Child Window*

Summary

In this chapter, you took a brief look at some of the common form controls that are provided with Silverlight. In addition, you looked at how to use a modal window in Silverlight, a feature new to Silverlight 3. The chapter was meant only as an introduction to the controls. You will be looking at these controls in more advanced capacities in the upcoming chapters.

In the next chapter, you will look at the Silverlight list controls: ListBox and DataGrid.

CHAPTER 5

Data Binding and Silverlight List Controls

The previous chapter focused on the form controls contained in Silverlight. In this chapter, you will look at two controls that are made to display lists of data: the `ListBox` and `DataGrid`. These controls are typically bound to data through a technique known as *data binding*, which I'll explore first.

Data Binding

Through data binding, UI elements (called *targets*) are "bound" to data from a data source (called the *source*), as illustrated in Figure 5-1. When the data sources change, the UI elements bound to those data sources update automatically to reflect the changes. The data can come from different types of sources, and the target can be just about any UI element, including standard Silverlight controls.

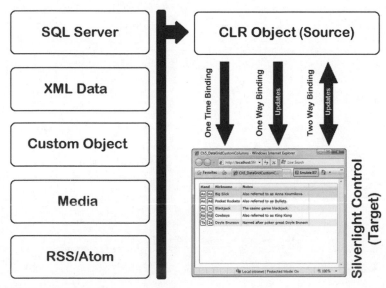

Figure 5-1. *Data binding in Silverlight*

Data binding simplifies application development. Since changes are reflected automatically, you do not need to manually update the UI elements. Also, by using data binding, you are able to separate the UI from the data in your application, which allows for a cleaner UI and easier maintenance.

The Binding Class

Data binding in Silverlight is accomplished by using the Binding class. The Binding class has two components—the source and target—and a property that defines the way the two are bound, called the *binding mode*. The source is the data that is to be bound, the target is a property of the control that the data is to be bound to, and the mode defines how the data is passed between the source and the target (one-way, one-time, or two-way). You'll see how this works in the upcoming exercise.

To define the binding of a control's property, you use XAML markup extensions, such as {Binding *<path>*}. For example, to bind the Text property of a TextBox to a data source's FirstName element, you would use the following XAML:

```
<TextBox Text="{Binding FirstName }" />
```

Try It Out: Simple Data Binding in Silverlight

To help explain data binding in Silverlight, let's build a very simple application. The application will include a Book object that contains two properties: Title and ISBN. These properties will be bound to two TextBox controls. Figure 5-2 shows the end result of the example.

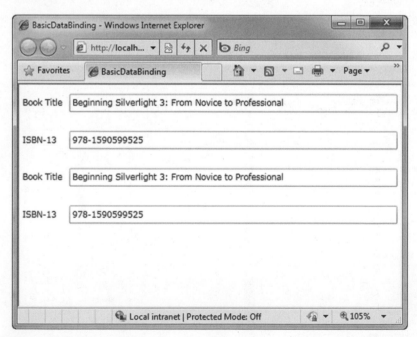

Figure 5-2. Simple data binding example

1. Create a new Silverlight application in Visual Studio 2008. Name the project BasicDataBinding, and allow Visual Studio to create a Web Site project to host your application.

2. Edit the MainPage.xaml file to define two columns and six grid rows. Place a TextBlock in each row in column 1 and a TextBox in each row in column 2. Also add some margins and some alignment assignments to improve the layout. The code for the page follows:

```
<UserControl x:Class="BasicDataBinding.MainPage"
    xmlns="http://schemas.microsoft.com/winfx/2006/xaml/presentation"
    xmlns:x="http://schemas.microsoft.com/winfx/2006/xaml"
    Width="400" Height="300">
    <Grid x:Name="LayoutRoot" Background="White">

        <Grid.ColumnDefinitions>
            <ColumnDefinition Width="Auto" />
            <ColumnDefinition />
        </Grid.ColumnDefinitions>
        <Grid.RowDefinitions>
            <RowDefinition />
            <RowDefinition />
            <RowDefinition />
            <RowDefinition />
            <RowDefinition />
            <RowDefinition />
        </Grid.RowDefinitions>

        <TextBlock Text="Book Title"
            VerticalAlignment="Center"
            Margin="5" />
        <TextBlock Text="ISBN-13"
            VerticalAlignment="Center"
            Margin="5"
            Grid.Row="1" />

        <TextBox Text="{Binding Title}"
            Height="24"
            Margin="5"
            Grid.Column="1" />
        <TextBox Text="{Binding ISBN}"
            Height="24"
            Margin="5"
            Grid.Column="1" Grid.Row="1" />

        <TextBlock Text="Book Title"
            VerticalAlignment="Center"
            Margin="5"
            Grid.Row="2" />
        <TextBlock Text="ISBN-13"
            VerticalAlignment="Center"
```

```
            Margin="5"
            Grid.Row="3" />

    <TextBox Text="{Binding Title}"
            Height="24"
            Margin="5"
            Grid.Column="1" Grid.Row="2" />
    <TextBox Text="{Binding ISBN}"
            Height="24"
            Margin="5"
            Grid.Column="1" Grid.Row="3" />

    </Grid>
</UserControl>
```

3. Next, edit the code behind, `MainPage.xaml.cs`. Add a Loaded event handler for the application, which will fire when the application is loaded by the client. This is accomplished with the following source code:

```
public partial class MainPage : UserControl
{
    public MainPage()
    {
        InitializeComponent();
        this.Loaded += new RoutedEventHandler(Page_Loaded);
    }

    void Page_Loaded(object sender, RoutedEventArgs e)
    {

    }
}
```

Now you need to add a class to define a `Book` object. Below the `MainPage` class, add the following class definition:

```
namespace BasicDataBinding
{
    public partial class MainPage : UserControl
    {
        public MainPage()
        {
            InitializeComponent();
            this.Loaded += new RoutedEventHandler(Page_Loaded);
        }

        void Page_Loaded(object sender, RoutedEventArgs e)
        {

        }
    }

    public class Book
```

```
{
    public string Title { get; set; }
    public string ISBN { get; set; }
}
}
```

4. Now that you have Book defined, you need to create an instance of Book and set it to the LayoutRoot's DataContext, as follows:

```
void Page_Loaded(object sender, RoutedEventArgs e)
{
    Book b = new Book() {
        Title = "Beginning Silverlight 3: From Novice to Professional",
        ISBN = "978-1590599525" };

    this.LayoutRoot.DataContext = b;
}
```

When you set up binding definitions for different controls, the controls do not know where they are going to get their data. The DataContext property sets the data context for a control that is participating in data binding. The DataContext property can be set directly on the control. If a given control does not have a DataContext property specified, it will look to its parent for its data context. The nice thing about this model is that if you look above in the XAML for the page, you will see little indication of where the controls are getting their data. This provides an extreme level of code separation, allowing designers to design XAML UIs and developers to work alongside the designers, defining the specifics of how the controls are bound to their data sources.

5. At this point, you can go ahead and start debugging the application. If all goes well, you will see the four text boxes populated with the data from the Book's instance (see Figure 5-2).

6. With the application running, change the book title in the first text box to just "Beginning Silverlight," by removing the "From Novice to Professional."

You might expect that, since the third text box is bound to the same data, it will automatically update to reflect this change. However, a couple of things need to be done to get this type of two-way binding to work.

One problem is that, currently, the Book class does not support notifying bound clients of changes to its properties. In other words, when a property changes in Book, the class will not notify the TextBox instances that are bound to the class of the change. You could take care of this by creating a change event for each property. This is far from ideal; fortunately, there is an interface that a class can implement that handles this for you. This interface is known as INotifyPropertyChanged. Let's use it.

7. Modify the Book class definition to inherit from INotifyPropertyChanged. Notice that when you inherit from INotifyPropertyChanged, you need to add using System.ComponentModel. Luckily, Visual Studio will help you with this, as shown in Figure 5-3.

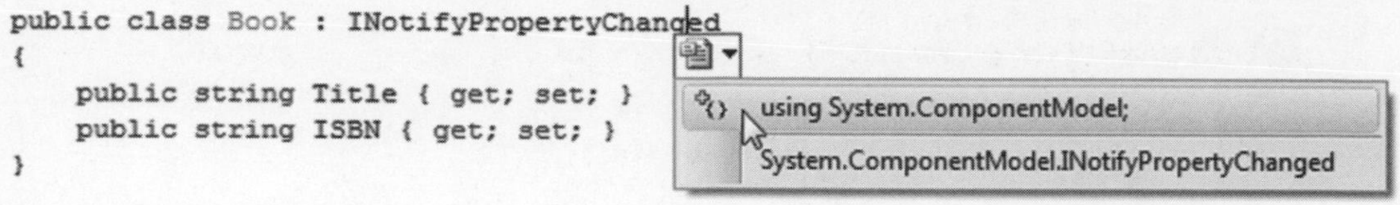

```
public class Book : INotifyPropertyChanged
{
    public string Title { get; set; }
    public string ISBN { get; set; }
}
```

using System.ComponentModel;

System.ComponentModel.INotifyPropertyChanged

Figure 5-3. Visual Studio assists when you need to add the System.ComponentModel namespace.

Next, you can let Visual Studio do some more work for you. After adding the using System.ComponentModel statement, right-click INotifyPropertyChanged and choose the Explicitly implement interface INotifyPropertyChanged option, as shown in Figure 5-4.

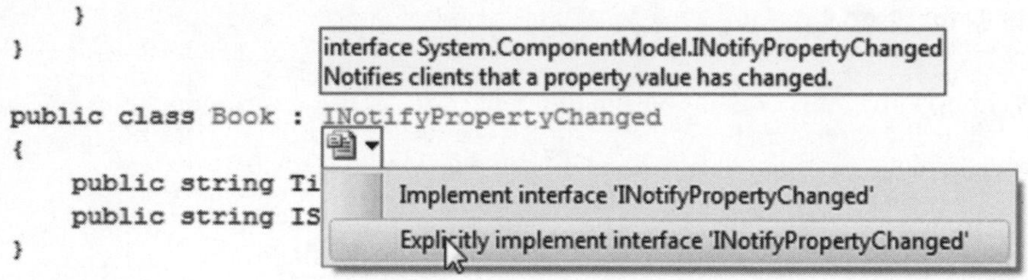

```
        }
    }

    public class Book : INotifyPropertyChanged
    {
        public string Ti
        public string IS
    }
```

interface System.ComponentModel.INotifyPropertyChanged
Notifies clients that a property value has changed.

Implement interface 'INotifyPropertyChanged'

Explicitly implement interface 'INotifyPropertyChanged'

Figure 5-4. Visual Studio also assists in implementing the INotifiyPropertyChanged interface.

Now Visual Studio has added a new public event to your class:

```
public class Book : INotifyPropertyChanged
{
    public string Title { get; set; }
    public string ISBN { get; set; }

    #region INotifyPropertyChanged Members

    public event PropertyChangedEventHandler PropertyChanged;

    #endregion
}
```

8. Next, you need to create a convenience method that will fire the PropertyChanged event. Call it FirePropertyChanged, as shown in the following code.

```
public class Book : INotifyPropertyChanged
{
    public string Title { get; set; }
    public string ISBN { get; set; }

    #region INotifyPropertyChanged Members

    void FirePropertyChanged(string property)
```

```
    {
        if (PropertyChanged != null)
        {
            PropertyChanged(this,
                new PropertyChangedEventArgs(property));
        }
    }

    public event PropertyChangedEventHandler PropertyChanged;

    #endregion
}
```

9. Now you need to extend the simplified properties by adding private members and full get/set definitions to define the get and set operations, as shown in the following code. The get is just like a normal get operation, where you simply return the internal member value. For the set, you first set the internal member value, and then call the FirePropertyChanged method, passing it the name of the property.

```
public class Book : INotifyPropertyChanged
{
    private string _title;
    private string _isbn;

    public string Title
    {
        get
        {
            return _title;
        }
        set
        {
            _title = value;
            FirePropertyChanged("Title");
        }
    }

    public string ISBN
    {
        get
        {
            return _isbn;
        }
        set
        {
            _isbn = value;
            FirePropertyChanged("ISBN");
        }
    }
```

```
#region INotifyPropertyChanged Members

void FirePropertyChanged(string property)
{
    if (PropertyChanged != null)
    {
        PropertyChanged(this,
            new PropertyChangedEventArgs(property));
    }
}

public event PropertyChangedEventHandler PropertyChanged;

#endregion
}
```

With this completed, your class is set up to notify bound clients of changes to the Title and ISBN properties. But you still need to take one more step. By default, when you bind a source to a target, the BindingMode is set to OneWay binding, which means that the source will send the data to the target, but the target will not send data changes back to the source. In order to get the target to update the source, you need to implement two-way (TwoWay) binding.

■ **Note** Earlier, I mentioned that there are three options for BindingMode. The third option is OneTime binding. In this mode, the values are sent to the target control property when the object is set to the DataContext. However, the values of the target property are not updated when the source value changes.

---

10. To change to two-way binding, add the Mode=TwoWay parameter when defining the {Binding} on a control, as follows:

```
<TextBlock Text="Book Title"
    VerticalAlignment="Center"
    Margin="5" />
<TextBlock Text="ISBN-13"
    VerticalAlignment="Center"
    Margin="5"
    Grid.Row="1" />

<TextBox Text="{Binding Title, Mode=TwoWay}"
    Height="24"
    Margin="5"
    Grid.Column="1" />
<TextBox Text="{Binding ISBN, Mode=TwoWay }"
    Height="24"
    Margin="5"
    Grid.Column="1" Grid.Row="1" />

<TextBlock Text="Book Title"
```

```
    VerticalAlignment="Center"
    Margin="5"
    Grid.Row="2" />
<TextBlock Text="ISBN-13"
    VerticalAlignment="Center"
    Margin="5"
    Grid.Row="3" />

<TextBox Text="{Binding Title, Mode=TwoWay }"
    Height="24"
    Margin="5"
    Grid.Column="1" Grid.Row="2" />
<TextBox Text="{Binding ISBN, Mode=TwoWay }"
    Height="24"
    Margin="5"
    Grid.Column="1" Grid.Row="3" />
```

11. Rebuild and run your application. Update any of the fields, and leave the focus on the control. You'll see that the two-way binding is triggered, and the corresponding field is also updated, as shown in Figure 5-5.

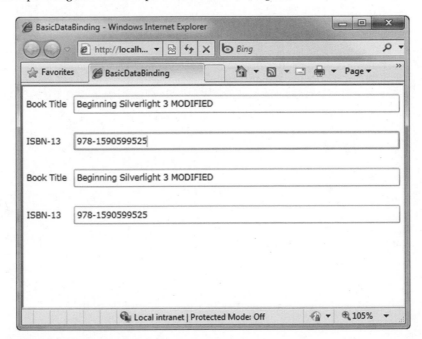

Figure 5-5. *Two-way binding in action*

Congratulations! You have just created a Silverlight application that allows for two-way data binding. We will now move on to look at data binding lists of data to the two list controls provided in Silverlight: DataGrid and ListBox.

Element to Element Binding

In addition to binding to data, elements can be bound directly to other elements, which can significantly improve the readability and efficiency of your code. The syntax for binding to an element is very similar to binding to a data item, the only difference is that in the binding an ElementName is specified, which is very much like setting the ItemsSource to the Element. As an example, if you wanted to bind the IsEnabled property of a control to a checkbox's IsChecked property. Assuming the checkbox is named EnableButton, the binding syntax would be the following.

```
IsEnabled="{Binding IsChecked, Mode=OneWay, ElementName=EnableButton}"
```

Notice that the binding is the same as it would be when binding to a data source, except that we have added the ElementName=EnableButton. Let's try this out in an exercise.

Try It Out: Element to Element Binding

To help explain element to element binding in Silverlight, let's build a very simple application. The application will include a button and a checkbox. When the checkbox is checked, the button is enabled, when the checkbox is unchecked, the button is disabled. Let's get started.

1. Create a new Silverlight application in Visual Studio 2008. Name the project Ch5_ElementBinding, and allow Visual Studio to create a Web Site project to host your application.

2. Edit the MainPage.xaml file to add a StackPanel to the root Grid. Place a ToggleButton and CheckBox named EnableButton within that StackPanel so the ToggleButton appears above the CheckBox. Add a margin of 20 on the StackPanel and 5 on the ToggleButton and CheckBox to add some spacing between the controls. The code for the page follows:

```
<Grid x:Name="LayoutRoot" Background="White">
    <StackPanel Margin="20">

        <ToggleButton
            Margin="5" Content="Click to Toggle" />

        <CheckBox
            x:Name="EnableButton" IsChecked="true"
            Margin="5" Content="Enable Button" />

    </StackPanel>
</Grid>
```

3. Next, we need to bind the ToggleButton's IsEnabled property to the CheckBox's IsChecked property. We will do this with one way binding as described earlier in this chapter, and we will set the ElementName to EnableButton, which is the name we gave our CheckBox. The updated source code should now look like the following.

```
<Grid x:Name="LayoutRoot" Background="White">
    <StackPanel Margin="20">

        <ToggleButton
            Margin="5" Content="Click to Toggle"
```

```
    IsEnabled="{Binding IsChecked, Mode=OneWay,
        ElementName=EnableButton}" />

<CheckBox
    x:Name="EnableButton" IsChecked="true"
    Margin="5" Content="Enable Button" />

</StackPanel>
</Grid>
```

4. That is it! No coding is required for this demo. Run the sample and will see that the `ToggleButton` is enabled, as shown in Figure 5-6.

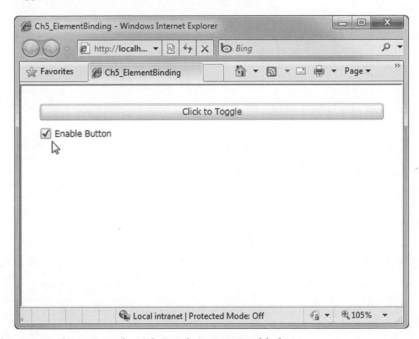

Figure 5-6. *Element Binding example with Toggle Button Enabled*

5. Now press uncheck the Enable Button checkbox and you will see that the `ToggleButton` is no longer enabled, as shown in Figure 5-7.

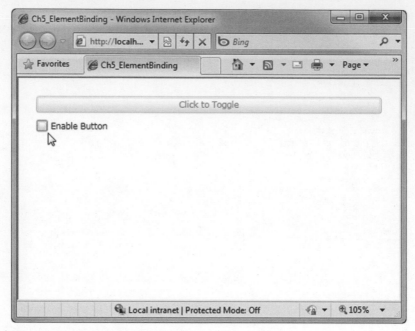

Figure 5-7. *Element Binding Example with Toggle Button Disabled*

The DataGrid Control

The data grid type of control has been around for ages and has been the primary choice for developers who need to display large amounts of data. The DataGrid control provided by Silverlight is not just a standard data grid, however. It contains a great deal of rich user functionality that, in the past, has been present only in third-party data grid components. For example, the Silverlight DataGrid handles resizing and reordering of grid columns.

Figure 5-8 shows an example of a very simple DataGrid, where the columns were automatically generated. Notice how the column titled Male is a check box. The DataGrid control has built-in intelligence to automatically show Boolean data types as check box cells.

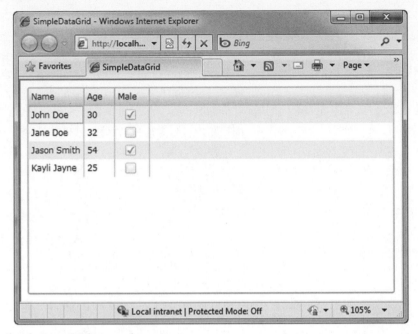

Figure 5-8. *A simple DataGrid example*

Try It Out: Building a Simple DataGrid

Let's run through a simple DataGrid example.

1.   Create a new Silverlight application in Visual Studio 2008. Name the project SimpleDataGrid, and have Visual Studio create a hosting web site application for you.

2.   Add the DataGrid to your application. To do this, simply add the DataGrid to the root Grid in your XAML, and set the Margin property to 10 to get some spacing around the grid. In addition, give the DataGrid the name grid. Note that, by default, the Grid's AutoGenerateColumns property is set to true. If you were going to define the columns manually, you would want to set this property to false. However, since you want the grid to create the columns automatically, you can simply omit the property. The DataGrid definition follows:

```
<Grid x:Name="LayoutRoot" Background="White">
    <data:DataGrid x:Name="grid" Margin="10" />
</Grid>
```

■ **Note** Why use <data:DataGrid>? As discussed in Chapter 4, the DataGrid is contained in an assembly called System.Windows.Controls.Data, which is not added to Silverlight applications by default. This way, if your application does not need any of the extended controls, the file size of your Silverlight application can be smaller. However, in order to add a DataGrid to your application, you need to reference the new assembly and add an xmlns reference to the assembly in the UserControl definition. As you might expect by now, Visual Studio can do all the work for you. To use this functionality in Visual Studio, drag the DataGrid control from the Toolbox to add it to your application. Visual Studio will add a new xmlns reference in the UserControl at the top of the .xaml page called data, which references the System.Windows.Controls.Data assembly. For the DataGrid, you will see the xml namespace referenced in the DataGrid definition <data:DataGrid>.

3. Next, build the class that will be bound to the DataGrid. Call the class GridData for simplicity, and give it three properties: Name (string), Age (int), and Male (Boolean). Also for simplicity, create a static method that will return an ObservableCollection containing some sample data that will be bound to the grid. In addition, define the class directly in the MainPage.xaml.cs file. This is not really a good idea in the real world, but for the sake of an example, it will work just fine. Ideally, you will want to define your classes in separate files or even in completely separate projects and assemblies. The code for the GridData class follows:

```
namespace SimpleDataGrid
{
    public partial class MainPage : UserControl
    {
        public MainPage()
        {
            InitializeComponent();
        }
    }

    public class GridData
    {
        public string Name { get; set; }
        public int Age { get; set; }
        public bool Male { get; set; }

        public static ObservableCollection<GridData> GetData()
        {
            ObservableCollection<GridData> data =
                new ObservableCollection<GridData>();

            data.Add(new GridData() {
                Name = "John Doe",
                Age = 30,
                Male = true });
```

```
        data.Add(new GridData() {
            Name = "Jane Doe",
            Age = 32,
            Male = false});

        data.Add(new GridData() {
            Name = "Jason Smith",
            Age = 54,
            Male = true });

        data.Add(new GridData() {
            Name = "Kayli Jayne",
            Age = 25,
            Male = false });

        return data;
        }
    }
}
```

■ **Note** When you are binding a collection of data to a DataGrid or ListBox, you may be tempted to use the List generic class. The problem with using the List class is that it does not have built-in change notifications for the collection. In order to bind a DataGrid and ListBox to dynamic data that will be updated, you should use the ObservableCollection generic class. The ObservableCollection class represents a collection of dynamic data that provides built-in notification when items in the collection are added, removed, or refreshed.

4. Now that you have the XAML and the class defined, you can wire them up. To do this, first create an event handler for the Loaded event of the page, as follows:

```
public partial class MainPage : UserControl
{
    public MainPage()
    {
        InitializeComponent();
        this.Loaded += new RoutedEventHandler(Page_Loaded);
    }

    void Page_Loaded(object sender, RoutedEventArgs e)
    {

    }
}
```

5. When the page is loaded, you want to call GetData() from the GridData class and bind that to the DataGrid's ItemsSource property, as follows:

```csharp
public partial class MainPage : UserControl
{
    public MainPage()
    {
        InitializeComponent();
        this.Loaded += new RoutedEventHandler(Page_Loaded);
    }

    void Page_Loaded(object sender, RoutedEventArgs e)
    {
        this.grid.ItemsSource = GridData.GetData();
    }
}
```

6. Build and run the application. If all is well, you should see the DataGrid displayed (see Figure 5-6).

Let's take a few moments and play around with this DataGrid to explore some of its features. First of all, if you click any of the column headers, you will notice that sorting is automatically available, as shown in Figure 5-9.

Next, if you place your cursor at the edge of one of the columns, you can use the mouse to click and drag the column's edge to resize the column, as shown in Figure 5-10. Again, this functionality is provided for free with the DataGrid's rich client-side functionality.

Finally, if you click and hold the mouse on one of the column headers, then drag it left or right to another column header's edge, you will see a little red triangle appear above the columns. For instance, click and drag the Name column so the little red triangle appears to the far right, as shown in Figure 5-11. When the red triangle is where you want it, release the mouse, and you will see that the Name column now appears as the last column in the DataGrid.

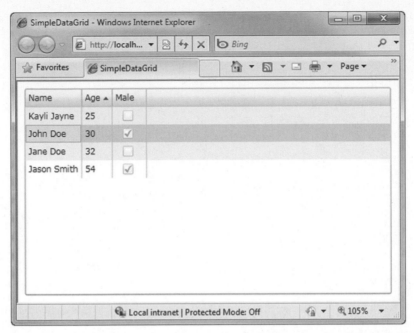

Figure 5-9. *Sorting in the DataGrid*

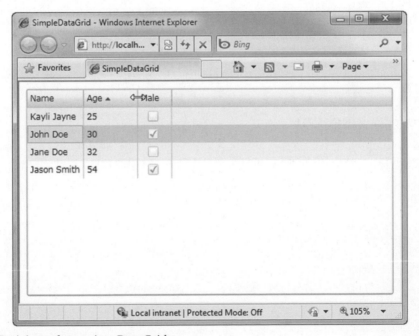

Figure 5-10. *Resizing columns in a DataGrid*

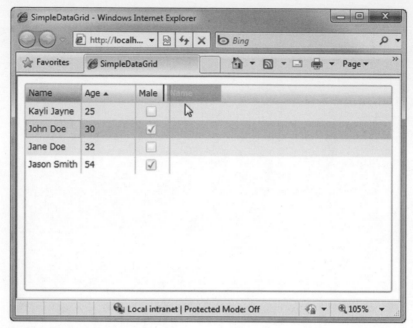

Figure 5-11. Column reordering in action

You'll agree that this is pretty nice out-of-the-box functionality for simply defining a `DataGrid` with this code:

```
<data:DataGrid x:Name="grid" Margin="10" />
```

Now that you have implemented a simple `DataGrid` example, let's explore some of the additional options available.

The Columns Collection

In the previous example, you allowed the `DataGrid` to automatically generate columns based on the data to which it was bound. This is not a new concept—it has been around in data grid components since the initial release of ASP.NET. But what if you want to have some additional control over the columns that are created in your `DataGrid`? What if you want to add a column that contains some more complex information, such as an image? You can do this by first setting the `AutoGenerateColumns` property on the grid to `false`. Then you need to generate the columns manually.

Columns are defined in a `DataGrid` using the `Columns` collection. The following is an example of setting the `Columns` collection in XAML. Notice that it sets the `AutogenerateColumns` property to `False`. If you neglect to do this, you will get all of the autogenerated columns in addition to the columns you define within the `Columns` collection.

```
<my:DataGrid x:Name="grid" Margin="10" AutoGenerateColumns="False">
    <my:DataGrid.Columns>

    </my:DataGrid.Columns>
</my:DataGrid>
```

You can place three types of columns within a Columns collection: a text column (DataGridTextColumn), a check box column (DataGridCheckBoxColumn), and a template column (DataGridTemplateColumn). All of the column types inherit from type DataGridColumn. A number of notable properties apply to all three column types, as shown in Table 5-1.

Table 5-1. DataGridColumn properties

Property	Description
CanUserReorder	Turns on and off the ability for the user to drag columns to reorder them
CanUserResize	Turns on or off the ability for the user to resize the column's width with the mouse
DisplayIndex	Determines the order in which the column appears in the DataGrid
Header	Defines the content of the column's header
IsReadOnly	Determines if the column can be edited by the user
MaxWidth	Sets the maximum column width in pixels
MinWidth	Sets the minimum column width in pixels
Visibility	Determines whether or not the column will be visible to the user
Width	Sets the width of the column, or can be set to automatic sizing mode

DataGridTextColumn

The DataGridTextColumn defines a column in your grid for plain text. This is the equivalent to BoundColumn in the ASP.NET DataGrid. The primary properties that can be set for a DataGridTextColumn are the Header, which defines the text that will be displayed in the columns header, and the DisplayMemberBinding property, which defines the property in the data source bound to the column.

The following example defines a text column with the header Name and is bound to the data source's Name property.

```
<my:DataGrid x:Name="grid" Margin="10" AutoGenerateColumns="False">
    <my:DataGrid.Columns>
        <my:DataGridTextColumn
                Header="Name"
                DisplayMemberBinding="{Binding Name}" />
        </my:DataGrid.Columns>
</my:DataGrid>
```

DataGridCheckBoxColumn

As you would expect, the DataGridCheckBoxColumn contains a check box. If you have data that you want to display as a check box in your grid, this is the control to use. Here is an example of the DataGridCheckBoxColumn that contains the header Male? and is bound to the data source's Male property:

```
<my:DataGrid x:Name="grid" Margin="10" AutoGenerateColumns="False">
    <my:DataGrid.Columns>
        <my:DataGridCheckBoxColumn
                Header="Male?"
                DisplayMemberBinding="{Binding Male}" />
            </my:DataGrid.Columns>
</my:DataGrid>
```

DataGridTemplateColumn

If you want data in your grid column that is not plain text and is not a check box, the
DataGridTemplateColumn provides a way for you to define the content for your column.
The DataGridTemplateColumn contains a CellTemplate and CellEditingTemplate, which determine what
content is displayed, depending on whether the grid is in normal view mode or in editing mode.

Note that while you get features such as automatic sorting in the other types of DataGrid columns,
that is not true of the DataGridTemplateColumn. These columns will need to have additional logic in place
to allow for sorting.

Let's consider an example that has two fields: FirstName and LastName. Suppose that when you are in
normal view mode, you want the data to be displayed side by side in TextBlock controls. However, when
the user is editing the column, you want to display two TextBox controls that allow the user to edit the
FirstName and LastName columns independently.

```
<my:DataGridTemplateColumn Header="Name">
    <my:DataGridTemplateColumn.CellTemplate>
        <DataTemplate>
            <StackPanel Orientation="Horizontal">
                <TextBlock Padding="5,0,5,0"
                    Text="{Binding FirstName}"/>
                <TextBlock Text="{Binding LastName}"/>
            </StackPanel>
        </DataTemplate>
    </my:DataGridTemplateColumn.CellTemplate>
    <my:DataGridTemplateColumn.CellEditingTemplate>
        <DataTemplate>
            <StackPanel Orientation="Horizontal">
                <TextBox Padding="5,0,5,0"
                    Text="{Binding FirstName}"/>
                <TextBox Text="{Binding LastName}"/>
            </StackPanel>
        </DataTemplate>
    </my:DataGridTemplateColumn.CellEditingTemplate>
</my:DataGridTemplateColumn>
```

Now that we have covered the basics of manually defining the grids in a DataGrid, let's try it out.

Try It Out: Building a DataGrid with Custom Columns

I thought it would be fun to build a DataGrid that contains a list of starting hands in poker. If you have
ever watched poker on TV, you most likely heard the players refer to things like "pocket rockets" and
"cowboys." These are simply nicknames they have given to starting hands. The DataGrid you are going to
build in this example will look like Figure 5-12.

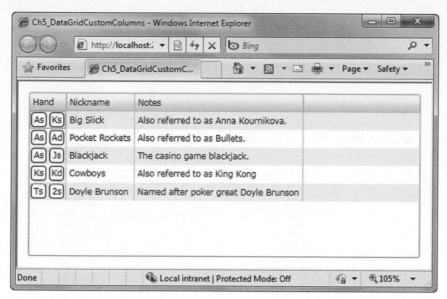

Figure 5-12. DataGrid with custom columns

1. Create a new Silverlight application called Ch5_DataGridCustomColumns. Allow Visual Studio to create a Web Site project to host the application.

2. After the project is loaded, right-click the Ch5_DataGridCustomColumns project and select Add New Item. In the Add New Item dialog box, select Class for the template, and name the class StartingHands.cs, as shown in Figure 5-13. Click the Add button to add the class to the project.

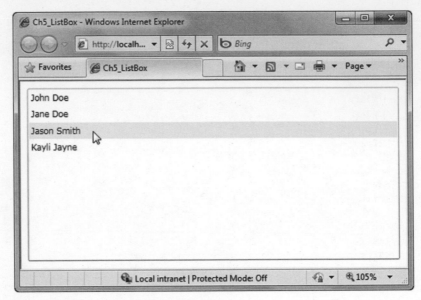

Figure 5-13. Adding a new class to the Silverlight project

3. Now define the StartingHands class. The class will contain four properties: Nickname (string), Notes (string), Card1 (string), and Card2 (string). Also create a static method in the class called GetHands(), which returns an ObservableCollection of StartingHands instances. The code follows:

```
using System;
using System.Net;
using System.Windows;
using System.Windows.Controls;
using System.Windows.Documents;
using System.Windows.Ink;
using System.Windows.Input;
using System.Windows.Media;
using System.Windows.Media.Animation;
using System.Windows.Shapes;
using System.Collections.ObjectModel;

namespace Ch5_DataGridCustomColumns
{
    public class StartingHands
    {
        public string Nickname { get; set; }
        public string Notes { get; set; }
        public string Card1 { get; set; }
        public string Card2 { get; set; }

        public static ObservableCollection<StartingHands> GetHands()
        {
```

```
ObservableCollection<StartingHands> hands =
new ObservableCollection<StartingHands>();

hands.Add(
    new StartingHands()
    {
        Nickname = "Big Slick",
        Notes = "Also referred to as Anna Kournikova.",
        Card1 = "As",
        Card2 = "Ks"
    });

hands.Add(
new StartingHands()
{
    Nickname = "Pocket Rockets",
    Notes = "Also referred to as Bullets.",
    Card1 = "As",
    Card2 = "Ad"
});

hands.Add(
    new StartingHands()
    {
        Nickname = "Blackjack",
        Notes = "The casino game blackjack.",
        Card1 = "As",
        Card2 = "Js"
    });

hands.Add(
    new StartingHands()
    {
        Nickname = "Cowboys",
        Notes = "Also referred to as King Kong",
        Card1 = "Ks",
        Card2 = "Kd"
    });

hands.Add(
    new StartingHands()
    {
        Nickname = "Doyle Brunson",
        Notes = "Named after poker great Doyle Brunson",
        Card1 = "Ts",
        Card2 = "2s"
    });


return hands;
```

```
            }
        }
}
```

4. Now that the class is built, in the MainPage.xaml file, change the width of the
    UserControl to be 500 and add a DataGrid named grdData to the root Grid by
    double-clicking the DataGrid control in the Toolbox. Add a 15-pixel margin
    around the DataGrid for some spacing, and set the AutoGenerateColumns
    property to False. The code follows:

```
<UserControl
    xmlns:data="clr-namespace:System.Windows.Controls;  ↵
assembly=System.Windows.Controls.Data"
    x:Class="Ch5_DataGridCustomColumns.Page"
    xmlns="http://schemas.microsoft.com/winfx/2006/xaml/presentation"
    xmlns:x="http://schemas.microsoft.com/winfx/2006/xaml"
    Width="500" Height="300">
    <Grid x:Name="LayoutRoot" Background="White">
        <data:DataGrid Margin="15" AutoGenerateColumns="False"></data:DataGrid>
    </Grid>
</UserControl>
```

5. Next, define the columns in the DataGrid. To do this, add the DataGrid.Columns
    collection, as follows:

```
<data:DataGrid x:Name="grdData" Margin="15" AutoGenerateColumns="False">
    <data:DataGrid.Columns>

    </data:DataGrid.Columns>
</data:DataGrid>
```

Referring back to Figure 5-12, the first column in the Grid contains the two
cards in the hand. To build this, you use a DataGridTemplateColumn. Within the
DataGridTemplateColumn, add a CellTemplate containing a Grid with two
columns, each containing a Border, Rectangle, and TextBlock, which will
overlap each other. Bind the two TextBlock controls to the Card1 and Card2
properties from the data source. Enter the following code:

```
<data:DataGrid x:Name="grdData" Margin="15" AutoGenerateColumns="False">
    <data:DataGrid.Columns>
        <data:DataGridTemplateColumn Header="Hand">
            <data:DataGridTemplateColumn.CellTemplate>
                <DataTemplate>
                    <Grid>

                        <Grid.ColumnDefinitions>
                            <ColumnDefinition />
                            <ColumnDefinition />
                        </Grid.ColumnDefinitions>

                        <Border
                            Margin="2" CornerRadius="4"
                            BorderBrush="Black" BorderThickness="1" />
```

```
                    <Rectangle
                        Margin="4" Fill="White" Grid.Column="0" />
                    <Border
                        Margin="2" CornerRadius="4" BorderBrush="Black"
                        BorderThickness="1" Grid.Column="1" />
                    <Rectangle
                        Margin="4" Fill="White" Grid.Column="1" />
                    <TextBlock
                        Text="{Binding Card1}" HorizontalAlignment="Center"
                        VerticalAlignment="Center" Grid.Column="0" />
                    <TextBlock
                        Text="{Binding Card2}" HorizontalAlignment="Center"
                        VerticalAlignment="Center" Grid.Column="1" />


                </Grid>
            </DataTemplate>
        </data:DataGridTemplateColumn.CellTemplate>
      </data:DataGridTemplateColumn>
    </data:DataGrid.Columns>
</data:DataGrid>
```

Again, referring back to Figure 5-12, the next two columns contain the nickname of the starting hand and notes about the starting hand. To implement this, use two DataGridTextColumn columns. Set the Headers of the columns to Nickname and Notes accordingly.

```
<data:DataGrid x:Name="grdData" Margin="15" AutoGenerateColumns="False">
    <data:DataGrid.Columns>
        <data:DataGridTemplateColumn Header="Hand">
            <data:DataGridTemplateColumn.CellTemplate>
                <DataTemplate>
                    <Grid>

                        <Grid.ColumnDefinitions>
                            <ColumnDefinition />
                            <ColumnDefinition />
                        </Grid.ColumnDefinitions>

                        <Border
                            Margin="2" CornerRadius="4"
                            BorderBrush="Black" BorderThickness="1" />
                        <Rectangle
                            Margin="4" Fill="White" Grid.Column="0" />
                        <Border
                            Margin="2" CornerRadius="4" BorderBrush="Black"
                            BorderThickness="1" Grid.Column="1" />
                        <Rectangle
                            Margin="4" Fill="White" Grid.Column="1" />
                        <TextBlock
                            Text="{Binding Card1}" HorizontalAlignment="Center"
                            VerticalAlignment="Center" Grid.Column="0" />
                        <TextBlock
```

```
                         Text="{Binding Card2}" HorizontalAlignment="Center"
                         VerticalAlignment="Center" Grid.Column="1" />

                </Grid>
            </DataTemplate>
        </data:DataGridTemplateColumn.CellTemplate>
    </data:DataGridTemplateColumn>

    <data:DataGridTextColumn
        Header="Nickname"
        Binding="{Binding Nickname}"  />
    <data:DataGridTextColumn
        Header="Notes"
        Binding="{Binding Notes}" />

    </data:DataGrid.Columns>
</data:DataGrid>
```

6. Finally, wire up the controls to the data source. To do this, navigate to the `MainPage.xaml.cs` file and add an event handler to the Page Loaded event. Within that Loaded event, simply set the DataGrid's ItemsSource property equal to the return value of the StartingHands.GetHands() static method. Here's the code:

```
public partial class MainPage : UserControl
{
    public MainPage()
    {
        InitializeComponent();
        this.Loaded += new RoutedEventHandler(Page_Loaded);
    }

    void Page_Loaded(object sender, RoutedEventArgs e)
    {
        this.grdData.ItemsSource = StartingHands.GetHands();
    }
}
```

7. Compile and run your application. If all goes well, your application should appear, as shown earlier in Figure 5-12.

This completes our DataGrid with custom columns example. Naturally, in a real-world application, you would be getting the data for these hands from an external data source, such as a web service or an XML file. We will be looking at that in Chapter 6. Now, let's take a look at the ListBox control.

The ListBox Control

In the past, the list box type of control has been considered one of the common controls in programming—no more special than a drop-down list. However, in Silverlight, this has all changed. The ListBox is perhaps one of the most flexible controls used to display lists of data. In fact, referring back to ASP.NET controls, the Silverlight ListBox is more a cousin to the DataList control than the ASP.NET ListBox control. Let's take a peek at this powerful control.

Default and Custom ListBox Items

If we wire up the `ListBox` to our `Person` data from our earlier `DataGrid` example, you will see that, by default, the `ListBox` really is just a standard `ListBox`.

```
<ListBox Margin="10" x:Name="list" DisplayMemberPath="Name" />
```

One additional property you may have noticed in this `ListBox` definition is `DisplayMemberPath`. If you are defining a simple text-based `ListBox`, the `ListBox` needs to know which data member to display. Since the `Person` class contains three properties (`Name`, `Age`, and `Male`), we need to tell it that we want the `Name` to be displayed. Figure 5-14 shows the results.

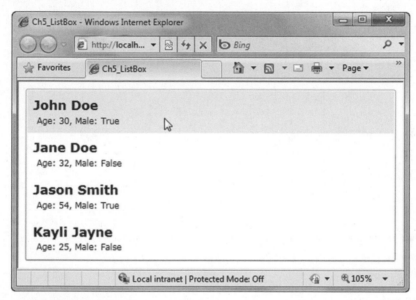

Figure 5-14. *A simple default ListBox*

However, the `ListBox` control can contain much more than plain text. In fact, if you define a custom `ItemTemplate` for the `ListBox`, you can present the items in a more interesting way. Here's an example using the same `Person` data:

```
<ListBox Margin="10" x:Name="list" DisplayMemberPath="Name">
    <ListBox.ItemTemplate>
        <DataTemplate>
            <StackPanel Margin="5" Orientation="Vertical">
                <TextBlock
                    FontSize="17"
                    FontWeight="Bold"
                    Text="{Binding Name}" />
                <StackPanel Margin="5,0,0,0" Orientation="Horizontal">
                    <TextBlock Text="Age: " />
                    <TextBlock Text="{Binding Age}" />
                    <TextBlock Text=", Male: " />
                    <TextBlock Text="{Binding Male}" />
```

```
          </StackPanel>
        </StackPanel>
      </DataTemplate>
    </ListBox.ItemTemplate>
</ListBox>
```

Figure 5-15 shows how this custom `ListBox` appears in a browser.

Figure 5-15. *A customized ListBox example*

Try It Out: Building a ListBox with Custom Content

Let's take the same data that displayed poker starting hands from the previous exercise and see what type of cool ListBox you can build with it. Figure 5-15 shows the custom ListBox you'll create in this exercise.

1. Start out by creating a new Silverlight application called Ch5_ListBoxCustom and allow Visual Studio to create a hosting web site.

2. You will use the same class that you built in the earlier DataGrid exercise. Right-click the Silverlight project, choose Add Existing Item, and browse to StartingHands.cs to add that class to the project.

3. When you add the existing StartingHands.cs class, it is in a different namespace than your current project. You can reference that namespace by adding a using statement at the top of your Silverlight application, or you can just change the namespace, as follows:

```
namespace Ch5_ListBoxCustom
{
    public class StartingHands
    {
        public string Nickname { get; set; }
        public string Notes { get; set; }
        public string Card1 { get; set; }
        public string Card2 { get; set; }

        ...
    }
}
```

4. Next, you need to define the ListBox's ItemTemplate. The ItemTemplate will contain a horizontal-oriented StackPanel including the grid to display the two cards. It will also include a nested vertical-oriented StackPanel that will contain two TextBlock controls to display the Nickname and Notes data. Here is the code:

```
<Grid x:Name="LayoutRoot" Background="White">
    <ListBox Margin="10" x:Name="list">
        <ListBox.ItemTemplate>
            <DataTemplate>
                <StackPanel Margin="5" Orientation="Horizontal">
                    <Grid>
                        <Grid.ColumnDefinitions>
                            <ColumnDefinition />
                            <ColumnDefinition />
                        </Grid.ColumnDefinitions>

                        <Border
                            Margin="2" CornerRadius="4"
                            BorderBrush="Black" BorderThickness="1" />
                        <Rectangle Margin="4" Fill="White"
                            Grid.Column="0" Width="20" />
```

```xml
            <Border
                Margin="2" CornerRadius="4" BorderBrush="Black"
                BorderThickness="1" Grid.Column="1" />
            <Rectangle Margin="4" Fill="White"
                Grid.Column="1" Width="20" />
            <TextBlock
                Text="{Binding Card1}" HorizontalAlignment="Center"
                VerticalAlignment="Center" Grid.Column="0" />
            <TextBlock
                Text="{Binding Card2}" HorizontalAlignment="Center"
                VerticalAlignment="Center" Grid.Column="1" />
        </Grid>

        <StackPanel Orientation="Vertical">
            <TextBlock
                Text="{Binding Nickname}"
                FontSize="16"
                FontWeight="Bold" />
            <TextBlock
                Text="{Binding Notes}" />
        </StackPanel>
      </StackPanel>
    </DataTemplate>
  </ListBox.ItemTemplate>
</ListBox>
</Grid>
```

5. The only thing left to do is to wire up the ListBox to the data source. To do this,
    navigate to the page.xaml.cs code behind, and add an event handler for the
    Page Loaded event. Then, within that Loaded event handler, add the following
    code to set the ListBox's ItemsSource to the return value from the
    StartingHands.GetHands() method, as you did earlier in the DataGrid example.

```csharp
namespace Ch5_ListBoxCustom
{
    public partial class MainPage : UserControl
    {
        public MainPage()
        {
            InitializeComponent();
            this.Loaded += new RoutedEventHandler(Page_Loaded);
        }

        void Page_Loaded(object sender, RoutedEventArgs e)
        {
            list.ItemsSource = StartingHands.GetHands();
        }
    }
}
```

6. Run the application. If all goes well, you will see the ListBox shown in Figure 5-
    16.

As you can see, the ListBox control's flexibility lets developers display lists of data in some very cool ways.

Summary

In this chapter, you looked at how to bind lists of data to Silverlight controls. Then you focused on two controls typically bound to data: the DataGrid control and the ListBox control. You saw how these controls are flexible and can show data in unique ways. However, in all of these examples, the classes contained static data. In real-world examples, the data that you will normally list in a DataGrid or ListBox will be coming from some external data source, such as an XML file or a web service. In the next chapter, you will look at how to get data from these external data sources and how to use that data to bind to your Silverlight applications.

CHAPTER 6

■■■

Data Access and Networking

Data access in Silverlight applications works differently than it does in traditional applications. You'll need to be aware of how it works and the limitations. In this chapter, you will look at what makes data access different, and then explore mechanisms for accessing data in a Silverlight application.

Data Access in Silverlight Applications

As discussed in Chapter 1, RIAs bridge the gap between Windows-based smart clients and web-based applications. When moving to this type of environment, data access and networking can be confusing.

In a Windows-based smart client, the application has access to the database at all times. It can create a connection to the database, maintain state with the database, and remain connected.

On the other hand, a web application is what is known as a *pseudo-conversational* environment, which is, for the most part, a completely stateless and disconnected environment. When a client makes a request to the web server, the web server processes the request and returns a response to the client. After that response has been sent, the connection between the client and the server is disconnected, and the server moves on to the next client request. No connection or state is maintained between the two.

In Silverlight applications, we have one additional layer of complexity. The application runs from the client's machine. However, it is still a disconnected environment, because it is hosted within a web browser. There is no concept of posting back for each request or creating a round-trip to the server for data processing. Therefore, data access is limited to a small number of options.

In addition, a Silverlight application has a number of security restrictions placed on it to protect the users from the application gaining too much control over their machine. For instance, the Silverlight application has access to only an isolated storage space to store its disconnected data. It has no access whatsoever to the client's hard disk outside its "sandbox." Silverlight's isolated storage is discussed in more detail in Chapter 9.

What are your options for accessing data in a Silverlight application? The following main mechanisms are available:

- The most common mechanism to access data from a Silverlight application is through web services, typically a WCF service.

- Silverlight applications can access data using ADO.NET Data Services, which provides access to data through a URI syntax.

- Silverlight also has built-in socket support, which allows applications to connect directly to a server through TCP sockets.

- Silverlight has out-of-the-box support for JavaScript Object Notation (JSON), as well as RSS 2.0 and Atom 1.0 syndication feed formats.

Of these mechanisms, I'll explore accessing WCF services from Silverlight 2 in depth, and then have a high-level look at using sockets. For examples and more information on accessing other data services, refer to *Pro Silverlight 3 in C# 2008* by Matthew MacDonald (Apress, 2009).

Accessing Data Through Web Services

One of the ways that a Silverlight application can access data is through web services. These can be ASP.NET Web Services (ASMX), Windows Communication Foundation (WCF) services, or representational state transfer (REST) services. Here, you will concentrate on using a WCF service, which is the preferred way of accessing data in a Silverlight application through web services.

Try It Out: Accessing Data Through a WCF Service

To demonstrate accessing data from a WCF service, you will build the same application that you built in Chapter 5 to try out the DataGrid. (For more information about any part of this exercise regarding the DataGrid, refer back to Chapter 5.) The difference will be that the application will get the data through a web service.

As you'll recall, this application displays common starting hands in poker and the nicknames that have been given to those starting hands. The UI will have three columns: the first column will display two images of the cards in the hand, the second column will display the nickname, and the third column will contain notes about the hand. The completed application is shown in Figure 6-1.

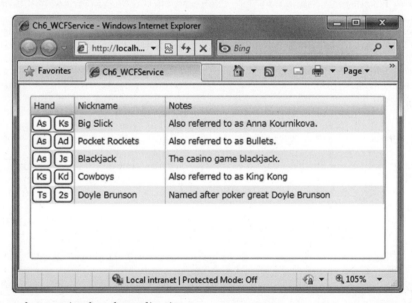

Figure 6-1. The poker starting hands application

1. Create a new Silverlight application in Visual Studio 2008. Call the application Ch6_WCFService, and allow Visual Studio to create a Web Application project named Ch6_WCFService.Web to host your application, as shown in Figure 6-2.

Figure 6-2. Adding the Silverlight application hosting project

Right-click the `Ch6_WCFService.Web` project and select Add → Class. Name the new class `StartingHands.cs`, as shown in Figure 6-3.

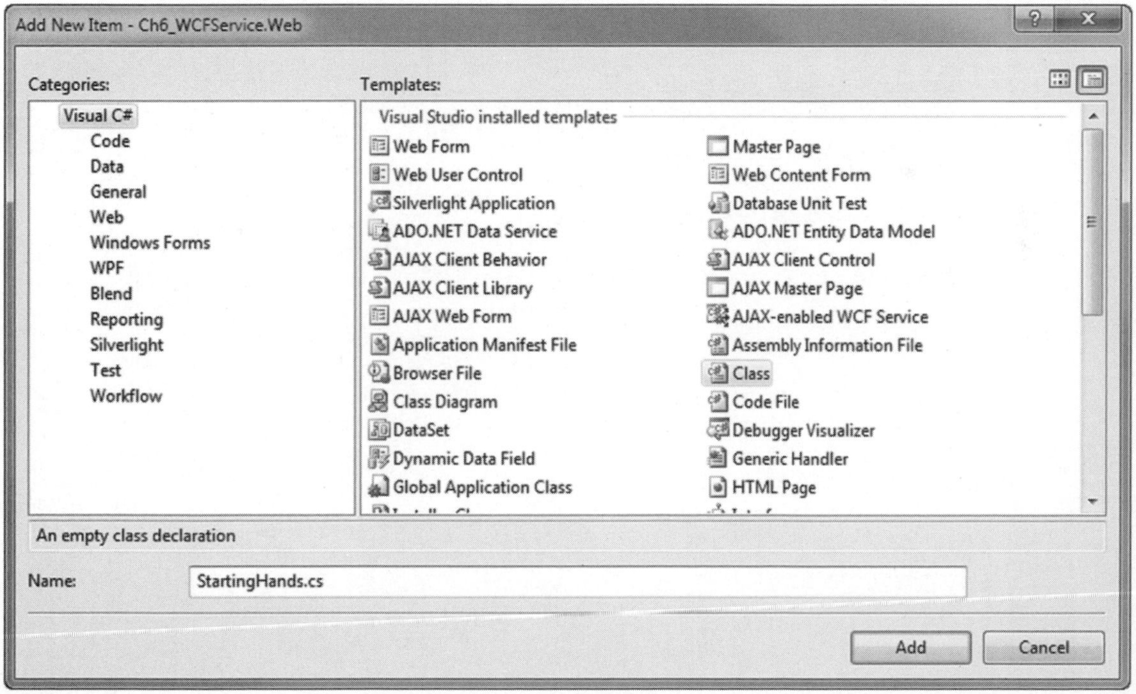

Figure 6-3. Adding the StartingHands.cs class to the project

2. Now you need to implement the StartingHands.cs class. It is very similar to the class used in Chapter 5's DataGrid example. To save yourself some typing, you can copy the code from that project. As shown in bold in the following code, the only differences are the namespace and the return type of the GetHands() method. Instead of using an ObservableCollection, it will return a simple List<StartingHands>.

■ **Note** In a real-world example, the StartingHands.cs class would be doing something like retrieving data from a SQL Server database and executing some business logic rules on the data. For simplicity, this example just returns a static collection.

```
using System;
using System.Collections.Generic;
using System.Linq;
using System.Web;

namespace Ch6_WCFService.Web
{
    public class StartingHands
    {
        public string Nickname { get; set; }
        public string Notes { get; set; }
        public string Card1 { get; set; }
        public string Card2 { get; set; }

        public static List<StartingHands> GetHands()
        {
            List<StartingHands> hands = new List<StartingHands>();

            hands.Add(
                new StartingHands()
                {
                    Nickname = "Big Slick",
                    Notes = "Also referred to as Anna Kournikova.",
                    Card1 = "As",
                    Card2 = "Ks"
                });

            hands.Add(
                new StartingHands()
                {
                    Nickname = "Pocket Rockets",
                    Notes = "Also referred to as Bullets.",
                    Card1 = "As",
                    Card2 = "Ad"
                });

            hands.Add(
```

```
        new StartingHands()
        {
            Nickname = "Blackjack",
            Notes = "The casino game blackjack.",
            Card1 = "As",
            Card2 = "Js"
        });

    hands.Add(
        new StartingHands()
        {
            Nickname = "Cowboys",
            Notes = "Also referred to as King Kong",
            Card1 = "Ks",
            Card2 = "Kd"
        });

    hands.Add(
        new StartingHands()
        {
            Nickname = "Doyle Brunson",
            Notes = "Named after poker great Doyle Brunson",
            Card1 = "Ts",
            Card2 = "2s"
        });


    return hands;
    }
  }
}
```

3. Next, you need to add the WCF service that will call the StartingHands.GetHands() method. Right-click the Ch6_WCFService.Web project and select Add ~TRA New Item. In the Add New Item dialog box, select the template named "Silverlight-enabled WCF Service" and name it StartingHandService.svc, as shown in Figure 6-4. Then click the Add button.

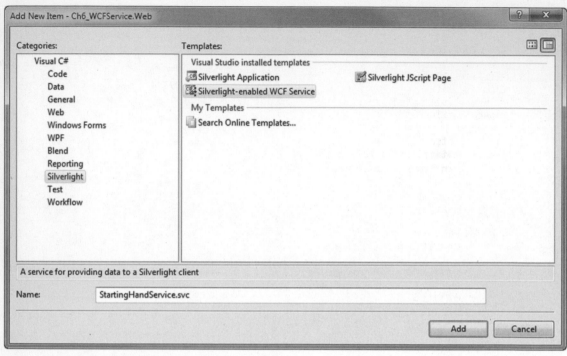

Figure 6-4. *Adding the Silverlight-enabled WCF service*

    4.   This will add a service named StartingHandService.svc to the project with an
attached code-behind file named StartingHandService.svc.cs. View that code
behind. You will see that Visual Studio has already created the base WCF
service, including a sample method called DoWork(), as follows:

```
namespace Ch6_WCFService.Web
{
    [ServiceContract(Namespace = "")]
    [AspNetCompatibilityRequirements(RequirementsMode =
        AspNetCompatibilityRequirementsMode.Allowed)]
    public class StartingHandService
    {
        [OperationContract]
        public void DoWork()
        {
            // Add your operation implementation here
            return;
        }

        // Add more operations here and mark them
        // with [OperationContract]
    }
}
```

5. Replace the DoWork() method with a GetHands() method that returns a List<StartingHands> collection, as follows:

```
namespace Ch6_WCFService.Web
{
    [ServiceContract(Namespace = "")]
    [AspNetCompatibilityRequirements(RequirementsMode =
        AspNetCompatibilityRequirementsMode.Allowed)]
    public class StartingHandService
    {
        [OperationContract]
        public List<StartingHands> GetHands()           {
                return StartingHands.GetHands();
        }
        // Add more operations here and mark them
        // with [OperationContract]
    }
}
```

This method simply returns the results from calling the StartingHands.GetHands() method.

Now that you have a Silverlight-enabled WCF service, you need to add a reference in your Silverlight project so that your Silverlight application can access the service. To do this, right-click References within the Ch6_WCFService in Solution Explorer and select Add Service Reference, as shown in Figure 6-5. This brings up the Add Service Reference dialog box.

Figure 6-5. Choosing to add a service reference

6. In the Add Service Reference dialog box, click the down arrow next to the Discover button and select Services in Solution, as shown in Figure 6-6.

7. Visual Studio will find the `StartingHandService.svc` and will populate the Services list in the Add Service Reference dialog box. Note that you may need to build the solution before Visual Studio will find your service. Expand the `StartingHandService.svc` node to show the `StartingHandService`. Click `StartingHandService` to see the `GetHands()` web method in the Operations listing, as shown in Figure 6-7. Enter `StartingHandServiceReference` as the Namespace field, and then click OK to continue.

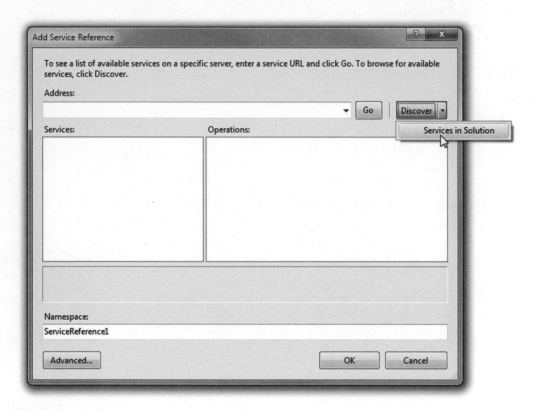

Figure 6-6. *Finding the services in the solution*

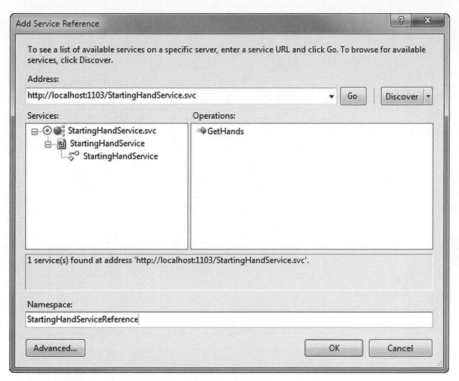

Figure 6-7. Adding a service reference for StartingHandService

Open the Visual Studio Object Browser by selecting View ~TRA Object Browser from the main menu. Navigate to the Ch6_WCFService entry and expand the tree. You will find Ch6_WCFService.StartingHandServiceReference under your project. Within that, you will see an object named StartingHandServiceClient. Select this object to examine it, as shown in Figure 6-8.

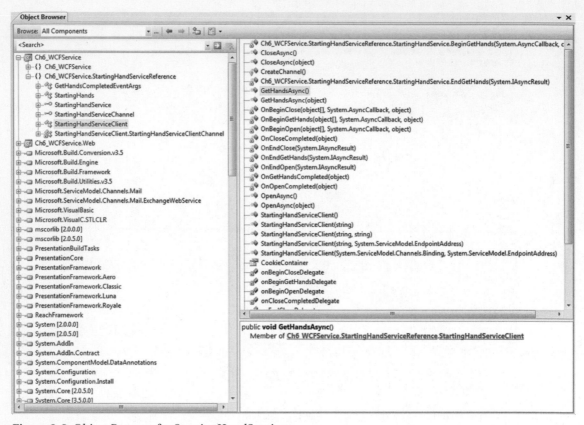

Figure 6-8. Object Browser for StartingHandService

8. Look at the members listed on the right side of the Object Browser. There are a number of items that are added, but take specific note of the method named `GetHandsAsync()` and the event named `GetHandsCompleted`. You will need to use both of these in order to call your web service from Silverlight.

9. Now it's time to create the Silverlight application's UI. Open the `MainPage.xaml` file in Visual Studio. Place the cursor within the root `Grid` and double-click the `DataGrid` control in the Toolbox. This adds the following XAML:

```
<Grid x:Name="LayoutRoot" Background="White">
    <data:DataGrid></data:DataGrid>
</Grid>
```

10. Highlight the `DataGrid` definition in the solution and replace it with the following `DataGrid` definition, which is from the previous `DataGrid` exercise in Chapter 5. The `DataGrid` contains three columns: one template column containing the two cards in the hand and two text columns containing the nickname and notes about the hand.

```xml
<data:DataGrid x:Name="grdData" Margin="15" AutoGenerateColumns="False">
    <data:DataGrid.Columns>
        <data:DataGridTemplateColumn Header="Hand">
            <data:DataGridTemplateColumn.CellTemplate>
                <DataTemplate>
                    <Grid>

                        <Grid.ColumnDefinitions>
                            <ColumnDefinition />
                            <ColumnDefinition />
                        </Grid.ColumnDefinitions>

                        <Border
                            Margin="2" CornerRadius="4"
                            BorderBrush="Black" BorderThickness="1" />
                        <Rectangle
                            Margin="4" Fill="White" Grid.Column="0" />
                        <Border
                            Margin="2" CornerRadius="4" BorderBrush="Black"
                            BorderThickness="1" Grid.Column="1" />
                        <Rectangle
                            Margin="4" Fill="White" Grid.Column="1" />
                        <TextBlock
                            Text="{Binding Card1}" HorizontalAlignment="Center"
                            VerticalAlignment="Center" Grid.Column="0" />
                        <TextBlock
                            Text="{Binding Card2}" HorizontalAlignment="Center"
                            VerticalAlignment="Center" Grid.Column="1" />

                    </Grid>
                </DataTemplate>
            </data:DataGridTemplateColumn.CellTemplate>
        </data:DataGridTemplateColumn>

        <data:DataGridTextColumn
            Header="Nickname"
            Binding="{Binding Nickname}"  />
        <data:DataGridTextColumn
            Header="Notes"
            Binding="{Binding Notes}" />

    </data:DataGrid.Columns>
</data:DataGrid>
```

11. Save the MainPage.xaml file and navigate to the code behind for the application, located in the MainPage.xaml.cs file. Wire up the Loaded event handler for the page, as follows:

```csharp
namespace Ch6_WCFService
{
    public partial class MainPage : UserControl
    {
        public MainPage()
        {
```

```
        InitializeComponent();
        this.Loaded += new RoutedEventHandler(Page_Loaded);
    }

    void Page_Loaded(object sender, RoutedEventArgs e)
    {
        throw new NotImplementedException();
    }
  }
}
```

Next, you need to call the WCF service. In Silverlight, web services can be called only asynchronously, so the browser's execution is not blocked by the transaction. In order to do this, you need to get an instance of the service reference (commonly referred to as the *web service proxy class*) named StartingHandService, which you added earlier. You will then wire up an event handler for the service's GetHandsCompleted event, which you examined in the Object Browser (in step 11). This is the event handler that will be called when the service has completed execution. Finally, you will execute the GetHandsAsync() method.

■ **Tip** In a real-world scenario, you will want to present the user with a progress bar or animation while the service is being called, since the duration of a web service call can be lengthy.

---

12. Within the Page_Loaded event handler, first obtain an instance of StartingHandService. Then, in the GetHandsCompleted event handler, bind the ItemsSource of the DataGrid to the result returned from the service call, as shown in the following code. Note that normally you will want to check the result to make certain that the web service call was successful, and alert the user accordingly in case of failure.

```
using Ch6_WCFService.StartingHandServiceReference;

namespace Ch6_WCFService
{
    public partial class Page : UserControl
    {
        public Page()
        {
            InitializeComponent();
            this.Loaded += new RoutedEventHandler(Page_Loaded);
        }

        void Page_Loaded(object sender, RoutedEventArgs e)
        {
            StartingHandServiceClient service = new StartingHandServiceClient();
            service.GetHandsCompleted += new
```

```
                EventHandler<GetHandsCompletedEventArgs>(service_GetHandsCompleted);
            service.GetHandsAsync();
        }

        void service_GetHandsCompleted(object sender, GetHandsCompletedEventArgs e)
        {
            this.grdData.ItemsSource = e.Result;
        }
    }
}
```

13. Test your application. If all goes well, you should see the populated DataGrid, as shown earlier in Figure 6-1.

This example demonstrated how to use the Silverlight-enabled WCF service provided in Visual Studio to allow your Silverlight application to access data remotely. As noted earlier in chapter in the section "Data Access in Silverlight Applications", this is one of the most common approaches to data access with Silverlight.

Accessing Services from Other Domains

In the previous example, the web service was on the same domain as your Silverlight application. What if you want to call a service that is on a different domain?

In fact, as a best practice, it is preferred to have your web services stored on a domain separate from your web application. Even for applications where you control both the web service and the Silverlight application, you may be dealing with different domains.

If you attempt to access a service from a different domain in Silverlight, you will notice that it fails. This is because, by default, a Silverlight application cannot call services that are on a different domain, unless it is permitted to do so by the service host. In order for Silverlight to determine if it has permission to access a service on a certain domain, it will look for one of two files in the root of the target domain: clientaccesspolicy.xml or crossdomain.xml.

First, Silverlight will look for a file named clientaccesspolicy.xml in the domain's root. This is Silverlight's client-access policy file. If you are publishing your own services that you want to be accessible by Silverlight applications, this is the file that you want to use, as it provides the most options for Silverlight application policy permissions. The following is a sample clientaccesspolicy.xml file:

```xml
<?xml version="1.0" encoding="utf-8"?>
<access-policy>
  <cross-domain-access>
    <policy>
      <allow-from http-request-headers="*">
        <domain uri="*"/>
      </allow-from>
      <grant-to>
        <resource path="/" include-subpaths="true"/>
      </grant-to>
    </policy>
  </cross-domain-access>
</access-policy>
```

149

The important elements are <allow-from> and <grant-to>. The <allow-from> element defines which domains are permitted to access the resources specified in the <grant-to> element.

If Silverlight cannot find a clientaccesspolicy.xml file at the root of the domain from which you are attempting to access a service, it will then look for a file named crossdomain.xml in the root. This is the XML policy file that has been used to provide access for Flash applications to access cross-domain services, and Silverlight supports this file as well. The following is an example of a crossdomain.xml file:

```
<?xml version="1.0"?>
<!DOCTYPE cross-domain-policy
    SYSTEM "http://www.macromedia.com/xml/dtds/cross-domain-policy.dtd">
<cross-domain-policy>
  <allow-http-request-headers-from domain="*" headers="*"/>
</cross-domain-policy>
```

Again, even though Silverlight supports crossdomain.xml, using clientaccesspolicy.xml for Silverlight applications is the preferred and best practice.

Accessing Data Through Sockets

In the majority of cases, your Silverlight applications will access data through web services. However, Silverlight provides another mechanism that, though rarely used, can be quite powerful. This mechanism is socket communications. In this section, you will look at a greatly simplified example of communicating with a server via sockets and TCP. The main purpose here is to give you a taste of using sockets in Silverlight so you have a basic understanding of the process and can consider whether you would like to take this approach. If so, you can refer to a more advanced resource, such as *Pro Silverlight 3 in C# 2008* by Matthew MacDonald (Apress, 2009).

For this example, let's assume that you have a socket server running at the IP address 192.168.1.100 on port 4500. The socket server simply accepts text inputs and does something with them. In Silverlight, you want to connect to that socket server and send it text from a TextBox control.

First, you make a connection to the socket server. To do this, you create an instance of a System.Net.Sockets.Socket object for IP version 4 (AddressFamily.InterNetwork). The type will be Stream, meaning it will accept a stream of bytes, and the protocol will be TCP.

```
Socket socket;
socket = new Socket(
    AddressFamily.InterNetwork,
    SocketType.Stream,
    ProtocolType.Tcp);
```

You need to execute the socket's ConnectAsync() method, but first you must create an instance of SocketAsyncEventArgs to pass to the method, using a statement similar to the following:

```
SocketAsyncEventArgs socketArgs = new SocketAsyncEventArgs()
{
    RemoteEndPoint = new IPEndPoint(
        IPAddress.Parse("192.168.1.100"),
        4500)
};
```

This statement sets the target for the socket connection as 192.168.1.100 on port 4500.

In addition, since this is an asynchronous connection, you need to have notification when the connection has been established. To get this notification, you wire up an event handler to be triggered on the SocketAsyncEventArgs.Completed event. Once you have that wired up, you simply call the ConnectAsync() method, passing it your SocketAsyncEventArgs instance.

```
socketArgs.Completed += new
    EventHandler<SocketAsyncEventArgs>(socketArgs_Completed);
socket.ConnectAsync(socketArgs);
```

The method for this event handler will first remove the event handler, and then it will examine the response from the socket server. If it is successful, it will send a stream of bytes from your TextBox control to the socket server through your established connection.

```
void socketArgs_Completed(object sender, SocketAsyncEventArgs e)
{
    e.Completed -= socketArgs_Completed;

    if (e.SocketError == SocketError.Success)
    {
        SocketAsyncEventArgs args = new SocketAsyncEventArgs();
        args.SetBuffer(bytes, 0, bytes.Length);
        args.Completed += new EventHandler<SocketAsyncEventArgs>(OnSendCompleted);
        socket.SendAsync(args);
    }
}
```

Once again, since the calls to the socket are asynchronous, you wire up another event handler called OnSendCompleted, which will fire when your SendAsync() method is completed. This event handler will do nothing more than close the socket.

```
void OnSendCompleted(object sender, SocketAsyncEventArgs e)
{
    socket.Close();
}
```

Although this seems pretty simple, it is complicated by client-access policy permissions. In the same way that a Silverlight application can call a web service on a separate domain only if it has the proper client-access policy permissions, a Silverlight application can call a socket server only if that server contains the proper client-access policy permissions. The following is an example of a client-access policy for a socket server:

```
<?xml version="1.0" encoding ="utf-8"?>
<access-policy>
  <cross-domain-access>
    <policy>
      <allow-from>
        <domain uri="*" />
      </allow-from>
      <grant-to>
        <socket-resource port="4500-4550" protocol="tcp" />
      </grant-to>
    </policy>
  </cross-domain-access>
</access-policy>
```

Recall that when you're using a web service, the client-access policy is contained in a file named `clientaccesspolicy.xml`, which is placed in the domain's root. In a socket access situation, things are a bit more complex.

Before Silverlight will make a socket request to a server on whatever port is requested by the application, it will first make a socket request of its own to the server on port 943, requesting a policy file. Therefore, your server must have a socket service set up to listen to requests on port 943 and serve up the contents of the client-access policy in order for Silverlight applications to be able to make a socket connection.

Summary

In this chapter, you focused on accessing data from your Silverlight applications through WCF services. I also discussed accessing data from different domains and cross-domain policy files. In addition, you looked at using sockets in Silverlight from a high level.

In the next chapter, you will look at data validation within Silverlight.

CHAPTER 7

■■■

Navigation Framework

The Navigation Framework is a new feature in Silverlight 3 that allows developers to implement a way to navigate through different pages within a Silverlight application, creating an experience similar to browsing through different pages of a web site. The framework also allows developers to create a history that can integrate with the browser enabling users to navigate forward and backward through the history using the browser's back and forward buttons.

In this chapter, you will explore the new Navigation Framework within Silverlight 3 and try out a couple of examples involving the different aspects of the framework.

Frame and Page Object

The two main objects that are contained in the Navigation Framework is the Frame and Page objects (see Figure 7-1). The Frame object is very similar to a ContentPlaceHolder in ASP.NET master pages and is the place holder for the different views to be loaded onto the page.

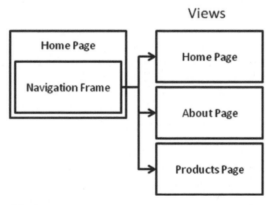

Figure 7-1. Frame and Page objects

Try It Out: Creating a Silverlight Navigation Application

This exercise demonstrates creating a Silverlight application with navigation support from scratch using the Navigation Framework. In the exercise, you will build a simple application that will contain two HyperlinkButtons and a Frame. Clicking the links will load one of two Pages into the Frame. Let's get started.

1. Start Visual Studio 2008 and select File → New → Project from the main menu.

2. In the New Project dialog box, select Silverlight as the project type and Silverlight Application as the template. Name the project Ch7_NavAppFromScratch, as shown in Figure 7-2.

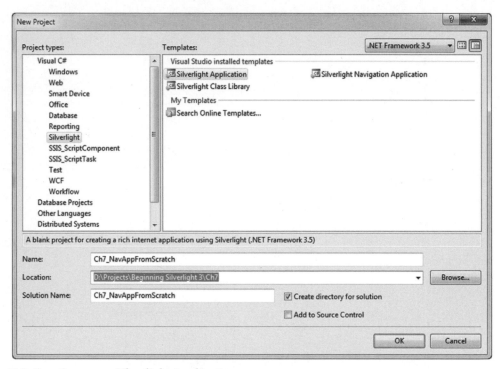

Figure 7-2. *Creating a new Silverlight Application*

3. When the New Silverlight Application dialog appears, select the default to host the Silverlight application in a new ASP.NET web application named Ch7_ NavAppFromScratch.Web. Press OK to continue.

4. By default the MainPage.xaml file will be created and opened for editing. You will start by editing that file. In the Grid definition, add ShowGridLines="True" so you can see how your cells are laid out. You can turn this property off later so your application is cleaner.

5. Next you want to define the Grid cells. You will simply have two rows, one for the links and one for the navigated content.

```
<Grid ShowGridLines="True" x:Name="LayoutRoot" Background="White">

    <Grid.RowDefinitions>
        <RowDefinition Height="30" />
        <RowDefinition></RowDefinition>
    </Grid.RowDefinitions>

</Grid>
```

6.   Now that you have the two rows, you want to add your HyperlinkButtons that
      will be used to navigate to the different views. You will do this in a horizontal
      StackPanel. For the Click property, create an event handler called LinkClick.

```
<Grid ShowGridLines="True" x:Name="LayoutRoot" Background="White">

    <Grid.RowDefinitions>
        <RowDefinition Height="30" />
        <RowDefinition></RowDefinition>
    </Grid.RowDefinitions>

    <StackPanel Orientation="Horizontal" HorizontalAlignment="Center">

        <HyperlinkButton Content="View 1"
                         Click="LinkClick"
                         Padding="5" />
        <HyperlinkButton Content="View 2"
                         Click="LinkClick"
                         Padding="5" />

    </StackPanel>

</Grid>
```

7.   The next step will be to add support for the Navigation Framework in your
      project. The first step is to add a reference to System.Windows.Controls.
      Navigation.dll by right clicking on the References folder in your Silverlight
      project and choosing Add Reference as shown in Figure 7-3.

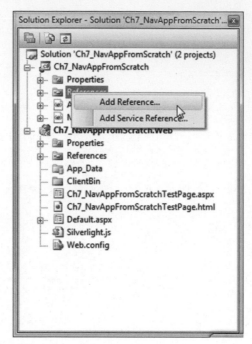

Figure 7-3. *The Silverlight navigation application Contents*

8. When the Add Reference dialog appears, be sure the .NET tab is selected and then browse through the list until you find System.Windows.Controls. Navigation, as shown in Figure 7-4. Select the entry and press OK to add the reference to the project.

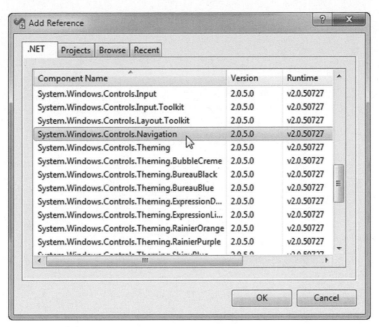

Figure 7-4. The Silverlight Navigation Application References

9. When the assembly is added you will see it appear under References in the
   Solution Explorer, as shown in Figure 7-5.

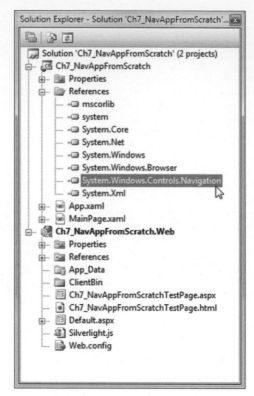

Figure 7-5. *The Silverlight Navigation Application Contents with Reference*

10. Now that you have added the reference to the Navigation Framework, you need to add the navigation objects to your application. You will start by adding the XML namespace for System.Windows.Controls.Navigation to the UserControl definition.

```
<UserControl x:Class="Ch8_NavAppFromScratch.MainPage"
    xmlns="http://schemas.microsoft.com/winfx/2006/xaml/presentation"
    xmlns:x="http://schemas.microsoft.com/winfx/2006/xaml"
    xmlns:navigation="clr-namespace:System.Windows.Controls; ⤸
assembly=System.Windows.Controls.Navigation"
    Width="400" Height="300">

<Grid ShowGridLines="True" x:Name="LayoutRoot" Background="White">

    …

</Grid>

</UserControl>
```

11. You can now add a Frame to the bottom row of the root grid named ContentFrame. You will also set the HorizontalContentAlignment and VerticalContentAlignment to Stretch so the Frame will consume the entire Grid Cell. You will also give the Frame a 10 pixel Margin and a BorderThickness to 2 pixels.

```
<Grid ShowGridLines="True" x:Name="LayoutRoot" Background="White">

    <Grid.RowDefinitions>
        <RowDefinition Height="30" />
        <RowDefinition></RowDefinition>
    </Grid.RowDefinitions>

    <StackPanel Orientation="Horizontal" HorizontalAlignment="Center">

        <HyperlinkButton Content="View 1"
                         Click="LinkClick"
                         Padding="5" />
        <HyperlinkButton Content="View 2"
                         Click="LinkClick"
                         Padding="5" />

    </StackPanel>

    <navigation:Frame x:Name="ContentFrame"
                      HorizontalContentAlignment="Stretch"
                      VerticalContentAlignment="Stretch"
                      Margin="10"
                      Grid.Row="1"
                      BorderThickness="2"
                      BorderBrush="Black" />

</Grid>
```

12. Next, you will add the different views to the project. Right-click on the Silverlight project and select Add New Item.

13. On the Add New Item dialog, select the Silverlight Page template, name the page View1.xaml and click on the Add button.

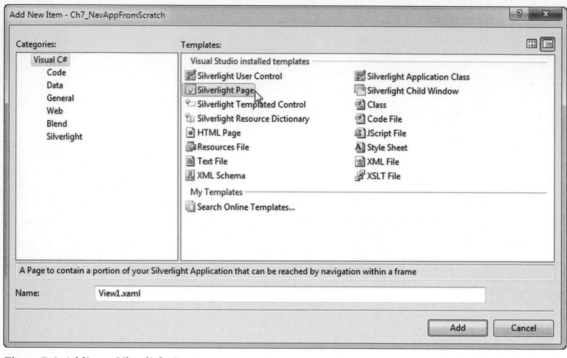

Figure 7-6. *Adding a Silverlight Page*

14. Once View1.xaml has been added, repeat steps 11 and 12 to add another Silverlight Page named View2.xaml.

15. Open View1.xaml up in design mode and add the following XAML to the root Grid.

```
<Grid x:Name="LayoutRoot" Background="White">
    <TextBlock Text="View 1"
               FontSize="60"
               Foreground="Green"
               HorizontalAlignment="Center"
               VerticalAlignment="Center" />
</Grid>
```

16. Open View2.xaml up in design mode and add the following XAML to the root Grid.

```
<Grid x:Name="LayoutRoot" Background="White">
    <TextBlock Text="View 2"
               FontSize="60"
               Foreground="Red"
               HorizontalAlignment="Center"
               VerticalAlignment="Center" />
</Grid>
```

17. You now have the main page containing the Frame and the two views that you will load into the Frame. Next, you need to actually load the views into the Frame. You will do this on the click event of the two HyperlinkButtons you added in step 6. While you can easily do this with two click event handlers, you will actually do it with one. You can set the Tag property of the HyperlinkButton to be the page view source file. Then the click event handler will be able to retrieve the source file from the Tag.

```
<StackPanel Orientation="Horizontal" HorizontalAlignment="Center">

    <HyperlinkButton Content="View 1"
                     Click="LinkClick"
                     Tag="/View1.xaml"
                     Padding="5" />
    <HyperlinkButton Content="View 2"
                     Click="LinkClick"
                     Tag="/View2.xaml"
                     Padding="5" />

</StackPanel>
```

18. Right click on LinkClick in the Click attribute and select Navigate to Event Handler in order to create the LinkClick event handler. Within the event add the following code to retrieve the view's source file.

```
private void LinkClick(object sender, RoutedEventArgs e)
{
    HyperlinkButton button = (HyperlinkButton)sender;
    string viewSource = button.Tag.ToString();
}
```

19. Now that you have the view's source file, you can use the Frame's Navigate method to navigate to the proper view.

```
private void LinkClick(object sender, RoutedEventArgs e)
{
    HyperlinkButton button = (HyperlinkButton)sender;
    string viewSource = button.Tag.ToString();
    ContentFrame.Navigate(new Uri(viewSource, UriKind.Relative));
}
```

20. You are now ready to run the solution. Select Debug → Start Debugging or press F5 to run the application. Internet Explorer will open and the application will be displayed, as shown in Figure 7-7.

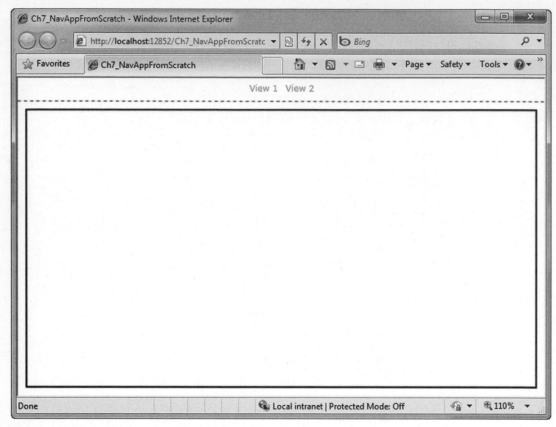

Figure 7-7. *Testing the Silverlight Navigation Application*

21. Press the View 1 HyperlinkButton at the top of the screen. The content frame will navigate to the View1.xaml content, as shown in Figure 7-8.

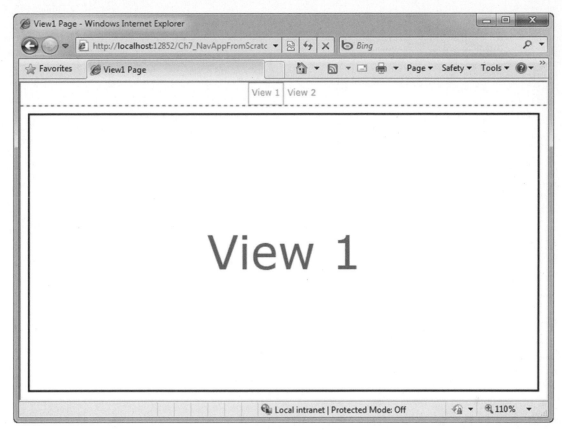

Figure 7-8. *Testing the Silverlight Navigation Application Template View 1*

22. You can then click on the View 2 link for similar results, as shown in Figure 7-9.

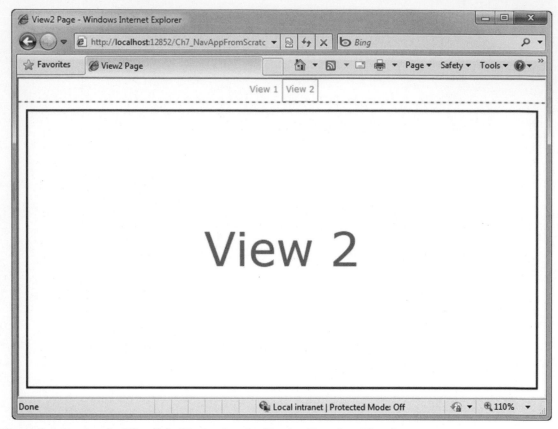

Figure 7-9. Testing the Silverlight Navigation Application Template View 2

23. Notice that you can press the browser's back button to navigate backward in history from View 2, to View 1, and back to the default.

Benefits of the Navigation Framework

While the functionality of the Navigation Framework may have been achieved in previous versions of Silverlight, the amount of work that it required was very significant and normally would require you to purchase a third party control or library. Clearly having this functionally built into Silverlight 3 is a major advantage. It reduces the amount of code required to achieve the same affects and produces much cleaner and maintainable code. In addition, it provides a number of additional benefits such as browser history support and deep linking.

Deep Linking

Another benefit of the Navigation Framework in Silverlight 3 is Deep Linking support. Deep linking is the ability to link to an application at a specific state.

To illustrate deep linking, consider an application when it is loaded a home page is displayed. When the user clicks on a link from the home page, the application navigates to the product listings page. The user can then on a product to navigate a page containing the details for that product. This application could be represented by the diagram shown in Figure 7-10.

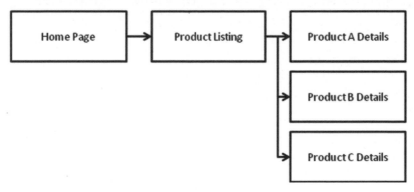

Figure 7-10. *Deep Linking in Silverlight 3*

Let's say you wanted to generate a link directly to the Product B Details page in the application. Using the Navigation Framework, Silverlight allows developers to link to different states in their application.

The NavigationService Object

As you have seen in this chapter, you change different views using the Frame object's Navigate method. There are times when you need to gain access to the Frame from within the page itself. For example, if you consider the diagram in Figure 7-11, you can easily navigate to View 1 from the Navigation Frame on the Home Page. However, if you want to navigate to Inner View 1 from the code behind on View 1, you need to get access to the navigation frame that is hosting View 1 in order to navigate to a different view.

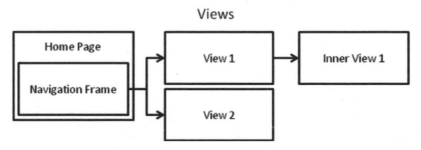

Figure 7-11. *NavigationService Object in Silverlight 3*

Luckily, the Navigation Framework contains an object that allows a view to access its hosting frame. That object is the `NavigationService`. Let's explore the use of the `NavigationService` object by running through the following exercise.

Try it Out: Using the NavigationService Object

In this exercise, you will expand on the example you built earlier in the chapter. You will add a button to the View1 Page and on the click event of that button you will navigate to a new Page called Inner View 1 using the NavigationService object. Let's get started.

1. Begin by opening the project Ch7_NavAppFromScratch you just completed in the previous section.

2. Open the XAML for View1.xaml and modify the source to include a button under the TextBlock.

```
<Grid x:Name="LayoutRoot" Background="White">
    <StackPanel>

        <TextBlock Text="View 1"
                   FontSize="60"
                   Foreground="Green"
                   HorizontalAlignment="Center"
                   VerticalAlignment="Center" />

        <Button Click="Button_Click"
                Padding="10"
                Content="Navigate to Inner View"
                HorizontalAlignment="Center" />

    </StackPanel>
</Grid>
```

3. You now need to add the new view that you will navigate to use the NavigationService. Right click on the Silverlight project and choose Add → New Item. Select Silverlight Page as the template and name the file InnerView1.xaml.

4. In the XAML for InnerView1.xaml, add a simple TextBlock.

```
<Grid x:Name="LayoutRoot" Background="White">
    <TextBlock Text="Inner View 1"
               FontSize="40"
               Foreground="Blue"
               HorizontalAlignment="Center"
               VerticalAlignment="Center" />
</Grid>
```

5. Next, add the Button_Click event handler in the View1.xaml code behind and add the following code

```
private void Button_Click(object sender, RoutedEventArgs e)
{
    NavigationService.Navigate(
        new Uri("/InnerView1.xaml", UriKind.Relative));
}
```

6.   You are now ready to run the solution. Select Debug → Start Debugging or press F5 to run the application. When Internet Explorer opens the application, click on the View 1 link at the top. The application should appear as shown in Figure 7-12.

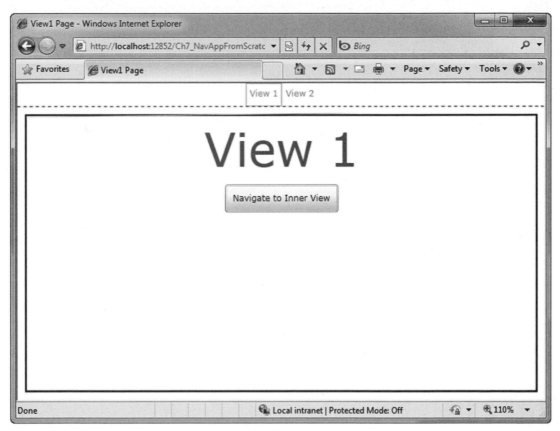

Figure 7-12. Testing the NavigationService Object

7.   If you click on the "Navigate to Inner View" button, the application should now show the InnerView1.xaml content in the top frame, as seen in Figure 7-13.

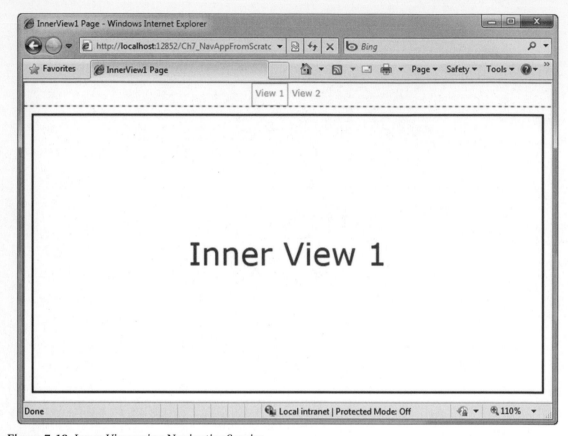

Figure 7-13. *Inner View using NavigationService*

In this section, you learned how to use the NavigationService object to access the navigation frame from a Silverlight Page. In the next section, you will learn how to pass data to navigation pages using another object contained in the Navigation Framework, the NetworkContext object.

Passing Data to Navigation Pages

In this section, you will discuss passing data to page views within a navigation framework solution. In HTML pages, data is passed to other pages using the QueryString. The same is true for pages within a Silverlight navigation application through the use of the NavigationContext object. As an example, if you want to retrieve the QueryString property ProductID, you would use the following syntax:

```
string productId = NavigationContext.QueryString["ProductID"].ToString();
```

Let's explore how to use the NavigationContext object to pass data to views.

Try it Out: Passing Data to Navigation Pages

In this exercise, you will expand on the project that you continued working on in the previous section. You will pass some additional data to the InnerView1.xaml file, retrieve that data using the NavigationContext object and then display the view content dependent on that data.

1. Begin by opening the project Ch7_NavAppFromScratch you were working on in the previous section.

2. Open the XAML for View1.xaml and modify the source to include a ComboBox under the Button.

```
<Grid x:Name="LayoutRoot" Background="White">
    <StackPanel>

        <TextBlock Text="View 1"
                FontSize="60"
                Foreground="Green"
                HorizontalAlignment="Center"
                VerticalAlignment="Center" />

        <Button Click="Button_Click"
                Padding="10"
                Content="Navigate to Inner View"
                HorizontalAlignment="Center" />

        <ComboBox Padding="10" Margin="10" x:Name="Color" Width="100">
            <ComboBoxItem Content="Blue" IsSelected="True" />
            <ComboBoxItem Content="Red" />
            <ComboBoxItem Content="Green" />
        </ComboBox>

    </StackPanel>
</Grid>
```

3. Next open the code behind for View1.xaml and edit the Button_Click event handler to pass the selected color in the query string of the Uri passed to the Navigate method.

```
private void Button_Click(object sender, RoutedEventArgs e)
{
    string color = Color.SelectionBoxItem.ToString();

    NavigationService.Navigate(
        new Uri(string.Format("/InnerView1.xaml?Color={0}", color),
            UriKind.Relative));
}
```

4. Open the InnerView1.xaml file and add a second TextBlock below the existing TextBlock using a StackPanel.

```
<Grid x:Name="LayoutRoot" Background="White">
<StackPanel Orientation="Vertical">
    <TextBlock Text="Inner View 1"
```

```
                    x:Name="ViewHeader"
                    FontSize="40"
                    Foreground="Blue"
                    HorizontalAlignment="Center"
                    VerticalAlignment="Center" />
    <TextBlock Text="(Blue)"
                    x:Name="ViewColor"
                    FontSize="30"
                    Foreground="Blue"
                    HorizontalAlignment="Center"
                    VerticalAlignment="Center" />
</StackPanel>
```

5. Open the code behind for InnerView1.xaml and retrieve the passed color using the NavigationContext object. Then add a switch statement to change the color of the TextBlocks and edit the Text for the second TextBlock.

```
protected override void OnNavigatedTo(NavigationEventArgs e)
{
    string color = NavigationContext.QueryString["Color"].ToString();
    Brush b;

    switch (color)
    {
        case "Red":
            b = new SolidColorBrush(Color.FromArgb(255,255,0,0));
            ViewHeader.Foreground = b;
            ViewColor.Foreground = b;
            ViewColor.Text = "(Red)";
            break;

        case "Green":
            b = new SolidColorBrush(Color.FromArgb(255, 0, 255, 0));
            ViewHeader.Foreground = b;
            ViewColor.Foreground = b;
            ViewColor.Text = "(Green)";
            break;

        default:
            b = new SolidColorBrush(Color.FromArgb(255, 0, 0, 255));
            ViewHeader.Foreground = b;
            ViewColor.Foreground = b;
            ViewColor.Text = "(Blue)";
            break;
    }

}
```

6. You are now ready to run the solution. Select Debug → Start Debugging or press F5 to run the application. When Internet Explorer opens the application, click on the View 1 link at the top. The application should appear, as shown in Figure 7-14.

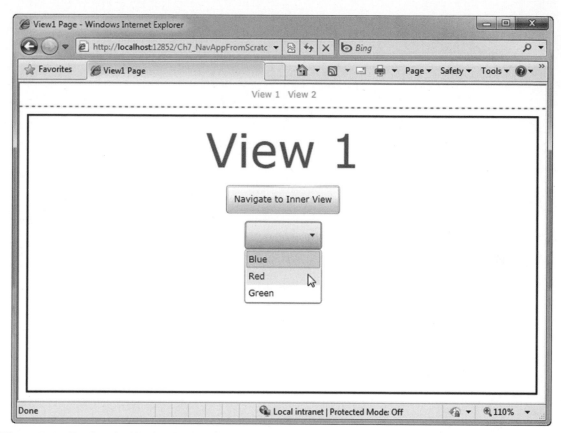

Figure 7-14. *Testing the Navigation Application Passing Data*

7. Select Red in the ComboBox and click on the "Navigate to Inner View" button. You will see the content of the InnerView1.xaml is displayed with red text and with the text "(Red)" displayed, as shown in Figure 7-15.

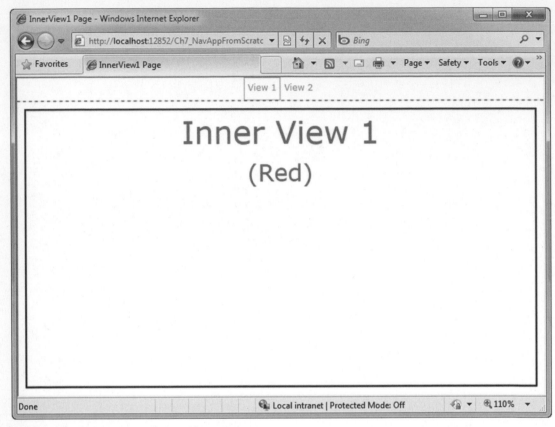

Figure 7-15. Navigation Result with Data Passed

In this section, you learned how to use the `NavigationContext` object to pass data to navigation views using the query string. In the next section, I will discuss Uri Mapping and how it can be used to create user friendly Uri's to your navigation views.

Uri Mapping

In the preceding examples, you may have noticed the URL changing as you navigated to different views in a frame. You may have also noticed that the URLs were not very pretty and contained some information that you may not want to display. As an example, consider the following URL:

`http://www.domain.com/Catalog.aspx#ProductDetails.xaml?ID=4`

For starters, this URL is not very pleasant to look at, and not very user-friendly either. It also may contain information that you would prefer not to provide the user, such as the exact filename and the query string name. A much more appropriate URL would look like the following:

`http://www.domain.com/Catalog.aspx#Product/4`

This URL is much easier to read and is more user-friendly. In addition, it doesn't give away any details about your solution. You can obtain this URL using a feature known as Uri Mapping. Let's work through an example to further explore Uri Mapping with the Navigation Framework.

Try it Out: Uri Mapping and the Navigation Framework

In this example, you will work through implementing Uri Mapping with the project that you have been working with earlier in the chapter .

1. Begin by opening the project Ch7_NavAppFromScratch you were working on in the previous section.

2. There are three views in your solution that you would like to add Uri Mapping for: View1.xaml, View2.xaml, and InnerView1.xaml. For these, you will add simple Uri Maps that point these to View1, View2, and InnerView. Start by opening the App.xaml file and adding the xml namespace for the navigation framework.

```
<Application
    xmlns="http://schemas.microsoft.com/winfx/2006/xaml/presentation"
     xmlns:x="http://schemas.microsoft.com/winfx/2006/xaml"
     x:Class="Ch8_NavAppFromScratch.App"
xmlns:nav="clr-
namespace:System.Windows.Navigation;assembly=System.Windows.Controls.Navigation">
    <Application.Resources>

    </Application.Resources>
</Application>
```

3. Now that the namespace is added, you need to add the UriMapper section to the Application Resources.

```
<Application.Resources>
    <nav:UriMapper x:Key="uriMapper">

    </nav:UriMapper>
</Application.Resources>
```

4. Within the UriMapper section you now need to add two UriMapping elements, one for View1.xaml and one for View2.xaml. Each mapping will contain two attributes: The Uri attribute is the name representing the mapping that will appear in the browser address bar, and the MappedUri attribute represents the actual Uri mapped to by the UriMapping.

```
<Application.Resources>
    <nav:UriMapper x:Key="uriMapper">
        <nav:UriMapping Uri="View1" MappedUri="/View1.xaml" />
        <nav:UriMapping Uri="View2" MappedUri="/View2.xaml" />
    </nav:UriMapper>
</Application.Resources>
```

5. You now can update MainPage.xaml to navigate to the views using the UriMappings.

```
<StackPanel Orientation="Horizontal" HorizontalAlignment="Center">

    <HyperlinkButton Content="View 1"
                     Click="LinkClick"
                     Tag="View1"
                     Padding="5" />
    <HyperlinkButton Content="View 2"
                     Click="LinkClick"
                     Tag="View2"
                     Padding="5" />

</StackPanel>
```

6. Next, you will shift your attention to the InnerView1.xaml. If you recall in the previous section on passing data to a navigation view, you are passing the color to InnerView1.xaml via the QuervString. Because of this, you need that to be taken into account in your UriMapping. Open up the code behind for View1.xaml and modify the Button_Click method so it navigates to InnerView/{0}.

```
private void Button_Click(object sender, RoutedEventArgs e)
{
    string color = Color.SelectionBoxItem.ToString();

    NavigationService.Navigate(
        new Uri(string.Format("InnerView/{0}", color),
            UriKind.Relative));
}
```

7. In order for this navigate to work, you need to add an additional UriMapping to the Application.Resources.

```
<Application.Resources>
    <nav:UriMapper x:Key="uriMapper">
        <nav:UriMapping Uri="View1" MappedUri="/View1.xaml" />
        <nav:UriMapping Uri="View2" MappedUri="/View2.xaml" />
        <nav:UriMapping Uri="InnerView/{c}"
                        MappedUri="/InnerView1.xaml?Color={c}" />
    </nav:UriMapper>
</Application.Resources>
```

8. Next, in the MainPage.xaml, add the UriMapper property to the Navigation Frame object.

```
<navigation:Frame x:Name="ContentFrame"
                  HorizontalContentAlignment="Stretch"
                  VerticalContentAlignment="Stretch"
                  Margin="10"
                  Grid.Row="1"
                  BorderThickness="2"
                  BorderBrush="Black"
                  UriMapper="{StaticResource uriMapper}" />
```

9. You are now ready to run the solution. Select Debug → Start Debugging or press F5 to run the application. When Internet Explorer opens the application, click on the View 1 link at the top. Notice that the URL now reads:

```
Ch8_NavAppFromScratchTestPage.aspx#View1
```

10. Now select Red and click on the Navigate to Inner View and once again inspect the URL:

```
Ch8_NavAppFromScratchTestPage.aspx#InnerView/Red
```

As you have seen in this example, UriMapping provide a way to create more user friendly Url addresses and also provide a way to hide application specific information from appearing in your application.

URI ROUTING

In addition to Uri Mapping, the Navigation Framework in Silverlight 3 supports Uri Routing. For example, if you placed all of your navigation views in a subdirectory named Views, you can follow a naming convention that you set. Then setup Uri Routes such as the following:

```
<nav:UriMapping Uri="{}{p}" MappedUri="/Views/{p}.xaml" />
```

This mapping will map all files within the Views directory to its filename minus the extension. For example, /Views/View1.xaml would map to View1 and /Views/AboutPage.xaml would map to AboutPage. As you can see if you are able to set a naming convention that you can follow, Uri Routing can really help you handle default mappings with the navigation framework.

Silverlight Navigation Application Template

While it is very possible to utilize the Navigation Framework from within a standard Silverlight application, Visual Studio 2008 contains a project template that will create a base Silverlight Navigation Application.

Try it Out: Using the Silverlight Navigation Application Template

In this example, you will create a base Silverlight application with navigation support using the built in Silverlight Navigation Application template included in Visual Studio 2008.

1. Start Visual Studio 2008 and select File → New → Project from the main menu.

2. In the New Project dialog box, select Silverlight as the project type and Silverlight Navigation Application as the template. Name the project Ch7_UsingNavTemplate, as shown in Figure 7-16.

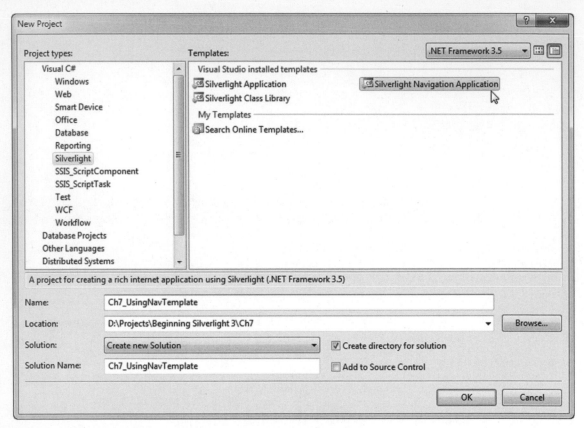

Figure 7-16. The Silverlight Navigation Application Project Template

3.   When the New Silverlight Application dialog appears, select the default to host the Silverlight application in a new ASP.NET web application named Ch7_UsingNavTemplate.Web. Press OK to continue.

4.   When the project is created by Visual Studio, you will notice that a number of pages have already been created for you, as shown in Figure 7-17. The base navigation project contains a main page called MainPage.xaml that hosts the navigation Frame, and two navigation Pages in the Views folder: AboutPage.xaml and HomePage.xaml.

Figure 7-17. *The base navigation project*

5. Select Debug → Start Debugging or press F5 to run the application. Internet Explorer will open and the application will be displayed, as shown in Figure 7-18.

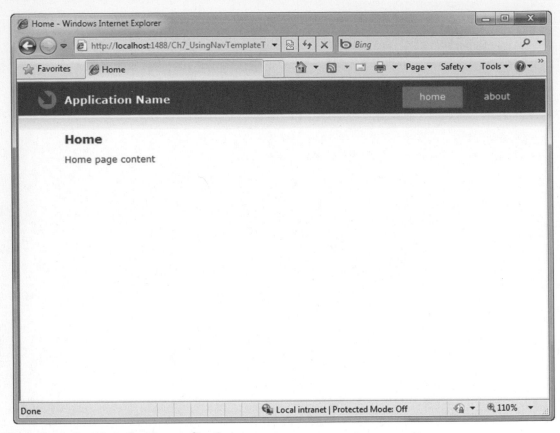

Figure 7-18. Creating a hosting application

6. You will notice at the top right-hand corner of the application there are two links: home and about. Click on the about button, the navigation frame will load in the AboutPage.xaml page into the white content box, as shown in Figure 7-19.

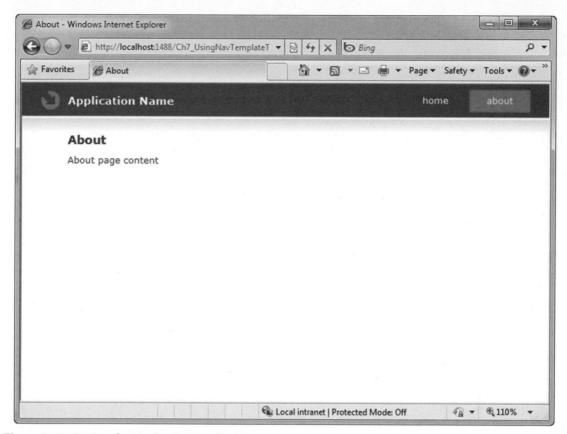

Figure 7-19. *Testing the Navigation Application*

As you have seen, the Silverlight Navigation Application VS.NET template can be used to give you a base application with navigation support to build on.

Using Multiple Frames

In all the examples you have worked through in this chapter, you have only dealt with a single Frame. However, there is no limit on the number of frames that you can include in your application. There are some restrictions, though. First of all, only one frame can integrate with the browser. Because of this, if you use multiple frames you will need to indicate what frame will be integrated with the browser. This is done using the JournalOwnership property on the Frame object. Consider the following example.

```
<navigation:Frame x:Name="ContentFrame"  />
<navigation:Frame x:Name="BottomFrame" JournalOwnership="OwnsJournal" />
```

In the preceding, the ContentFrame will have full integration with the browser, but the BottomFrame won't. Let's see this in action in the following exercise.

Try it Out: Using Multiple Frames

In this example, you will add a second Frame to the project you have been working on throughout this chapter.

1. Begin by opening the project Ch7_NavAppFromScratch you were working on in the previous section.

2. You will start by adding a new view to the project. Right click on the Silverlight project and choose Add → New Item. Select Silverlight Page as the template and name the file BottomView.xaml.

3. In the XAML for BottomView.xaml, add a simple TextBlock.

```
<Grid x:Name="LayoutRoot" Background="White">
    <TextBlock Text="Bottom View 1"
            FontSize="30"
            Foreground="Green"
            HorizontalAlignment="Center"
            VerticalAlignment="Center" />
</Grid>
```

4. With the new view created, you now need to edit the MainPage.xaml file to add a third row to the Grid and add a new frame within that new row. The second frame will not integrate with the browser so you will set the JournalOwnership property to OwnsJournal.

```
<Grid ShowGridLines="True" x:Name="LayoutRoot" Background="White">

    <Grid.RowDefinitions>
        <RowDefinition Height="30" />
        <RowDefinition></RowDefinition>
        <RowDefinition Height="65" />
    </Grid.RowDefinitions>

<StackPanel Orientation="Horizontal" HorizontalAlignment="Center">

    <HyperlinkButton Content="View 1"
                Click="LinkClick"
                Tag="View1"
                Padding="5" />
    <HyperlinkButton Content="View 2"
                Click="LinkClick"
                Tag="View2"
                Padding="5" />

</StackPanel>

        <navigation:Frame x:Name="ContentFrame"
                    HorizontalContentAlignment="Stretch"
                    VerticalContentAlignment="Stretch"
                    Margin="10"
                    Grid.Row="1"
                    BorderThickness="2"
```

```
                    BorderBrush="Black"
                    UriMapper="{StaticResource uriMapper}" />

        <navigation:Frame x:Name="BottomFrame"
                    HorizontalContentAlignment="Stretch"
                    VerticalContentAlignment="Stretch"
                    Margin="10"
                    Grid.Row="2"
                    JournalOwnership="OwnsJournal"
                    BorderThickness="2"
                    BorderBrush="Black" />
</Grid>
```

5. Next view the code behind for MainPage.xaml and add a Navigate call for BottomFrame.

```
private void LinkClick(object sender, RoutedEventArgs e)
{
    HyperlinkButton button = (HyperlinkButton)sender;
    string viewSource = button.Tag.ToString();
    ContentFrame.Navigate(new Uri(viewSource, UriKind.Relative));
    BottomFrame.Navigate(new Uri("/BottomView.xaml", UriKind.Relative));
}
```

6. You are now ready to run the solution. Select Debug → Start Debugging or press F5 to run the application. Click on the View 1 link at the top and the application will appear, as shown in Figure 7-20 with the second frame at the bottom.

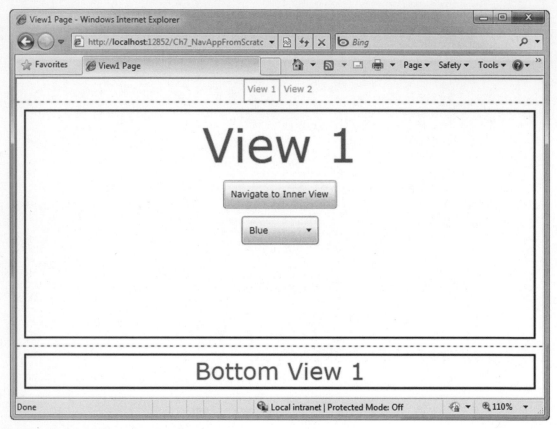

Figure 7-20. Multiple navigation frames

Summary

In this chapter, you looked at the Navigation Framework in-depth and saw how it can be used to build Silverlight applications that contain multiple page views. You explored the different objects within the Navigation Framework, such as the NavigationContext and NavigationService, as well as how to implement Uri Mapping within your applications.

CHAPTER 8

■ ■ ■

Local Storage in Silverlight

Localized storage in Silverlight is handled by its *isolated storage* feature, which is a virtual file system that can be used to store application data on the client's machine. As just a few examples, you might use local storage in your application to store user settings, undo information, shopping cart contents, or a local cache for your commonly used objects. Implementations of this feature are really limited only by your imagination.

In this chapter, you will explore Silverlight's isolated storage. I will walk you through building a virtual storage explorer to view the directories and files contained within isolated storage for an application. In addition, you will look at the isolated storage quota and how to increase the quota size for your Silverlight applications.

Working with Isolated Storage

Storing application information has always been a challenge for developers of traditional web applications. Often, implementing such storage means storing information in cookies or on the server, which requires using a postback to retrieve the data. In the case of desktop applications, implementing storage for application information is significantly easier, as developers have more access to the user's hard drive. Once again, Silverlight bridges the gap between desktop applications and web applications by offering isolated storage.

Using the Silverlight classes for working with isolated storage, you can not only store settings locally, but also create files and directories, as well as read and write files within isolated storage.

Using the Isolated Storage API

The classes for accessing isolated storage are contained within the System.IO.IsolatedStorage namespace. This namespace contains the following three classes:

- IsolatedStorageFile
- IsolatedStorageFileStream
- IsolatedStorageSettings

You'll look at each class to see what it represents.

IsolatedStorageFile

The IsolatedStorageFile class represents the isolated storage area, and the files and directories contained within it. This class provides the majority of the properties and methods used when working with isolated storage in Silverlight. As an example, in order to get an instance of the user's isolated storage for a given application, use the static method GetUserStoreForApplication(), as follows:

```
using (var store = IsolatedStorageFile.GetUserStoreForApplication())
{
    //...
}
```

Once the storage instance has been retrieved, a number of operations are available, including CreateDirectory(), CreateFile(), GetDirectoryNames(), and GetFileNames(). Also, the class has properties, such as Quota and AvailableFreeSpace. The following example creates a directory in isolated storage called Directory1, and then it retrieves the total and available free space in isolated storage:

```
using (var store = IsolatedStorageFile.GetUserStoreForApplication())
{
    store.CreateDirectory("Directory1");
    long quota = store.Quota;
    long availableSpace = store.AvailableFreeSpace;
}
```

IsolatedStorageFileStream

The IsolatedStorageFileStream class represents a given file. It is used to read, write, and create files within isolated storage. The class extends the FileStream class, and in most cases, developers will use a StreamReader and StreamWriter to work with the stream. As an example, the following code creates a new file named TextFile.txt and writes a string to the file:

```
using (var store = IsolatedStorageFile.GetUserStoreForApplication())
{
    IsolatedStorageFileStream stream = store.CreateFile("TextFile.txt");
    StreamWriter sw = new StreamWriter(stream);
    sw.Write("Contents of the File);
    sw.Close();
}
```

IsolatedStorageSettings

The IsolatedStorageSettings class allows developers to store key/value pairs in isolated storage. The key/value pairs are user-specific and provide a very convenient way to store settings locally. The following example demonstrates storing the user's name in IsolatedStorageSettings.

```
public partial class MainPage : UserControl
{
    private IsolatedStorageSettings isSettings =
        IsolatedStorageSettings.ApplicationSettings;
```

```csharp
public MainPage()
{
    InitializeComponent();
    this.Loaded += new RoutedEventHandler(Page_Loaded);
    this.cmdSave.Click += new RoutedEventHandler(cmdSave_Click);
}

void cmdSave_Click(object sender, RoutedEventArgs e)
{
    isSettings["name"] = this.txtName.Text;
    SetWelcomeMessage();
}

void Page_Loaded(object sender, RoutedEventArgs e)
{
    SetWelcomeMessage();
}

private void SetWelcomeMessage()
{
    if (isSettings.Contains("name"))
    {
        string name = (string)isSettings["name"];
        this.txtWelcome.Text = "Welcome " + name;
    }
    else
    {
        txtWelcome.Text =
            "Welcome! Enter Your Name and Press Save.";
    }
}
}
```

The first time users access the application, they will see the message "Welcome! Enter Your Name and Press Save." They can then enter their name and click the Save Name button. The name will be saved in local storage under the key/value pair called name. The next time the user accesses the application, his name will still be stored in local storage, and he will see the friendly welcome message, as shown in Figure 8-1.

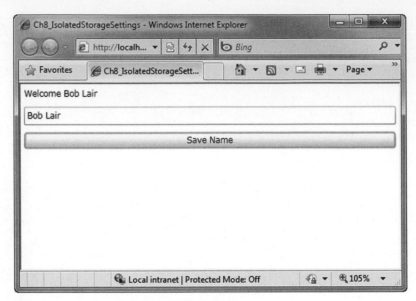

Figure 8-1. *Saving a user's name with IsolatedStorageSettings*

Now that you have briefly looked at some of the key classes associated with Silverlight's isolated storage, let's try building an application that uses this storage.

Try It Out: Creating a File Explorer for Isolated Storage

In this example, you will create a file explorer that will allow a user to navigate through an application's virtual storage within Silverlight's isolated storage. The file explorer will allow users to view, modify, and create new files within the given directories. Keep in mind that a Silverlight application has its own isolated storage, so the file explorer will be unique to the application. The end result will appear as shown in Figure 8-2.

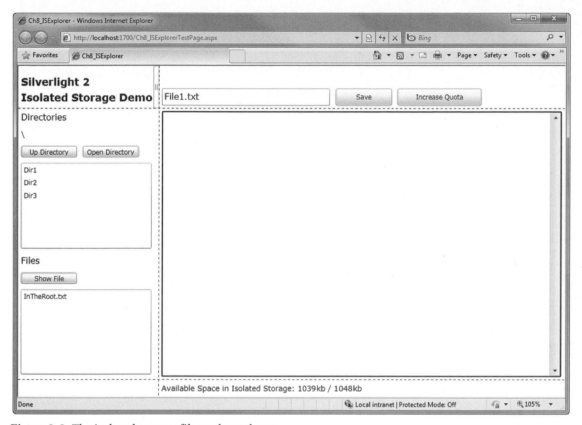

Figure 8-2. The isolated storage file explorer demo

Creating the Application Layout

Let's get started by setting up the application layout.

1. Create a new Silverlight application in Visual Studio 2008. Name it
    Ch8_ISExplorer and allow Visual Studio to create an ASP.NET web application
    called Ch8_ISExplorer.Web to host your application.

2. When the project is created, you should be looking at the MainPage.xaml file. If
    you do not see the XAML source, switch to that view so that you can edit the
    XAML. The application should take up the entire browser window, so begin by
    removing the Width and Height properties from your base UserControl.

```
<UserControl x:Class="Ch8_ISExplorer.MainPage"
    xmlns="http://schemas.microsoft.com/winfx/2006/xaml/presentation"
    xmlns:x="http://schemas.microsoft.com/winfx/2006/xaml">
    <Grid x:Name="LayoutRoot" Background="White">

    </Grid>
</UserControl>
```

187

3. Next, define a Grid for the form layout. Add two columns and three rows to the Grid. Set the Width property of the first column to 250. Set the Height property of the top row to 75 and the bottom row to 30. Also, in order to better see your Grid layout, set the ShowGridLines property to True.

```
<Grid x:Name="LayoutRoot" Background="White" ShowGridLines="True">
    <Grid.ColumnDefinitions>
        <ColumnDefinition Width="250" />
        <ColumnDefinition />
    </Grid.ColumnDefinitions>
    <Grid.RowDefinitions>
        <RowDefinition Height="75" />
        <RowDefinition />
        <RowDefinition Height="30" />
    </Grid.RowDefinitions>
</Grid>
```

4. Run your application. It should look like Figure 8-3.

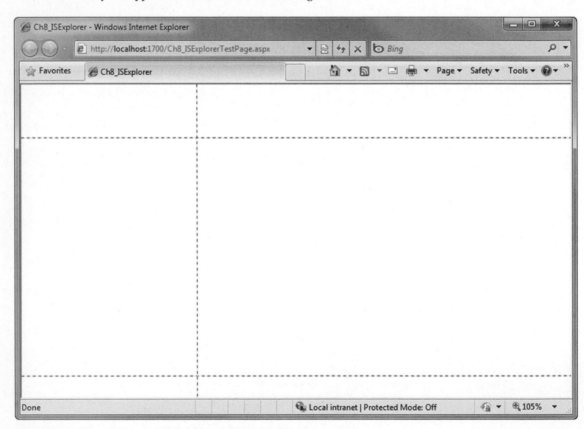

Figure 8-3. *The grid layout of the file explorer application*

Next, add a GridSplitter to allow the user to resize the left and right columns. Set the Grid.RowSpan to 3 and HorizontalAlignment to Right.

```
<Grid x:Name="LayoutRoot" Background="White" ShowGridLines="True">
    <Grid.ColumnDefinitions>
        <ColumnDefinition Width="250" />
        <ColumnDefinition />
    </Grid.ColumnDefinitions>
    <Grid.RowDefinitions>
        <RowDefinition Height="75" />
        <RowDefinition />
        <RowDefinition Height="30" />
    </Grid.RowDefinitions>

    <basics:GridSplitter
        Grid.RowSpan="3"
        HorizontalAlignment="Right" />
</Grid>
```

Now you will start filling the Grid cells with controls. You will add quite a few controls, using nested StackPanel components to assist in getting the desired layout. These controls have been discussed in detail in Chapters 4 and 5, and you can refer back to those chapters for more information about any of the controls used here.

5. In Grid.Row and Grid.Column (0,0), place a StackPanel that contains a couple cosmetic TextBlock controls that will serve as your application title, as follows (with some of the existing code omitted for brevity):

```
<Grid x:Name="LayoutRoot" Background="White" ShowGridLines="True">
    ...
    <basics:GridSplitter ...

    <StackPanel
        VerticalAlignment="Bottom"
        Orientation="Vertical"
        Margin="5">

        <TextBlock
            FontSize="18"
            FontWeight="Bold"
            Text="Silverlight 2">
        </TextBlock>
        <TextBlock
            FontSize="18"
            FontWeight="Bold"
            Text="Isolated Storage Demo">
        </TextBlock>

    </StackPanel>
</Grid>
```

Referring to Figure 8-2, you will notice that the content is divided into two sections: one for directories (top) and one for files (bottom). Let's first take care of the section for directories.

6. In Grid.Row and Grid.Column (1,0), place another StackPanel, which spans two rows, with a couple TextBlock controls, three Button controls, and two ListBox controls. The XAML should appear as follows (again, with some of the source code omitted, but the changes are shown):

```xml
<Grid x:Name="LayoutRoot" Background="White" ShowGridLines="True">
    ...
    <basics:GridSplitter ...

    <StackPanel
        VerticalAlignment="Bottom"
        Orientation="Vertical"
        Margin="5">

        <TextBlock
            FontSize="18"
            FontWeight="Bold"
            Text="Silverlight 2">
        </TextBlock>
        <TextBlock
            FontSize="18"
            FontWeight="Bold"
            Text="Isolated Storage Demo">
        </TextBlock>

    </StackPanel>

    <StackPanel
        Grid.Row="1"
        Grid.RowSpan="2"
        Orientation="Vertical">

        <TextBlock
            FontSize="15"
            Text="Directories"
            Margin="5">
        </TextBlock>

        <TextBlock
            x:Name="lblCurrentDirectory"
            FontSize="13"
            Text="Selected Directory"
            Margin="5">
        </TextBlock>

        <StackPanel Orientation="Horizontal">
            <Button
                x:Name="btnUpDir"
```

```
                Margin="5"
                Click="btnUpDir_Click"
                Content="Up Directory"
                Width="100"
                Height="20" />
            <Button
                x:Name="btnOpenDir"
                Margin="5"
                Click="btnOpenDir_Click"
                Content="Open Directory"
                Width="100"
                Height="20" />
        </StackPanel>

        <ListBox Height="150"
            x:Name="lstDirectoryListing"
            Margin="5,5,13,5">
        </ListBox>
    </StackPanel>
</Grid>
```

First is a simple cosmetic TextBlock for the section title. This is followed by the TextBlock named lblCurrentDirectory, which will be filled with the current directory. As the users navigate through the directories, it will be important to inform them which directory they are in.

Next are two Button controls (btnUpDir and btnOpenDir), which will be used for navigating through the directories. This is simplified into two basic tasks: moving up a directory and opening the currently selected directory. To get the buttons to appear visually as desired, they are contained in a StackPanel with horizontal orientation.

The final ListBox will be populated with directories named lstDirectoryListing. As the users navigate through the directories using the btnUpDir and btnOpenDir buttons, this ListBox will be repopulated automatically with the directories contained in the user's current location.

7. Next, still within Grid.Row and Grid.Column (1,0), add the files section, as follows:

```
<Grid x:Name="LayoutRoot" Background="White" ShowGridLines="True">

    ...
        <ListBox Height="100"
            x:Name="lstDirectoryListing"
            Margin="5,5,13,5">
        </ListBox>

        <TextBlock
            FontSize="15"
            Text="Files"
            Margin="5">
        </TextBlock>
```

```
    <StackPanel Orientation="Horizontal">
        <Button
            x:Name="btnOpenFile"
            Margin="5"
            Click="btnOpenFile_Click"
            Content="Show File"
            Width="100"
            Height="20" />
    </StackPanel>

    <ListBox Height="150"
        x:Name="lstFileListing"
        Margin="5,5,13,5">
    </ListBox>

</StackPanel>
</Grid>
```

As with the previous section, the first TextBlock holds the section title. Next is a Button control called btnOpenFile. Notice that even though there is only one button, it is still placed within a StackPanel for consistency. In the future, if you want to extend this application—for example, to add file deletion functionality—you may want to add buttons to this StackPanel. This is purely user preference; the StackPanel really was not required in this instance.

Finally, you have the ListBox that will be filled with the files in the current directory, in the same way that the directories ListBox will be filled in the top section.

8. To see what you have so far, press F5 (or choose Debug → Start Debugging from the menu bar) to start your Silverlight application.

Notice that Visual Studio will compile successfully and will open the browser instance. However, just when you think everything is going great and you are excited to see your beautiful form coming to life, you get an XamlParseException with a cryptic message:

```
AG_E_PARSER_BAD_PROPERTY_VALUE [Line: 66 Position: 34].
```

This is caused by the fact that, within the code behind, you have not declared the delegates that are referred to in your XAML.

■ **Note** The line and position noted in the error message you see may be slightly different from those shown here, depending on the spacing you included when adding the controls to the code.

---

9. Stop debugging by clicking the Stop button. Press F7 or select View → View Code. Sure enough, there are no event handlers.

At this point, you could go through and manually add the handlers in the code. But I think you've done enough typing already, so let's have Visual Studio do it for you.

10. Return to your XAML by clicking the `MainPage.xaml` file in the Files tab. Look at the controls you have added. You will notice that the code refers to three event handlers, one for each of the buttons: `btnUpDir_Click`, `btnOpenDir_Click`, and `btnOpenFile_Click`.

11. Find the first reference, `btnUpDir_Click`. Right-click it and select the Navigate to Event Handler option, as shown in Figure 8-4. Visual Studio will automatically create the event handler in the code behind, as follows:

```
public partial class MainPage : UserControl
{
    public MainPage()
    {
        InitializeComponent();
    }

    private void btnUpDir_Click(object sender, RoutedEventArgs e)
    {

    }
}
```

Figure 8-4. Choosing the Navigate to Event Handler option in Visual Studio

12. Repeat step 11 for the other two event handlers. At this point, your code behind should look as follows:

```
public partial class MainPage : UserControl
{
    public MainPage()
    {
        InitializeComponent();
    }

    private void btnUpDir_Click(object sender, RoutedEventArgs e)
    {
```

```
    }

    private void btnOpenDir_Click(object sender, RoutedEventArgs e)
    {

    }

    private void btnOpenFile_Click(object sender, RoutedEventArgs e)
    {

    }
}
```

13. Run the application. Once again, press F5 to start debugging. Barring any typos, the Silverlight application should appear as shown in Figure 8-5.

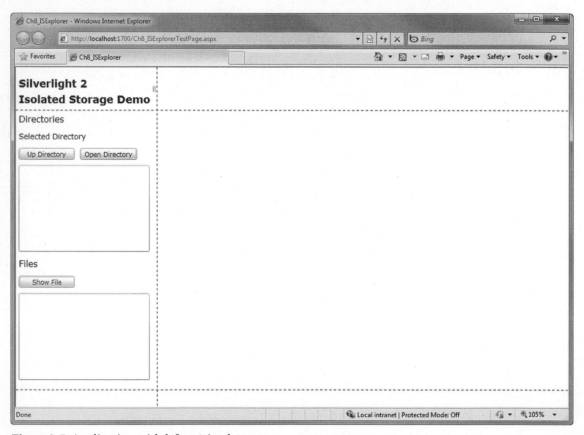

Figure 8-5. Application with left portion layout

It's looking good so far! You are almost finished with the application layout. Now, let's move on to the right column and add the final controls.

At the bottom of your Grid definition within Grid.Row and Grid.Column (0,1), place another StackPanel. Within it, add a TextBox named txtFileName that will contain the name of the file being edited, along with a Button control named btnSave, which will save the file referred to in txtFileName. Your XAML should look as follows:

```
<Grid x:Name="LayoutRoot" Background="White" ShowGridLines="True">

    ...

    </StackPanel>

    <StackPanel
        VerticalAlignment="Bottom"
        Orientation="Horizontal"
        Grid.Row="0"
        Grid.Column="1">

        <TextBox
            x:Name="txtFileName"
            Text="File1.txt"
            Margin="5"
            Width="300"
            Height="30"
            FontSize="15">
        </TextBox>
        <Button
            x:Name="btnSave"
            Margin="5"
            Content="Save"
            Width="100"
            Height="30"
            Click="btnSave_Click">
        </Button>

    </StackPanel>

</Grid>
```

14. While you are at it, go ahead and have Visual Studio create the event handler for btnSave_Click. Right-click it and choose the Navigate to Event Handler option to add the following handler:

```
public partial class MainPage : UserControl
{
    ...

    private void btnSave_Click(object sender, RoutedEventArgs e)
    {

    }
}
```

195

15. Navigate back to the XAML. Within Grid.Row and Grid.Column (1,1), add a TextBox named txtContents, which will display the contents of the opened file, as follows:

```
<Grid x:Name="LayoutRoot" Background="White" ShowGridLines="True">

    ...

    </StackPanel>

    <TextBox
        x:Name="txtContents"
        VerticalScrollBarVisibility="Visible"
        HorizontalScrollBarVisibility="Auto"
        AcceptsReturn="True"
        BorderBrush="Black" BorderThickness="2"
        Margin="5" Grid.Column="1" Grid.Row="1"
        FontSize="15" FontFamily="Courier">
    </TextBox>

</Grid>
```

Since this should be a multiline TextBox, you set the AcceptsReturn property to True. You also set the VerticalScrollBarVisibility property to Visible, which makes it always appear, and the HorizontalScrollBarVisibility property to Auto, which makes it appear only when there is enough text to require left and right scrolling.

16. Within Grid.Row and Grid.Column (1,2), place a StackPanel that contains five TextBlock controls, some that are simply cosmetic, and some that will be populated in the application's code, as follows:

```
<Grid x:Name="LayoutRoot" Background="White" ShowGridLines="True">

    ...

    </StackPanel>

    <TextBox
        x:Name="txtContents"
        VerticalScrollBarVisibility="Visible"
        HorizontalScrollBarVisibility="Auto"
        AcceptsReturn="True"
        BorderBrush="Black" BorderThickness="2"
        Margin="5" Grid.Column="1" Grid.Row="1"
        FontSize="15" FontFamily="Courier">
    </TextBox>

    <StackPanel
        VerticalAlignment="Bottom" Orientation="Horizontal"
        Margin="5" Grid.Column="1" Grid.Row="2">

        <TextBlock FontSize="13"
            Text="Available Space in Isolated Storage: " />
```

```
<TextBlock x:Name="txtAvalSpace" FontSize="13" Text="123" />
<TextBlock FontSize="13" Text="kb / " />
<TextBlock x:Name="txtQuota" FontSize="13" Text="123" />
<TextBlock FontSize="13" Text="kb" />
```

```
    </StackPanel>
```

```
</Grid>
```

With this, you are finished creating the application layout! You can now turn your attention to the code behind.

Coding the File Explorer

Now let's add the functionality that demonstrates accessing Silverlight's isolated storage.

1. When the file explorer is started, it will do two things. First, it will load some sample directories and files in isolated storage. Second, it will populate the directories and files ListBox controls, as well as update the informative TextBlock controls. You will encapsulate these tasks into two methods: LoadFilesAndDirs() and GetStorageData(). Create a Loaded event handler and add these two method calls to the event.

```
public partial class MainPage : UserControl
{
    public MainPage()
    {
        InitializeComponent();
        this.Loaded += new RoutedEventHandler(Page_Loaded);
    }

    void Page_Loaded(object sender, RoutedEventArgs e)
    {
        LoadFilesAndDirs();
        GetStorageData();
    }

    private void LoadFilesAndDirs()
    {

    }

    private void GetStorageData()
    {

    }

    private void btnUpDir_Click(object sender, RoutedEventArgs e)
    {

    }
```

```csharp
        private void btnOpenDir_Click(object sender, RoutedEventArgs e)
        {

        }

        private void btnOpenFile_Click(object sender, RoutedEventArgs e)
        {

        }

        private void btnSave_Click(object sender, RoutedEventArgs e)
        {

        }
}
```

2. Next, add references to two namespaces for your application. Also, create a global string variable called currentDir, which will store the current directory.

```csharp
using ...
using System.IO;
using System.IO.IsolatedStorage;

namespace Ch8_ISExplorer
{
    public partial class MainPage : UserControl
    {
        private string currentDir = "";

        public MainPage()
        {
            InitializeComponent();
            this.Loaded += new RoutedEventHandler(Page_Loaded);
        }

        ...
    }
}
```

3. Let's implement the LoadFilesAndDirs() method. The first step is to get an instance of the user's isolated storage for the application using the IsolatedStorageFile class's GetUserStoreForApplication() method. You will do this within a C# using statement so the instance is disposed of automatically.

```csharp
private void LoadFilesAndDirs()
{
    using (var store =
        IsolatedStorageFile.GetUserStoreForApplication())
    {
    }
}
```

4. Now that you have an instance of the isolated storage, create three root-level directories and three subdirectories, one in each of the root-level directories. Use the CreateDirectory() method to create the directories, as follows:

```
private void LoadFilesAndDirs()
{
    using (var store =
        IsolatedStorageFile.GetUserStoreForApplication())
    {
        // Create three directories in the root.
        store.CreateDirectory("Dir1");
        store.CreateDirectory("Dir2");
        store.CreateDirectory("Dir3");

        // Create three subdirectories under Dir1.
        string subdir1 = System.IO.Path.Combine("Dir1", "SubDir1");
        string subdir2 = System.IO.Path.Combine("Dir2", "SubDir2");
        string subdir3 = System.IO.Path.Combine("Dir3", "SubDir3");
        store.CreateDirectory(subdir1);
        store.CreateDirectory(subdir2);
        store.CreateDirectory(subdir3);
    }
}
```

5. Next, create two files: one in the root and one in a subdirectory. To do this, use the CreateFile() method, which returns an IsolatedStorageFileStream object. For now, you will leave the files empty, so after creating the files, simply close the stream.

```
private void LoadFilesAndDirs()
{
    using (var store =
        IsolatedStorageFile.GetUserStoreForApplication())
    {
        // Create three directories in the root.
        store.CreateDirectory("Dir1");
        store.CreateDirectory("Dir2");
        store.CreateDirectory("Dir3");

        // Create three subdirectories under Dir1.
        string subdir1 = System.IO.Path.Combine("Dir1", "SubDir1");
        string subdir2 = System.IO.Path.Combine("Dir2", "SubDir2");
        string subdir3 = System.IO.Path.Combine("Dir3", "SubDir3");
        store.CreateDirectory(subdir1);
        store.CreateDirectory(subdir2);
        store.CreateDirectory(subdir3);

        // Create a file in the root.
        IsolatedStorageFileStream rootFile =
            store.CreateFile("InTheRoot.txt");
        rootFile.Close();
```

```
        // Create a file in a subdirectory.
        IsolatedStorageFileStream subDirFile =
            store.CreateFile(
                System.IO.Path.Combine(subdir1, "SubDir1.txt"));
        subDirFile.Close();
    }
}
```

■ **Caution** Notice the `Path.Combine()` method call here is fully qualified (specified with the namespace). This is because there is another `Path` class in `System.Windows.Shapes`. If you don't fully qualify `Path`, the ambiguous name will cause an error.

That completes the `LoadFilesAndDirs()` method. Next, you will implement the `GetStorageData()` method, which will display the storage information in the application.

6. Since you will be populating the directories and files `ListBox` controls, you need to make sure you clear them each time the `GetStorageData()` method is called. You will do this by calling the `Items.Clear()` method on the two `ListBox` controls. Then you will get an instance of the user's isolated storage, in the same way as you did in the `LoadFilesAndDirs()` method.

```
private void GetStorageData()
{
    this.lstDirectoryListing.Items.Clear();
    this.lstFileListing.Items.Clear();

    using (var store =
        IsolatedStorageFile.GetUserStoreForApplication())
    {

    }
}
```

7. Next, you want to list all of the directories that are contained in the directory passed to the method. In order to do this, you will construct a search string using the `System.IO.Path.Combine()` method. You will then call the `GetDirectoryNames()` method along with the search string. This will return a string array, which you can then step through to manually populate the directories `ListBox`.

```
private void GetStorageData()
{
    this.lstDirectoryListing.Items.Clear();
    this.lstFileListing.Items.Clear();

    using (var store =
        IsolatedStorageFile.GetUserStoreForApplication())
```

```
    {
        string searchString =
            System.IO.Path.Combine(currentDir, "*.*");

        string[] directories =
            store.GetDirectoryNames(searchString);

        foreach (string sDir in directories)
        {
            this.lstDirectoryListing.Items.Add(sDir);
        }
    }
}
```

8. Now populate the files ListBox. You do this in the same way that you populated the directories ListBox, except this time, use the GetFileNames() method, which similarly returns a string array.

```
private void GetStorageData()
{
    this.lstDirectoryListing.Items.Clear();
    this.lstFileListing.Items.Clear();

    using (var store =
        IsolatedStorageFile.GetUserStoreForApplication())
    {
        string searchString =
            System.IO.Path.Combine(currentDir, "*.*");

        string[] directories =
            store.GetDirectoryNames(searchString);

        foreach (string sDir in directories)
        {
            this.lstDirectoryListing.Items.Add(sDir);
        }

        string[] files = store.GetFileNames(searchString);

        foreach (string sFile in files)
        {
            this.lstFileListing.Items.Add(sFile);
        }
    }
}
```

9. Now that the two ListBox controls are populated, you want to populate three additional TextBlock controls. One will show the current directory. The other two will display the amount of free space remaining in isolated storage and the available quota for the application. You get this information by using the Quota and AvailableFreeSpace properties, which return the total and free space in bytes, respectively.

```
private void GetStorageData()
{
    this.lstDirectoryListing.Items.Clear();
    this.lstFileListing.Items.Clear();

    using (var store =
        IsolatedStorageFile.GetUserStoreForApplication())
    {
        string searchString =
            System.IO.Path.Combine(currentDir, "*.*");

        string[] directories =
            store.GetDirectoryNames(searchString);

        foreach (string sDir in directories)
        {
            this.lstDirectoryListing.Items.Add(sDir);
        }

        string[] files = store.GetFileNames(searchString);

        foreach (string sFile in files)
        {
            this.lstFileListing.Items.Add(sFile);
        }

        long space = store.AvailableFreeSpace;
        txtAvalSpace.Text = (space / 1000).ToString();

        long quota = store.Quota;
        txtQuota.Text = (quota / 1000).ToString();

        this.lblCurrentDirectory.Text =
            String.Concat("\\", currentDir);
    }
}
```

■ **Note** For simplicity, you are dividing by 1000 instead of 1024. Therefore, the calculation will not be exact, but close enough for the purposes of this example.

---

10. Run the application. You will see that the current directory is set to \, and that the three directories and the file you created at the root level are displayed in the ListBox controls, as shown in Figure 8-6.

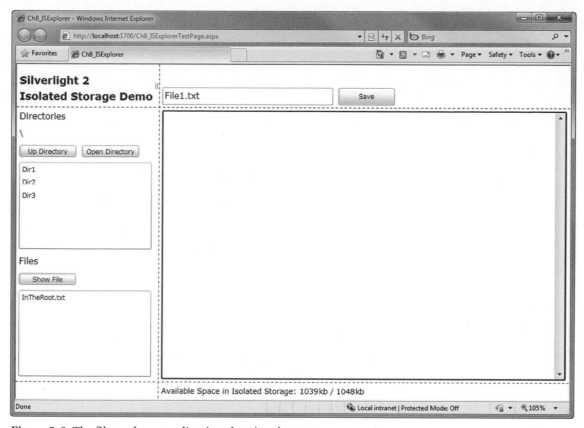

Figure 8-6. *The file explorer application showing the root*

Now you can implement the Button events, starting with the Up Directory and Open Directory buttons.

11. When the user clicks the Up Directory button, the system will find the current directory's parent directory using System.IO.Path.GetDirectoryName(), set the current directory to be that parent directory, and reexecute the GetStorageData() method.

```
private void btnUpDir_Click(object sender, RoutedEventArgs e)
{
    if (currentDir != "")
    {
        currentDir =
            System.IO.Path.GetDirectoryName(currentDir);
    }

    GetStorageData();
}
```

12. When the user clicks the Open Directory button, you will combine the current directory with the selected directory from the directory ListBox using the System.IO.Path.Combine() method, set the current directory to that new directory, and once again reexecute the GetStorageData() method.

```
private void btnOpenDir_Click(object sender, RoutedEventArgs e)
{
    if (this.lstDirectoryListing.SelectedItem != null)
    {
        currentDir =
            System.IO.Path.Combine(
                currentDir,
                this.lstDirectoryListing.SelectedItem.ToString());
    }
    GetStorageData();
}
```

13. Next, implement the Show File button's Click event, as follows:

```
private void btnOpenFile_Click(object sender, RoutedEventArgs e)
{
    if (this.lstFileListing.SelectedItem != null)
    {
        this.txtFileName.Text =
            this.lstFileListing.SelectedItem.ToString();

        using (var store =
            IsolatedStorageFile.GetUserStoreForApplication())
        {
            string filePath =
                System.IO.Path.Combine(
                    currentDir,
                    this.lstFileListing.SelectedItem.ToString());

            IsolatedStorageFileStream stream =
                store.OpenFile(filePath, FileMode.Open);
            StreamReader sr = new StreamReader(stream);

            this.txtContents.Text = sr.ReadToEnd();
            sr.Close();
        }
    }
}
```

When a user clicks the Show File button, the file from isolated storage opens, and its contents are displayed in txtContents. You achieve this by first getting an instance of the user's isolated storage, and then generating the path to the file by combining the current directory with the file name provided in txtFileName. After you have constructed the full file path, you open the file using OpenFile(), which returns a Stream containing the file contents. You attach a StreamReader to the Stream to assist in working with the stream, and then display the contents of the Stream using the StreamReader's ReadToEnd() method.

14. Finally, wire up the Save button, which will save the contents of txtContents to the file name specified in txtFileName. You want to make it so that if the user enters a file name that doesn't exist, the application will create a new file. If the user enters one that does exist, the application will override the contents of that file. Although this is not perfect for use in the real world, it serves as a fine demo for using isolated storage.

```
private void btnSave_Click(object sender, RoutedEventArgs e)
{
    string fileContents = this.txtContents.Text;

    using (var store =
        IsolatedStorageFile.GetUserStoreForApplication())
    {
        IsolatedStorageFileStream stream =
            store.OpenFile(
                System.IO.Path.Combine(
                    currentDir,
                    this.txtFileName.Text),
                FileMode.OpenOrCreate);

        StreamWriter sw = new StreamWriter(stream);
        sw.Write(fileContents);
        sw.Close();
        stream.Close();
    }

    GetStorageData();
}
```

This method is similar to the ShowFile() method. Basically, you get the isolated storage instance, and open the file using the OpenFile() method, passing it the full file path. However, this time, you pass the OpenFile() method FileMode.OpenOrCreate. This way, if the file doesn't exist, the application will create it. You then attach the returned stream to a StreamWriter, and write the contents to the Stream using the StreamWriter's Write() method.

After writing the file, you clean up the objects and call the GetStorageData() method, which will cause the newly created file to appear in the files ListBox (in the event a new file was created).

At this point, you're ready to test your completed application.

Testing the File Explorer

Now let's try out your new file explorer.

1. Fire up the application by pressing F5. If all goes well, you should see the application.

2. Highlight Dir1 in the Directories list box and click the Open Directory button. The application will navigate to that directory and refresh the list boxes to show the directories and files contained within that file.

3. Enter the file name SampleTextFile.txt in the txtFileName text box. For the contents, enter some arbitrary data. If you have Microsoft Word, you can generate a ton of random text using =Rand(10,20) and paste the content into the text box.

   After you enter the contents, click the Save button. You will see the file appear in the Files list box, as shown in Figure 8-7.

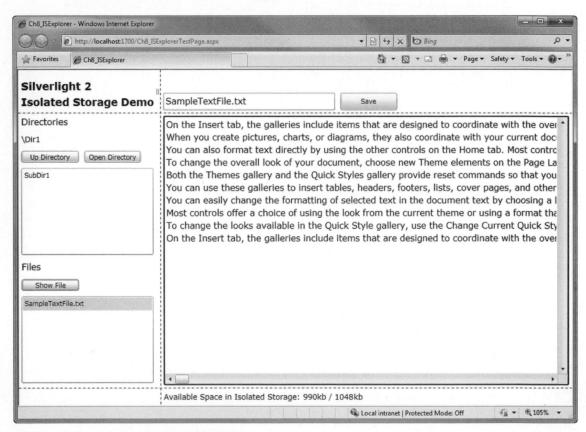

Figure 8-7. Testing the completed file explorer

4. Click the Up Directory button to navigate back to the root. You will notice that the current directory changes, as do the contents of the list boxes. For kicks, click Save again. This time, the application will save the same file in the root directory.

5. Highlight the InTheRoot.txt file and click the Show File button. Since you left the file empty, nothing will appear in the txtContents box. You can enter some text in the text box and click Save.

6. Highlight SampleTextFile.txt and click Show File. The contents of your file are still there. It really works!

7. Try adding some files (preferably with a large amount of text). Take a look at the display of the current free space and quota of the isolated storage at the bottom of the application. You should see the amount of free space decrease.

8. Stop debugging. Now restart debugging. Notice anything? Your files are still there! That is because isolated storage is persistent data, and it will remain until the user clears the isolated storage, as explained in the next section.

This exercise demonstrated how Silverlight's isolated storage works and how you can access it. In the following section, you will learn how to manage isolated storage, including changing its quota.

Managing Isolated Storage

By default, the amount of isolated storage space available for a Silverlight application is 1MB. You can view the available storage, clear it, and increase its size.

Viewing and Clearing Isolated Storage

In order to view the isolated storage saved on your machine, simply right-click any Silverlight application and select Silverlight Configuration from the pop-up menu. This will display the Microsoft Silverlight Configuration window. Navigate to the Application Storage tab, as shown in Figure 8-8. There, you can see your test application in the listing, and depending on what other Silverlight applications you have accessed, you may see other web sites listed.

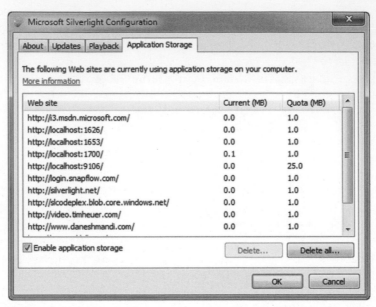

Figure 8-8. Viewing application storage information in the Microsoft Silverlight Configuration window

If users want to clear the storage space, they simply need to highlight the site they want to clear data for and click Delete. This will display a confirmation dialog box, as shown in Figure 8-9.

Figure 8-9. Deleting an application's isolated storage

What if you want more storage space for your application? Developers can request additional storage space by using the TryIncreaseQuotaTo() method. A restriction placed on this task is that it can be executed only in a user-triggered event, such as a Button control's Click event. This restriction is in place to prevent the application from increasing the quota without the user's knowledge.

Try It Out: Increasing the Isolated Storage Quota

To demonstrate how to increase the isolated storage quota, let's add a button to the file explorer demo to increase the quota to 4MB.

1. Open the IsolatedStorageExplorer project that you created in the previous exercise.

2. In the MainPage.xaml file, locate the definition of the Save button and add a new Button control called btnIncreaseQuota, with the caption Increase Quota, as follows:

```
<StackPanel
    VerticalAlignment="Bottom"
    Orientation="Horizontal"
    Grid.Row="0"
    Grid.Column="1">

    <TextBox
        x:Name="txtFileName"
        Text="File1.txt"
        Margin="5"
        Width="300"
        Height="30"
        FontSize="15">
    </TextBox>
    <Button
        x:Name="btnSave"
        Margin="5"
        Content="Save"
        Width="100"
        Height="30"
        Click="btnSave_Click">
    </Button>
    <Button
        x:Name="btnIncreaseQuota"
        Margin="5"
        Content="Increase Quota"
        Width="150"
        Height="30"
        Click="btnIncreaseQuota_Click">
    </Button>

</StackPanel>
```

3. You have wired up the Click event to a new event handler created by Visual Studio. Navigate to the code behind's definition of that event handler.

```
private void btnIncreaseQuota_Click(object sender, RoutedEventArgs e)
{
}
```

4. Next, you want to get an instance of the user's isolated storage, just as you did numerous times in creating the file explorer. Then call the IncreaseQuotaTo() method, passing it 4000000, which is roughly 4MB. Add the following to event handler:

```
private void btnIncreaseQuota_Click(object sender, RoutedEventArgs e)
{
    using (var store =
        IsolatedStorageFile.GetUserStoreForApplication())
    {
        if (store.IncreaseQuotaTo(4000000))
        {
            GetStorageData();
        }
        else
        {
            // The user rejected the request to increase the quota size
        }
    }
}
```

■ **Note** These numbers are not exact, which is fine for the demonstration here. You can increase the quota to 4MB exactly by multiplying 1024 by 4.

Notice that the IncreaseQuotaTo() method returns a Boolean value. Depending on whether the user accepted the application's request to increase the quota size, true or false will be returned. If the user accepted the request, you will want to redisplay the information displayed for the quota. The easiest way to do this is to simply call the GetStorageData() method, as you did in the event handler here.

5. Try out your new addition by running your application and clicking the new Increase Quota button. You will see the dialog box shown in Figure 8-10.

Figure 8-10. Dialog box to request to increase available storage

Click Yes. You will notice that the available quota is now increased in your application, as shown in Figure 8-11.

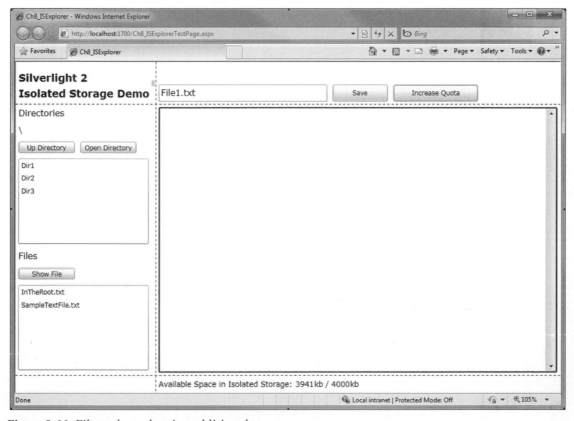

Figure 8-11. File explorer showing additional storage space

This completes the file explorer. Now you can apply these concepts to your own persistent storage implementations in your Silverlight applications.

Summary

In this chapter, you looked at Silverlight's isolated storage feature. As you saw, it is very straightforward to store user-specific data for your application and have that data persist over browser instances. This provides a very convenient way for developers to add offline content or save user settings.

In the next chapter, you will look at Microsoft Expression Blend 2, an application created for the sole purpose of visually editing XAML.

CHAPTER 9

∎∎∎

Introduction to Expression Blend

So far in this book, the primary focus has been on using Visual Studio 2008 to create Silverlight applications. Visual Studio provides developers with a strong IDE for developing RIAs. However, you may want your Silverlight applications to contain some complicated design elements, and in these cases, it's not much fun to edit the XAML manually. To address this problem, Microsoft has created Expression Blend, a product built to edit XAML documents visually.

Whereas Visual Studio has been designed to cater to the developer, Expression Blend has been built for the designer. As you've seen, Silverlight does a fantastic job of separating the appearance and logic of an application, so developers and designers can work side by side. ASP.NET took a few strides to achieve this separation, but still fell short in many ways. I think you will find that Silverlight has reached a new layer in this separation, making it much more practical for designers and developers to truly work in parallel in designing applications.

The first reaction most ASP.NET software developers will have when opening Expression Blend is shock. "Wow, this looks like no Microsoft development product I have ever seen!" And it is true that Expression Blend is quite different from the standard Visual Studio IDE type of product. The Microsoft developers have finally provided a product for the graphic designer audience, and they have attempted to make it very similar to the tools designers are accustomed to using. As software developers, we may need to play around a bit in Expression Blend to get the feel of it. Personally, I have found it quite cool to learn and use, and I think you will, too.

This chapter will get you started with Expression Blend. You'll learn about its key features and its workspace. Finally, I'll walk you through creating a grid layout with Expression Blend.

Key Features in Expression Blend

In this section, you will look at some of the notable features in Expression Blend, including the following:

- Visual XAML editor
- Visual Studio 2008 integration
- Split-view mode
- Visual State Manager and template editing support
- Timeline

■ **Note** One of the things that Microsoft has done better and better over the past few years is documentation. Expression Blend's documentation is quite comprehensive. For additional information about any of the items discussed in this chapter, refer to the User Guide provided with Expression Blend.

Visual XAML Editor

Clearly, the biggest feature of Expression Blend is that it provides a WYSIWYG editor for XAML. XAML is a very clean language, but it can also get quite complex quickly when you are working with your applications. This is especially true when you start to add animations and transformations, which are covered in Chapter 11.

Although it is possible to edit your XAML files completely in Visual Studio using IntelliSense, there is no substitute for a visual editor. In addition, the XAML that Expression Blend creates is very clean and developer-friendly. This should make developers happy, considering the terrible memories of earlier versions of FrontPage, where every change you made would result in your code being mangled beyond recognition.

In addition, when you start working with styles (covered in Chapter 10), IntelliSense support in Visual Studio becomes limited, so the XML is very difficult to edit manually. Expression Blend provides an extremely quick and easy way to edit and create styles, which is another reason it is an invaluable tool for editing your Silverlight applications.

Visual Studio 2008 Integration

Due to the strong push for developers and designers to work in parallel, and given the fact that XAML files are included directly within Visual Studio 2008 projects, a valid concern would be how well Expression Blend and Visual Studio work together. If there were conflicts between the two IDEs, there could be conflicts between the developers and designers, resulting in resistance to working in parallel.

The good news is that Expression Blend integrates with Visual Studio. Visual Studio 2008 projects can be opened directly in Expression Blend and vice versa. In addition, while Expression Blend creates Visual Studio 2008 projects by default, it is also capable of opening Visual Studio 2005 projects.

Split-View Mode

As is shown in Figure 9-1, Expression Blend allows you to work in design and source (XAML) mode simultaneously. For example, you can draw an object at the top in design mode, and the XAML in the source window will be updated automatically. In addition, you can just as easily edit the XAML, and the change will be reflected automatically in the design window.

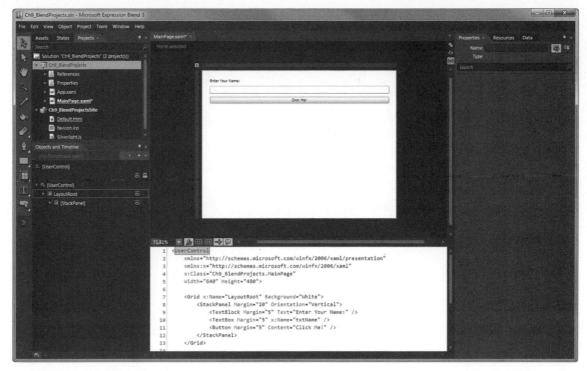

Figure 9-1. Expression Blend's split-view mode

Visual State Manager and Template Editing Support

One of the cool features of Silverlight is the fact that all controls released with it support the new Parts and State model, which requires strict separation between a control's logic and appearance. Microsoft recommends that all custom controls also support this model.

By separating the logic from the appearance of a control, a developer or designer can completely change the appearance of a control without affecting its behavior. This process is known as creating a template, or *skinning*, and is regulated by Visual State Manager (VSM). Expression Blend provides a very clean way to create and edit these parts and states, which makes skinning your applications a relatively simple task. You'll learn more about VSM and skinning in *Pro Silverlight 3 in C# 2008* by Matthew MacDonald (Apress, 2009).

World-Class Timeline

In Silverlight, animations are based on keyframes within a storyboard. These keyframes are set on a timeline, and they define the start and end points of a smooth visual transition. Figure 9-2 shows the Expression Blend timeline, which is located in the Objects and Timeline panel.

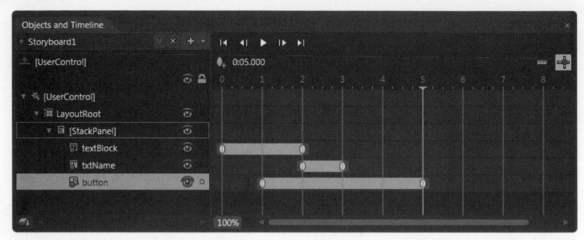

Figure 9-2. The Expression Blend timeline

The timeline provides you with structure for all of the animation sequences in your Silverlight application. Instead of the timeline being based on abstract frames, it is based on time, which makes it very straightforward and easy to understand. Also, as you develop your animations, you can quickly navigate to any given time on the timeline to check the appearance of your application at that point.

Try It Out: Working with Projects in Expression Blend

As you've learned, one of the key features of Expression Blend is that it integrates directly with Visual Studio 2008 projects. This exercise demonstrates how you can use the two products side by side while creating and editing projects.

1. Open Expression Blend. By default, when you open Expression Blend, you will see the splash screen shown in Figure 9-3. If you do not want this screen to appear when you start Expression Blend, you can simply uncheck the Run at startup check box at the bottom left. For now, if this screen appears, click Close to continue with the example.

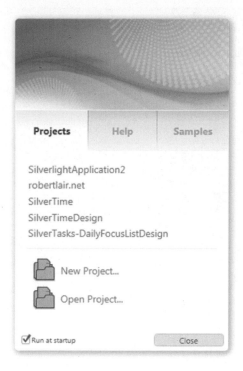

Figure 9-3. *Startup screen for Expression Blend*

2.   You should now have an empty Expression Blend workspace. From the main menu, click File → New Project. This will display the New Project dialog box.

3.   In the New Project dialog box, select Silverlight 3 Application + Website for the project type, and then enter Ch9_BlendProjects for the project name, as shown in Figure 9-4. Click OK to create the new project.

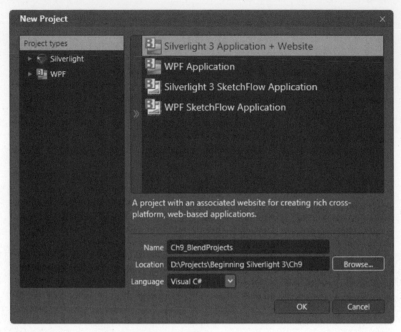

Figure 9-4. Creating a new project in Expression Blend

4.   By default, Expression Blend will open the MainPage.xaml file for editing. In the upper-right portion of the artboard (which contains the XML) are options to switch between design, XAML, and split-mode view. Click Split to see both the XAML and the design view at the same time, as shown in Figure 9-5.

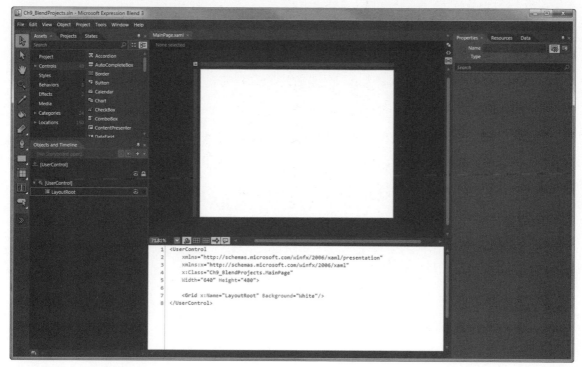

Figure 9-5. *Split-view mode in Expression Blend*

Now edit this project in Visual Studio. In the Project panel, right-click the
Ch9_BlendProjects project and select Edit in Visual Studio, as shown in Figure
9-6. This will automatically start Visual Studio 2008 and open your project.

■ **Note** Step 5 assumes that you have already installed Visual Studio 2008. If not, you will need to install that
to continue.

Figure 9-6. Editing a Expression Blend project in Visual Studio

5. In Visual Studio 2008, double-click `MainPage.xaml` in Solution Explorer. Let's make a simple change to the application in Visual Studio.

6. Modify the root `Grid` to add the following code shown in bold, to define a `StackPanel` with a `TextBlock`, `TextBox`, and `Button`.

```
<UserControl
    xmlns="http://schemas.microsoft.com/winfx/2006/xaml/presentation"
    xmlns:x="http://schemas.microsoft.com/winfx/2006/xaml"
    x:Class="Ch9_BlendProjects.MainPage"
    Width="640" Height="480">

    <Grid x:Name="LayoutRoot" Background="White">
        <StackPanel Margin="20" Orientation="Vertical">
            <TextBlock Margin="5" Text="Enter Your Name:" />
            <TextBox Margin="5" x:Name="txtName" />
            <Button Margin="5" Content="Click Me!" />
        </StackPanel>
    </Grid>
</UserControl>
```

7. From the main menu, click File → Save All, just to make sure everything is saved.

8. Switch back to Expression Blend. It will prompt you with the File Modified dialog box, as shown in Figure 9-7. Click Yes. You will see Expression Blend refresh the project so that it reflects the changes you made in Visual Studio 2008.

Figure 9-7. File modification notification in Expression Blend

Pretty nifty, right? The same file modification is offered when you do the reverse: make a change in Expression Blend and then go back into Visual Studio. Feel free to try this out yourself.

As this exercise demonstrated, Expression Blend and Visual Studio work together seamlessly. You can switch back and forth between the two products without fear of data loss or conflicts.

■ **Note** Although usually Expression Blend will be used together with Visual Studio, Expression Blend will actually pick up on changes to open files caused by edits in any editor.

Exploring the Workspace

Now that I have briefly discussed some of the key features of Expression Blend, let's take a look at the different elements of its workspace. Despite its radical appearance, developers will find many similarities between Visual Studio and Expression Blend.

Let's start out by looking at Expression Blend in Animation workspace mode. You enter this mode by selecting Window → Workspaces → Animation from the main menu. Starting at the left, you will see the Toolbox and the artboard, which contains the application and the XAML source. On the right is the Properties panel. Docked with the Properties panel are the Project and Resources panels. At the bottom of the workspace, you will see the VSM panel and Objects and Timeline panel. Let's take a closer look at some of these workspace elements.

Toolbox

The Expression Blend Toolbox provides the tools for adding and manipulating objects within your application. As shown in Figure 9-8, it is divided into five primary sections: selection tools, view tools, brush tools, object tools, and asset tools. The object tool group includes six submenus, which contain path tools, shape tools, layout tools, text controls, and common controls.

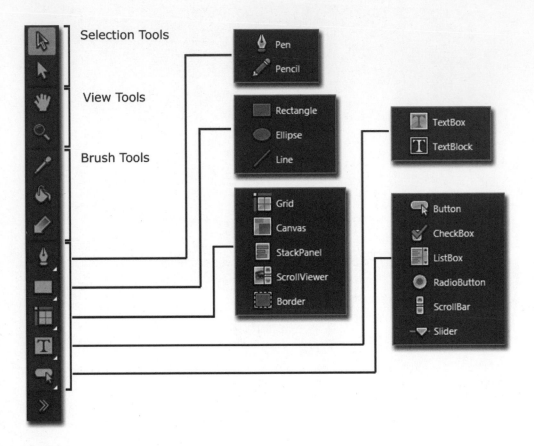

Figure 9-8. *The Expression Blend Toolbox*

Clicking the Asset Tools icon at the very bottom of the Toolbox opens the Asset Library window, which lists the Silverlight system controls, as shown in Figure 9-9.

Figure 9-9. The Asset Library window

Project Panel

The Project panel is very similar to Solution Explorer in Visual Studio. It lists all the files associated with the project.

The Project panel also displays project references and properties. See Figure 9-6 for an example of the Project panel.

Properties Panel

The Properties panel allows you to view and modify the properties of objects on the artboard. Figure 9-10 shows an example of the Properties panel when an Ellipse control is selected.

The Properties panel is divided into a number of sections to help you easily find specific properties. The sections displayed depend on the object you have selected. In addition, the Search box at the top of the Properties panel allows you to filter the listing by typing in the property name. Figure 9-11 shows an example of the Properties panel after searching for the Margin property.

Figure 9-10. *The Properties panel*

Figure 9-11. *Filtering the Properties panel*

Objects and Timeline Panel

All objects that are added to your Silverlight application are represented in the Objects and Timeline panel. Since items can be nested within other objects, a type of layering takes place. For objects that contain additional objects, an arrow will appear to the left of the item. Click this arrow to expand and collapse the display of the nested objects.

When animation is added to your Silverlight application, storyboards are created. Storyboards are represented in the timeline, as shown earlier in Figure 9-2. You'll learn more about the timeline in Chapter 11.

Laying Out an Application with Expression Blend

As discussed in Chapter 3, you have a number of options when it comes to laying out your Silverlight application. Although these layout controls can be added manually, Expression Blend offers a visual option. In this section, you will look at how Expression Blend can be used to easily work with the Grid layout control.

Working with the Grid Control in Expression Blend

In Expression Blend, you place dividers to create columns and rows in the grid. When a Grid control is defined, Expression Blend will show blue rulers above and to the left of the grid. When you move your cursor over the blue rulers, a row divider will appear. Clicking the blue ruler will place the divider, and dragging a placed divider will move it. You will have a chance to try this out in a moment.

In the top-left corner of the window is an icon that determines the grid's edit mode. There are two layout editing modes for a grid within Expression Blend:

> *Canvas layout mode*: In canvas layout mode, when column and row dividers are moved, elements inside those rows and columns stay in place.

> *Grid layout mode*: In grid layout mode, the elements move with the column and row dividers.

Try It Out: Editing a Layout Grid with Expression Blend

Let's give layout in Expression Blend a try. In this exercise, you will create a simple grid layout with three rows and two columns. Then you will nest a secondary grid within the right-center cell, and place two more rows within that grid. The end product will look like Figure 9-12.

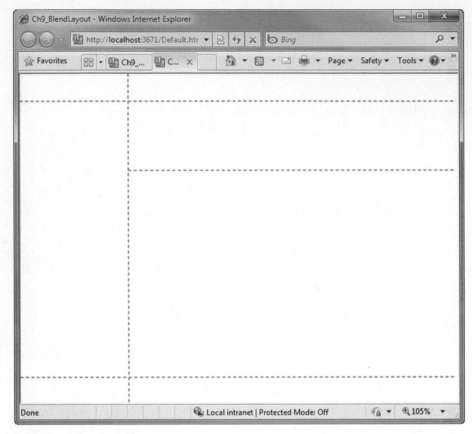

Figure 9-12. *The completed grid layout*

1. In Expression Blend, create a new Silverlight 3 Application + Website project named Ch9_BlendLayout. The MainPage.xaml file will be opened automatically, and as usual, a root Grid named LayoutRoot will be present.

2. First, create the column definitions. To do this, at about 25% from the left of the top blue grid ruler, click the ruler to place a grid divider, as shown in Figure 9-13. If you examine the XAML, you will notice that the <Grid.ColumnDefinitions> element has been added, along with two <ColumnDefinition> elements, as follows (note that your percentages do not need to be exact):

```
<UserControl
    xmlns="http://schemas.microsoft.com/winfx/2006/xaml/presentation"
    xmlns:x="http://schemas.microsoft.com/winfx/2006/xaml"
    x:Class="GridsInBlend.MainPage"
    Width="640" Height="480">

    <Grid x:Name="LayoutRoot" Background="White" >
        <Grid.ColumnDefinitions>
```

```xml
            <ColumnDefinition Width="0.25*"/>
            <ColumnDefinition Width="0.75*"/>
        </Grid.ColumnDefinitions>
    </Grid>
</UserControl>
```

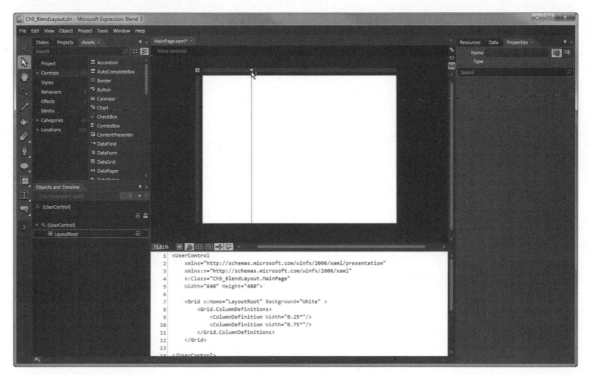

Figure 9-13. *Adding column definitions*

3. Next, create the rows. In the blue grid ruler on the left, click at about 10% from the top and 10% from the bottom to place two dividers. Your grid should now look like the one shown in Figure 9-14.

The source for the MainPage.xaml file should be very similar to the following (the actual heights and widths do not need to be exact):

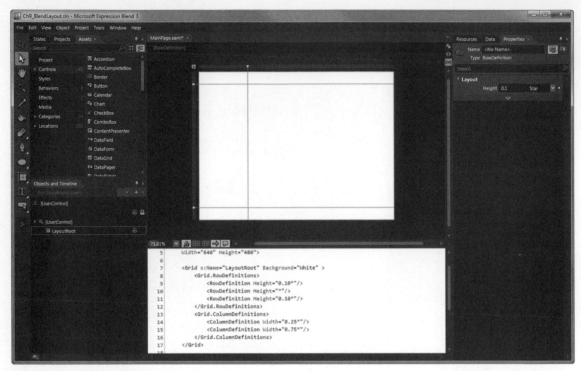

Figure 9-14. *Adding row definitions*

```
<UserControl
    xmlns="http://schemas.microsoft.com/winfx/2006/xaml/presentation"
    xmlns:x="http://schemas.microsoft.com/winfx/2006/xaml"
    x:Class="GridsInBlend.MainPage"
    Width="640" Height="480">

    <Grid x:Name="LayoutRoot" Background="White" >
        <Grid.RowDefinitions>
            <RowDefinition Height="0.1*"/>
            <RowDefinition Height="0.8*"/>
            <RowDefinition Height="0.1*"/>
        </Grid.RowDefinitions>
        <Grid.ColumnDefinitions>
            <ColumnDefinition Width="0.25*"/>
            <ColumnDefinition Width="0.75*"/>
        </Grid.ColumnDefinitions>
    </Grid>
</UserControl>
```

At this point, you have created a number of cells. Now, let's create a nested grid within the right-center cell. To do this, make certain that the LayoutRoot is selected in the Objects and Timeline panel, and then double-click the Grid control in the Toolbox. This will add a Grid of the default size to your application, as shown in Figure 9-15.

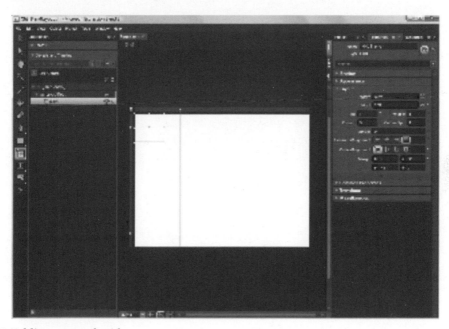

Figure 9-15. Adding a nested grid

4. With this new grid selected, edit its properties. In the Properties panel, set the properties as shown in Figure 9-16.

5. The nested grid should now take up the entire right-center cell. In the Objects and Timeline panel, double-click the innerGrid object you just added. The top and left grid rulers will now appear for the inner grid, as shown in Figure 9-17.

At this point, you could easily add rows and columns using the rulers, as you did with the LayoutRoot, but let's try a different method.

Figure 9-16. *Setting the nested grid properties*

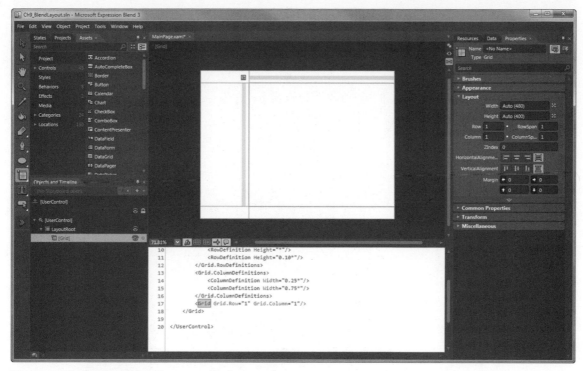

Figure 9-17. Nested grid with row and column rulers

With innerGrid selected, in the Properties panel's Search box, type **Definitions**. This will display the RowDefinitions and ColumnDefinitions properties, as shown in Figure 9-18.

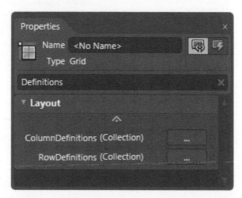

Figure 9-18. RowDefinition and ColumnDefinition property collections

6. Click the button to the right of RowDefinitions (Collection) to bring up the RowDefinition Collection Editor dialog box.

7. Click the "Add another item" button near the bottom of the RowDefinition Collection Editor dialog box and add two RowDefinition items. Set the Height property for the first RowDefinition to be .25 and the Height property for the second RowDefinition to .75, as shown in Figure 9-19. Then click OK to close the editor.

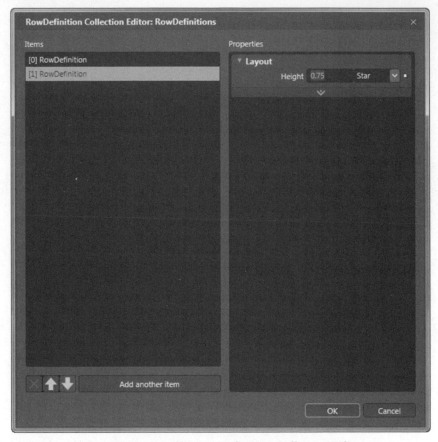

Figure 9-19. Adding RowDefinition items in the RowDefinition Collection Editor

In the Properties panel, set the ShowGridLines property for both Grids to True.

The final XAML should look like the following (again, the heights and widths only need to be close):

```
<UserControl
    xmlns="http://schemas.microsoft.com/winfx/2006/xaml/presentation"
    xmlns:x="http://schemas.microsoft.com/winfx/2006/xaml"
    x:Class="GridsInBlend.MainPage"
    Width="640" Height="480">

    <Grid x:Name="LayoutRoot" Background="White" ShowGridLines="True" >
```

```
    <Grid.RowDefinitions>
        <RowDefinition Height="0.1*"/>
        <RowDefinition Height="0.8*"/>
        <RowDefinition Height="0.1*"/>
    </Grid.RowDefinitions>
    <Grid.ColumnDefinitions>
        <ColumnDefinition Width="0.25*"/>
        <ColumnDefinition Width="0.75*"/>
    </Grid.ColumnDefinitions>
    <Grid Height="Auto"
        Margin="0,0,0,0"
        VerticalAlignment="Stretch"
        Grid.Row="1"
        x:Name="innerGrid"
        Grid.Column="1"
        ShowGridLines="True">
        <Grid.RowDefinitions>
            <RowDefinition Height="0.25*"/>
            <RowDefinition Height="0.75*"/>
        </Grid.RowDefinitions>
    </Grid>
    </Grid>
</UserControl>
```

8. Press F5 to test your application. The result should appear as shown earlier in Figure 9-12.

As you can see, once you get used to working with Expression Blend, it can save you quite a bit of typing. This will make laying out your applications a much faster and easier task.

Summary

In this chapter, you took a first look at Expression Blend and how it can be used alongside Visual Studio 2008 to help you design your Silverlight applications. You also looked at working with the Grid layout control to create complex layouts for your applications.

The upcoming chapters explain how to use Expression Blend to style your Silverlight applications, as well as add transformations and animations to your applications.

CHAPTER 10

Styling in Silverlight

Of course you will want to create a rich appearance for your Silverlight application. You'll make choices about your design. What font size and family will you use? How much space will you place between your objects? What size of text boxes and buttons will you use?

As you'll learn in this chapter, you can control the styles of your Silverlight application's UI elements in several ways. The first approach you will explore is the straightforward use of inline properties. Then you will look at how to define and apply Silverlight styles.

Inline Properties

You can simply define style properties directly in the object definitions. As an example, the following code snippet sets the FontFamily, FontSize, FontWeight, and Margin properties within the TextBlock itself.

```
<TextBlock
    Grid.Row="0"
    Grid.Column="0"
    Text="First Name"
    FontFamily="Verdana"
    FontSize="16"
    FontWeight="Bold"
    Margin="5" />
```

You can set inline properties using either Visual Studio or Expression Blend. Let's try out both.

Try It Out: Setting Inline Properties with Visual Studio

The following exercise demonstrates how to use Visual Studio 2008 to define the appearance of your Silverlight applications with inline properties. In this exercise, you will create the UI for a simple data-input application. You will not add any logic to the application, since the focus is on the appearance of the controls.

1. Open Visual Studio 2008 and create a new Silverlight application named Ch10_VSInlineStyling. Allow Visual Studio to create a Web Application project to host the application.

2. When the project is created, you should be looking at the `MainPage.xaml` file. If you do not see the XAML source, switch to that view. Start by adjusting the size of the `UserControl` to get some additional space in which to work. Set `Height` to 400 and `Width` to 600, as follows:

```
<UserControl x:Class="Ch10_VSInlineStyling.MainPage"
    xmlns="http://schemas.microsoft.com/winfx/2006/xaml/presentation"
    xmlns:x="http://schemas.microsoft.com/winfx/2006/xaml"
    Width="600" Height="400">
    <Grid x:Name="LayoutRoot" Background="White">

    </Grid>
</UserControl>
```

3. Add four rows and two columns to the root `Grid`. Set the width of the left column to 150, leaving the rest of the row and column definitions unspecified, as follows:

```
<Grid x:Name="LayoutRoot" Background="White">
    <Grid.RowDefinitions>
        <RowDefinition />
        <RowDefinition />
        <RowDefinition />
        <RowDefinition />
    </Grid.RowDefinitions>
    <Grid.ColumnDefinitions>
        <ColumnDefinition Width="150" />
        <ColumnDefinition />
    </Grid.ColumnDefinitions>
</Grid>
```

Next, add `TextBlock` controls in the three top-left columns and `TextBox` controls in the top-right columns, with the text `First Name`, `Last Name`, and `Age`. Then add three `Button` controls within a horizontal `StackPanel` in the bottom-right column. Give these buttons the labels `Save`, `Next`, and `Delete`. (Again, you won't be adding any logic to these controls; you will simply be modifying their appearance.) The code for this layout follows:

```
<Grid x:Name="LayoutRoot" Background="White">
    <Grid.RowDefinitions>
        <RowDefinition />
        <RowDefinition />
        <RowDefinition />
        <RowDefinition />
    </Grid.RowDefinitions>
    <Grid.ColumnDefinitions>
        <ColumnDefinition Width="150" />
        <ColumnDefinition />
    </Grid.ColumnDefinitions>

    <TextBlock Grid.Row="0" Grid.Column="0" Text="First Name" />
    <TextBlock Grid.Row="1" Grid.Column="0" Text="Last Name" />
    <TextBlock Grid.Row="2" Grid.Column="0" Text="Age" />
```

```
    <TextBox Grid.Row="0" Grid.Column="1" />
    <TextBox Grid.Row="1" Grid.Column="1" />
    <TextBox Grid.Row="2" Grid.Column="1"  />

    <StackPanel Grid.Row="3" Grid.Column="2" Orientation="Horizontal">
        <Button Content="Save" />
        <Button Content="Next" />
        <Button Content="Delete" />
    </StackPanel>
</Grid>
```

4. Press F5 to start the application. You will see that the UI you have created is far from attractive, as shown in Figure 10-1. So let's make this ugly UI look a bit nicer by adding some styling.

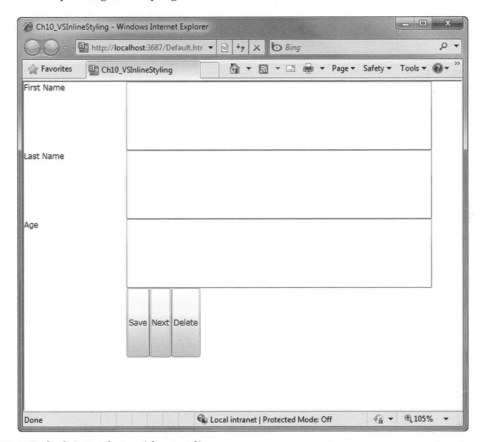

Figure 10-1. Default input form without styling

5. Start with the three TextBlock controls. Within Visual Studio, set the FontFamily, FontSize, FontWeight, and Margin properties directly within each TextBlock definition, as shown in the following code snippet. As you type the property names, you will notice that IntelliSense makes this task a bit less tedious. Once you have set the four properties on the First Name TextBlock, copy and paste the properties to the other two TextBlock controls.

```
<TextBlock Grid.Row="0" Grid.Column="0" Text="First Name"
    FontFamily="Verdana"
    FontSize="16"
    FontWeight="Bold"
    Margin="5" />
<TextBlock Grid.Row="1" Grid.Column="0" Text="Last Name"
    FontFamily="Verdana"
    FontSize="16"
    FontWeight="Bold"
    Margin="5" />
<TextBlock Grid.Row="2" Grid.Column="0" Text="Age"
    FontFamily="Verdana"
    FontSize="16"
    FontWeight="Bold"
    Margin="5" />
```

6. Run the application again. You can see the changes that have been made to the TextBlock labels, as shown in Figure 10-2.

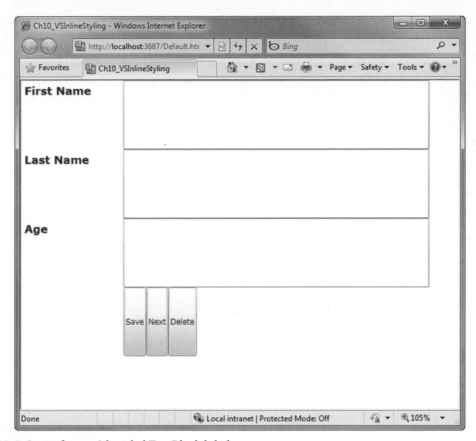

Figure 10-2. Input form with styled TextBlock labels

7. Now let's focus on the TextBox controls. Add the following style attributes to these controls.

```
<TextBox Grid.Row="0" Grid.Column="1"
    VerticalAlignment="Top"
    Height="24"
    Margin="5"
    FontSize="14"
    FontFamily="Verdana"
    Foreground="Blue"
    Background="Wheat" />

<TextBox Grid.Row="1" Grid.Column="1"
    VerticalAlignment="Top"
    Height="24"
    Margin="5"
    FontSize="14"
    FontFamily="Verdana"
```

```
    Foreground="Blue"
    Background="Wheat" />

<TextBox Grid.Row="2" Grid.Column="1"
    VerticalAlignment="Top"
    Height="24"
    Margin="5"
    FontSize="14"
    FontFamily="Verdana"
    Foreground="Blue"
    Background="Wheat" />
```

8. Run the application to see the effect. It should look like Figure 10-3.

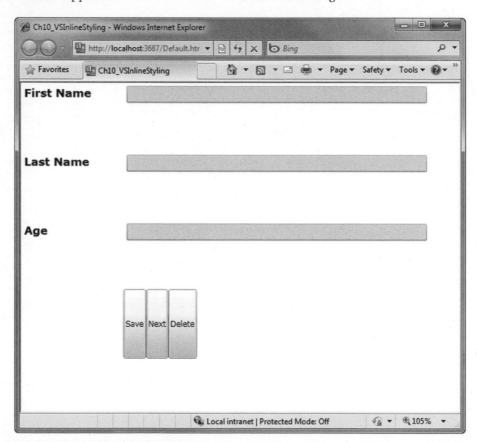

Figure 10-3. Input form with styled TextBox controls

Notice that the spacing between the rows is too large. Ideally, the spaces should only be large enough to allow the margins of the controls to provide the separation. To adjust this spacing, on each RowDefinition, change the Height property to Auto, as follows:

```
<Grid.RowDefinitions>
    <RowDefinition Height="Auto" />
    <RowDefinition Height="Auto" />
    <RowDefinition Height="Auto" />
    <RowDefinition Height="Auto" />
</Grid.RowDefinitions>
<Grid.ColumnDefinitions>
    <ColumnDefinition Width="150" />
    <ColumnDefinition />
</Grid.ColumnDefinitions>
```

9. Once more, run the application to see how it looks at this point. Figure 10-4 shows the results of the automatic height settings.

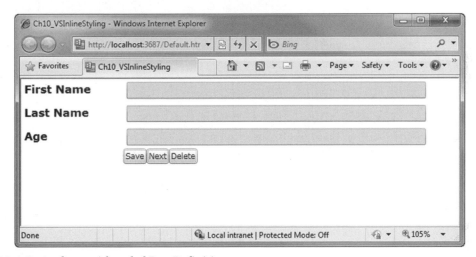

Figure 10-4. *Input form with styled RowDefinitions*

10. The next elements to tackle are the Button controls. Add the following style attributes to these three controls:

```
<Button Content="Save"
    FontFamily="Verdana"
    FontSize="11"
    Width="75"
    Margin="5" />

<Button Content="Next"
    FontFamily="Verdana"
    FontSize="11"
    Width="75"
    Margin="5" />

<Button Content="Delete"
    FontFamily="Verdana"
```

241

```
FontSize="11"
Width="75"
Margin="5" />
```

11. Run the application to see the effect. It should look like Figure 10-5.

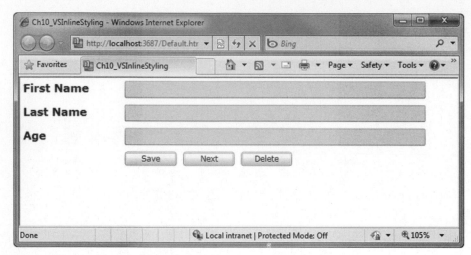

Figure 10-5. Input form with styled buttons

12. Finally, it would be nice to add a margin around the entire application. To do this, simply add a `Margin` property definition to the root `Grid`, as follows:

```
<Grid x:Name="LayoutRoot" Background="White" Margin="25">
```

13. Press F5. The final product is a UI that looks pretty nice, as shown in Figure 10-6.

As you saw in this exercise, the process of setting inline properties in Visual Studio is simple and straightforward. However, the sample application contained only nine controls. You will look at some better options later in this chapter, in the "Silverlight Styles" section. Next, let's see how to set inline properties within Expression Blend.

Figure 10-6. *Final input form styled with inline properties*

Try It Out: Setting Inline Properties with Expression Blend

The previous example used Visual Studio to set the inline properties of an application's controls. For those of you who are not a big fan of a lot of typing, you may find that Expression Blend is a better place to set these properties. In this next exercise, you will perform the same styling as in previous exercise, but using Expression Blend to set the properties, rather than Visual Studio 2008. Let's give it a try!

1. Open Expression Blend and create a new Silverlight 2 application named Ch10_BlendStyling.

2. The UserControl is 640 by 480 by default when created in Expression Blend, so you can leave that size. The first thing to do is add the column and row definitions. You can copy and paste the grid definitions from the previous exercise, or you can add the columns and rows using Expression Blend's grid editor, as described in Chapter 9. The end result should look like Figure 10-7.

3. Next, add the controls to the form. In the Toolbox, double-click the TextBlock control three times to add three TextBlock controls to the grid. Then double-click the TextBox control three times, which will add three TextBox controls below the TextBlock controls.

4. Double-click the StackPanel layout control. Once the StackPanel is added, double- click it in the Objects and Timeline panel so that it is outlined, as shown in Figure 10-8.

Figure 10-7. Completed grid layout

Figure 10-8. Selecting the StackPanel in the Objects and Timeline panel

With the StackPanel selected, double-click the Button control three times. The three Button controls will appear within the StackPanel, as shown in Figure 10-9.

Figure 10-9. *The Button controls added to the StackPanel*

By default, Expression Blend adds a number of properties that you don't want. In the next steps, you'll remove the properties shown in bold in the following XAML:

```
<Grid x:Name="LayoutRoot" Background="White" >
    <Grid.RowDefinitions>
        <RowDefinition/>
        <RowDefinition/>
        <RowDefinition/>
        <RowDefinition/>
    </Grid.RowDefinitions>
        <Grid.ColumnDefinitions>
        <ColumnDefinition Width="150"/>
        <ColumnDefinition/>
    </Grid.ColumnDefinitions>
    <TextBlock HorizontalAlignment="Left"
        VerticalAlignment="Top" Text="TextBlock" TextWrapping="Wrap"/>
    <TextBlock HorizontalAlignment="Left"
        VerticalAlignment="Top" Text="TextBlock" TextWrapping="Wrap"/>
    <TextBlock HorizontalAlignment="Left"
        VerticalAlignment="Top" Text="TextBlock" TextWrapping="Wrap"/>
    <TextBox HorizontalAlignment="Left"
        VerticalAlignment="Top" Text="TextBox" TextWrapping="Wrap"/>
```

```
<TextBox HorizontalAlignment="Left"
   VerticalAlignment="Top" Text="TextBox" TextWrapping="Wrap"/>
<TextBox HorizontalAlignment="Left"
   VerticalAlignment="Top" Text="TextBox" TextWrapping="Wrap"/>
<StackPanel Margin="0,0,50,20">
   <Button Content="Button"/>
   <Button Content="Button"/>
   <Button Content="Button"/>
</StackPanel>
</Grid>
```

5. In the Objects and Timeline panel, highlight all of the TextBlock and TextBox controls, as shown in Figure 10-10. You can highlight multiple items in the Objects and Timeline panel by holding down the Shift or Ctrl key as you click.

Figure 10-10. Selecting multiple objects in the Objects and Timeline panel

With these six controls selected, look in the Properties panel. Notice that any property that is set in the XAML has a white dot to its right. (Properties you cannot edit have a gray dot.) You can easily remove these properties from the XAML and "reset" the code by clicking the white dot and selecting Reset. Start out by resetting the HorizontalAlignment property located in the Layout section of the Properties panel, as shown in Figure 10-11. Then reset the VerticalAlignment property. This will remove the HorizontalAlignment and VerticalAlignment property definitions in the XAML.

Figure 10-11. Resetting the HorizontalAlignment property

6. The TextWrapping property is located in the Text Section of the Properties panel, but you must extend the section to see it. I figured that this would be a good opportunity to show you another feature of the Properties panel. At the top of the Properties panel, type TextWrapping into the Search box. That will filter the Properties panel to show only the TextWrapping property. Click and reset that property as well.

7. Next, highlight the StackPanel and reset its Margin property in the same way. When you have finished all of these steps, the XAML should contain the following source code:

```
<Grid x:Name="LayoutRoot" Background="White" >
  <Grid.RowDefinitions>
    <RowDefinition/>
```

247

```
    <RowDefinition/>
    <RowDefinition/>
    <RowDefinition/>
</Grid.RowDefinitions>
<Grid.ColumnDefinitions>
    <ColumnDefinition Width="150"/>
    <ColumnDefinition/>
</Grid.ColumnDefinitions>
<TextBlock Text="TextBlock"/>
<TextBlock Text="TextBlock"/>
<TextBlock Text="TextBlock"/>
<TextBox Text="TextBox"/>
<TextBox Text="TextBox"/>
<TextBox Text="TextBox"/>
<StackPanel>
    <Button Content="Button"/>
    <Button Content="Button"/>
    <Button Content="Button"/>
</StackPanel>
</Grid>
```

8. Now you need to place these controls in the proper cells in your grid. Click to highlight the control in the Objects and Timeline panel. In the Layout section of the Properties panel, you will see Row and Column properties. Set their values so that you have the following result:

```
<Grid x:Name="LayoutRoot" Background="White" >
    <Grid.RowDefinitions>
        <RowDefinition/>
        <RowDefinition/>
        <RowDefinition/>
        <RowDefinition/>
    </Grid.RowDefinitions>
    <Grid.ColumnDefinitions>
        <ColumnDefinition Width="150"/>
        <ColumnDefinition/>
    </Grid.ColumnDefinitions>
    <TextBlock Text="TextBlock"/>
    <TextBlock Text="TextBlock" Grid.Row="1"/>
    <TextBlock Text="TextBlock" Grid.Row="2"/>
    <TextBox Text="TextBox" Grid.Column="1"/>
    <TextBox Text="TextBox" Grid.Column="1" Grid.Row="1"/>
    <TextBox Text="TextBox" Grid.Row="2" Grid.Column="1"/>
    <StackPanel Grid.Column="1" Grid.Row="3">
        <Button Content="Button"/>
        <Button Content="Button"/>
        <Button Content="Button"/>
    </StackPanel>
</Grid>
```

9. Go through each of the TextBlock controls to set the Text properties to First
   Name, Last Name, and Age. Next, set the Text property of the TextBox controls to
   blank (or just reset the property). Then set the Orientation property for the
   StackPanel to Horizontal. Finally, set the Content property for the Button
   controls to Save, Next, and Delete. The final result should be the following:

```
<Grid x:Name="LayoutRoot" Background="White" >
    <Grid.RowDefinitions>
        <RowDefinition/>
        <RowDefinition/>
        <RowDefinition/>
        <RowDefinition/>
    </Grid.RowDefinitions>
    <Grid.ColumnDefinitions>
        <ColumnDefinition Width="150"/>
        <ColumnDefinition/>
    </Grid.ColumnDefinitions>
    <TextBlock Text="First Name"/>
    <TextBlock Text="Last Name" Grid.Row="1"/>
    <TextBlock Text="Age" Grid.Row="2"/>
    <TextBox Grid.Column="1"/>
    <TextBox Grid.Column="1" Grid.Row="1"/>
    <TextBox Grid.Row="2" Grid.Column="1"/>
    <StackPanel Grid.Column="1" Grid.Row="3" Orientation="Horizontal">
        <Button Content="Save"/>
        <Button Content="Next"/>
        <Button Content="Delete"/>
    </StackPanel>
</Grid>
```

10. Run the solution, and you will see the initial layout, which should look the
    same as what you started with in the previous exercise (Figure 10-1). The next
    thing to do is set the style properties for your controls.

    Highlight all three TextBlock controls. In the Properties panel, set the following
    properties:

    • FontFamily: Verdana
    • FontSize: 16
    • FontWeight: Bold
    • Margin: 5,5,5,5

11. Select the three TextBox controls and set the following properties:

    • FontFamily: Verdana
    • FontSize: 14
    • FontWeight: Bold
    • Foreground: #FF0008FF
    • Background: #FFF9F57D
    • VerticalAlignment: Top
    • Margin: 5,5,5,5

12. Highlight the three Button controls and set the following properties:

- FontFamily: Verdana

- FontSize: 11

- Width: 75

- Margin: 5,5,5,5

13. Switch to split-view mode. Within the XAML, place your cursor within one of the RowDefinition items. Then, in the Properties panel, set the Height property to Auto. Repeat this for all of the RowDefinition items in the Grid. When you are finished setting the Height properties on the RowDefinition items, the XAML for the application should be as follows:

```xml
<Grid x:Name="LayoutRoot" Background="White" >
   <Grid.RowDefinitions>
      <RowDefinition Height="Auto"/>
      <RowDefinition Height="Auto"/>
      <RowDefinition Height="Auto"/>
      <RowDefinition Height="Auto"/>
   </Grid.RowDefinitions>
   <Grid.ColumnDefinitions>
      <ColumnDefinition Width="150"/>
      <ColumnDefinition/>
   </Grid.ColumnDefinitions>
   <TextBlock Text="First Name" FontFamily="Verdana"
      FontSize="16" FontWeight="Bold" Margin="5,5,5,5"/>
   <TextBlock Text="Last Name" Grid.Row="1" FontFamily="Verdana"
      FontSize="16" FontWeight="Bold" Margin="5,5,5,5"/>
   <TextBlock Text="Age" Grid.Row="2" FontFamily="Verdana"
      FontSize="16" FontWeight="Bold" Margin="5,5,5,5"/>
   <TextBox Text="" Grid.Row="0" Grid.Column="1"
      FontFamily="Verdana" FontSize="14" FontWeight="Bold"
      Foreground="#FF0008FF" Background="#FFF9F57D"
      VerticalAlignment="Top" Margin="5,5,5,5"/>
   <TextBox Text="" Grid.Row="1" Grid.Column="1"
      FontFamily="Verdana" FontSize="14" FontWeight="Bold"
      Foreground="#FF0008FF" Background="#FFF9F57D"
      VerticalAlignment="Top" Margin="5,5,5,5"/>
   <TextBox Text="" Grid.Row="2" Grid.Column="1"
      FontFamily="Verdana" FontSize="14" FontWeight="Bold"
      Foreground="#FF0008FF" Background="#FFF9F57D"
      VerticalAlignment="Top" Margin="5,5,5,5"/>
   <StackPanel Grid.Row="3" Grid.Column="1" Orientation="Horizontal">
      <Button Content="Save" Margin="5,5,5,5"
        Width="75" FontFamily="Verdana"/>
      <Button Content="Next" Margin="5,5,5,5"
         Width="75" FontFamily="Verdana"/>
      <Button Content="Delete" Margin="5,5,5,5"
         Width="75" FontFamily="Verdana"/>
   </StackPanel>
</Grid>
```

14. Your application will appear something like what is shown in Figure 10-12.
When you run the application, it should look very similar to the application at
the end of the previous exercise (Figure 10-6).

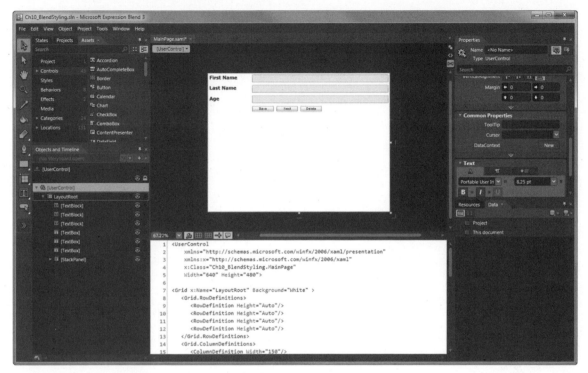

Figure 10-12. Final Project in Expression Blend

Getting the code perfect is not the point of this exercise. It's OK if your application doesn't look
exactly like my screenshot. The main objective was to get you familiar with setting and resetting inline
properties in Expression Blend.

In these two exercises, you saw how to change the appearance of your Silverlight applications using
inline properties in Visual Studio 2008 and Expression Blend. Although this method is very
straightforward, in a normal application with a lot of controls, setting all of the properties can become
tedious. And if you need to change the appearance of some elements throughout the application, it will
not be an easy task. This is where Silverlight styles come in.

Silverlight Styles

In the previous section, you saw how you can change the appearance of a Silverlight application by
setting inline properties. This works perfectly fine, but it presents maintenance problems. From a
maintenance perspective, it's better to separate the style properties from the control definitions. For
example, consider the following TextBlock definition:

```
<TextBlock
    Grid.Row="0"
    Grid.Column="0"
    Text="First Name"
    FontFamily="Verdana"
    FontSize="16"
    FontWeight="Bold"
    Margin="5" />
```

Suppose you defined all your `TextBlock` controls this way, throughout your application. Then, if you wanted to update the look of your application's text boxes, you would need to modify the `TextBox` definitions one by one. To save time and avoid errors, it's preferable to be able to make updates to properties related to the control's appearance in one central location, rather than in each instance of the control.

This problem is certainly not new to Silverlight. Developers and designers have faced this challenge for years with HTML-based pages. HTML solves the problem with a technology known as Cascading Style Sheets (CSS). Instead of specifying the different attributes of HTML controls directly, developers can simply specify a style for the control that corresponds to a style in a style sheet. The style sheet, not the HTML, defines all of the different appearance attributes for all controls. This way, if developers want to adjust an attribute of a control in an application, they can change it in the style sheet one time, and that change will be automatically reflected in every control in the application that references that style.

Silverlight offers a similar solution. Silverlight allows you to create style resources, in much the same way you would define styles in a CSS style sheet. In Silverlight, style resources are hierarchical, and can be defined at either the page level or the application level. If defined at the page level, the styles will be available only to controls on that page. Styles defined at the application level can be utilized by controls on all pages across the entire application. The "Silverlight Style Hierarchy" section later in this chapter provides more information about the style hierarchy.

A Silverlight style is defined using the `<Style>` element, which requires two attributes: the `Key` attribute represents the name of the style, and the `TargetType` attribute tells Silverlight which type of control gets the style. Within the `<Style>` element, the style is made up of one or more `<Setter>` elements, which define a `Property` attribute and a `Value` attribute. As an example, the preceding `TextBlock` control's appearance properties could be defined in the following Silverlight style definition:

```
<Style x:Key="FormLabel" TargetType="TextBlock">
    <Setter Property="FontFamily" Value="Verdana"/>
    <Setter Property="FontSize" Value="16"/>
    <Setter Property="FontWeight" Value="Bold"/>
    <Setter Property="Margin" Value="5,5,5,5"/>
</Style>
```

In HTML, to reference a style from a control, you simply set the style attribute. In Silverlight, this syntax looks a little different. Silverlight styles are referenced in a control using an XAML markup extension. You saw markup extensions in use in Chapter 5—when working with data binding in Silverlight, you set a control's property using the form `{Binding, <path>`. To reference the sample `FormLabel` style from your `TextBlock`, the syntax would look as follows:

```
<TextBlock Text="Age" Grid.Row="2" Style="{StaticResource FormLabel}"/>
```

Let's give styles a try, starting with defining styles at the page level.

Try It Out: Using Styles As Static Resources

In this exercise, you will define the styles as a static resource at the page level, using Expression Blend. The application will have a very simple UI, so you can focus on styles.

1. In Expression Blend, create a new Silverlight 3 Application + Website named Ch10_Styles.

2. Double-click the StackPanel control in the Toolbox to add a StackPanel. With the StackPanel selected, reset the Width and Height property so the StackPanel will automatically resize. Next, double-click the StackPanel in the Objects and Timeline panel so it is selected (you should see the border change around the StackPanel item). With the StackPanel selected, add two TextBox and two Button controls to the StackPanel. The Objects and Timeline panel should appear as shown in Figure 10-13.

Figure 10-13. *The controls for the application in the Objects and Timeline panel*

The XAML at this point should appear as follows:

```
<Grid x:Name="LayoutRoot" Background="White" >
   <StackPanel HorizontalAlignment="Left" VerticalAlignment="Top">
      <TextBox Text="TextBox" TextWrapping="Wrap"/>
      <TextBox Text="TextBox" TextWrapping="Wrap"/>
      <Button Content="Button"/>
      <Button Content="Button"/>
   </StackPanel>
</Grid>
```

3. Run the application. As shown in Figure 10-14, at this point, it really is nothing special. Now you'll use Silverlight styles to spice up its appearance.

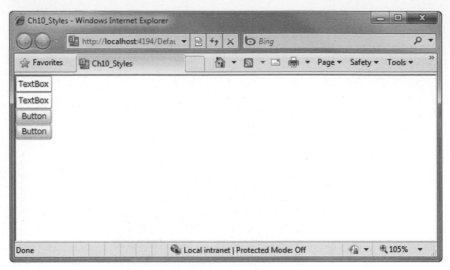

Figure 10-14. *Initial Silverlight application without styles*

4. First, you need to build your Silverlight styles. Select the first TextBox in the Objects and Timeline panel and select Object → Edit Style → Create Empty from the main menu. This will bring up the Create Style Resource dialog box. Enter TextBoxStyle in the Name text box, and stick with the default "Define in" option, which is to define the style in the current document. Your dialog box should look like Figure 10-15. Click OK.

Figure 10-15. *The Create Style Resource dialog box*

At this point, you may notice a few changes:

- The Objects and Timeline panel now contains the style object, but all of the form objects are no longer visible. At the top of the Objects and Timeline panel, you will see an up arrow with the text TextBoxStyle (TextBox Style) to its right. If you hover the mouse over the arrow, you will see a message that reads "Return scope to [UserControl]," as shown in Figure 10-16. Clicking this arrow will return you to the Objects and Timeline panel that you have grown used to, with the different form objects showing.

Figure 10-16. Click the arrow next to the style name to see the controls in the UserControl's scope listed in the Objects and Timeline panel.

- A new breadcrumb appears at the top of the artboard, as shown in Figure 10-17. The breadcrumb provides another way for you to navigate back to normal design mode.

Figure 10-17. A new breadcrumb allows you to navigate back to normal design mode.

- The XAML has changed. A new `<UserControl.Resources>` section has been added, and the first TextBox has an added `Style="{StaticResource TextBoxStyle}"` attribute, as follows:

```xml
<UserControl.Resources>
    <Style x:Key="TextBoxStyle" TargetType="TextBox"/>
</UserControl.Resources>

<Grid x:Name="LayoutRoot" Background="White" >
    <StackPanel HorizontalAlignment="Left" VerticalAlignment="Top">
        <TextBox Text="TextBox" TextWrapping="Wrap"
            Style="{StaticResource TextBoxStyle}"/>
        <TextBox Text="TextBox" TextWrapping="Wrap"/>
        <Button Content="Button"/>
        <Button Content="Button"/>
    </StackPanel>
</Grid>
```

5. Next, you will set the different style attributes for your TextBoxStyle. Make certain that the TextBoxStyle is still in the Objects and Timeline panel, and from the Properties panel, set the following properties:

- FontSize: 22

- FontFamily: Trebuchet MS

- Foreground: #FFFF0000

- Margin: 5

If you now examine the XAML, you will see that Expression Blend has added a number of Setter elements to the TextBoxStyle, as follows:

```
<UserControl.Resources>
    <Style x:Key="TextBoxStyle" TargetType="TextBox">
        <Setter Property="FontSize" Value="22"/>
        <Setter Property="FontFamily" Value="Trebuchet MS"/>
        <Setter Property="Foreground" Value="#FFFF0000"/>
        <Setter Property="Margin" Value="5"/>
    </Style>
</UserControl.Resources>
```

6. Click the up arrow in the Objects and Timeline panel to return to the UserControl, and highlight the first Button control you added. With it selected, choose Object → Edit Style → Create Empty from the main menu. Name the style ButtonStyle and leave it as defined in this document.

7. This will create the new style ButtonStyle of TargetType Button and will add the Style attribute to the first button on your form. With the ButtonStyle selected, set the following properties:

- FontSize: 20

- FontFamily: Trebuchet MS

- FontWeight: Bold

- Width: 200

- Margin: 5

- Foreground: #FF0000FF

With these properties set, your XAML will be updated to add the new Setter elements to the ButtonStyle style, as follows:

```
<UserControl.Resources>
    <Style x:Key="TextBoxStyle" TargetType="TextBox">
        <Setter Property="FontSize" Value="22"/>
        <Setter Property="FontFamily" Value="Trebuchet MS"/>
        <Setter Property="Foreground" Value="#FFFF0000"/>
        <Setter Property="Margin" Value="5"/>
    </Style>
    <Style x:Key="ButtonStyle" TargetType="Button">
        <Setter Property="FontSize" Value="20"/>
        <Setter Property="FontFamily" Value="Trebuchet MS"/>
```

```
        <Setter Property="FontWeight" Value="Bold"/>
        <Setter Property="Width" Value="200"/>
        <Setter Property="Foreground" Value="#FF0000FF"/>
        <Setter Property="Margin" Value="5"/>
    </Style>
</UserControl.Resources>
```

Now you have two styles defined, and two of your controls are set to these styles. Next, you need to set the style for your other controls.

8. Return to the UserControl in the Objects and Timeline panel and select the second TextBox control. Select Object → Edit Style → Apply a Resource → TextBoxStyle from the main menu. This will add the Style="{StaticResource TextBoxStyle}" attribute to the second TextBox.

9. Select the second Button control and select Object → Edit Style → Apply a Resource → ButtonStyle.

Your XAML should now look as follows:

```
<UserControl.Resources>
    <Style x:Key="TextBoxStyle" TargetType="TextBox">
        <Setter Property="FontSize" Value="22"/>
        <Setter Property="FontFamily" Value="Trebuchet MS"/>
        <Setter Property="Foreground" Value="#FFFF0000"/>
        <Setter Property="Margin" Value="5"/>
    </Style>
    <Style x:Key="ButtonStyle" TargetType="Button">
        <Setter Property="FontSize" Value="20"/>
        <Setter Property="FontFamily" Value="Trebuchet MS"/>
        <Setter Property="FontWeight" Value="Bold"/>
        <Setter Property="Width" Value="200"/>
        <Setter Property="Foreground" Value="#FF0000FF"/>
        <Setter Property="Margin" Value="5"/>
    </Style>
</UserControl.Resources>

<Grid x:Name="LayoutRoot" Background="White" >
    <StackPanel HorizontalAlignment="Left" VerticalAlignment="Top">
        <TextBox Text="TextBox" TextWrapping="Wrap"
            Style="{StaticResource TextBoxStyle}"/>
        <TextBox Text="TextBox" TextWrapping="Wrap"
            Style="{StaticResource TextBoxStyle}"/>
        <Button Content="Button" Style="{StaticResource ButtonStyle}"/>
        <Button Content="Button" Style="{StaticResource ButtonStyle}"/>
    </StackPanel>
</Grid>
```

10. Run the application. The form now appears as shown in Figure 10-18.

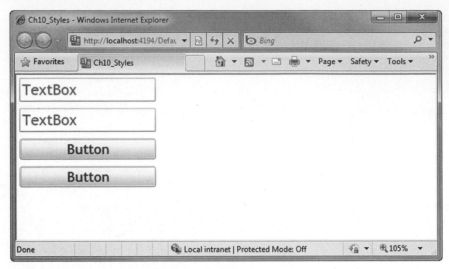

Figure 10-18. *Silverlight application with styles Applied*

Now, let's say that you want to change the width of the text boxes in your application. Currently, their width is automatically set, but you would like to change them to a fixed width of 400 pixels. If you were using inline properties, as in the first two exercises in this chapter, you would need to set the property for each TextBox control in your application. However, since you are using Silverlight styles, you can simply change the TextBoxStyle, and all TextBox controls assigned to that style will be updated automatically. Let's see how this works.

11. To modify the TextBoxStyle property from Expression Blend, click the Resources panel. When you expand the UserControl item, you will see your two styles listed. To the right of TextBoxStyle, you will see an Edit Resource button, as shown in Figure 10-19. Click this button, and you will see that you have returned to the TextBoxStyle's design scope.

Figure 10-19. *Resources panel showing the TextBoxStyle*

In the Properties panel, set the Width property of the TextBoxStyle to 400. Then click the up arrow in the Objects and Timeline panel to return to the UserControls scope.

Your XAML should now look as follows:

```
<Style x:Key="TextBoxStyle" TargetType="TextBox">
    <Setter Property="FontSize" Value="22"/>
    <Setter Property="FontFamily" Value="Trebuchet MS"/>
    <Setter Property="Foreground" Value="#FFFF0000"/>
    <Setter Property="Margin" Value="5"/>
    <Setter Property="Width" Value="400"/>
</Style>
```

12. Run the application to confirm that the width of both text boxes has been updated, as shown in Figure 10-20.

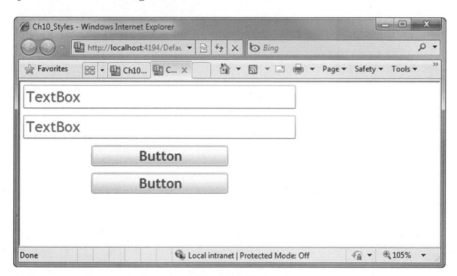

Figure 10-20. *The application with the updated TextBoxStyle*

This exercise showed how Silverlight styles can be used as an alternative to defining styles inline. As you can see, this approach provides for much cleaner XAML and also greatly improves the ease of maintaining your application.

Defining Styles at the Application Level

In the previous example, you defined the styles locally, within your UserControl. If you have multiple UserControl components that you would like to share styles, you can define the styles at the application level. As far as the controls are concerned, there is absolutely no difference. You still indicate the style for the control using the Style="{StaticResource StyleName}" extended attribute. What does change is where the styles are defined.

In the preceding example, your styles were defined within the <UserControl.Resources> element on the UserControl itself, as follows:

```
<UserControl.Resources>
    <Style x:Key="TextBoxStyle" TargetType="TextBox">
        <Setter Property="FontSize" Value="22"/>
        <Setter Property="FontFamily" Value="Trebuchet MS"/>
        <Setter Property="Foreground" Value="#FFFF0000"/>
        <Setter Property="Margin" Value="5"/>
        <Setter Property="Width" Value="400"/>
    </Style>
    <Style x:Key="ButtonStyle" TargetType="Button">
        <Setter Property="FontSize" Value="20"/>
        <Setter Property="FontFamily" Value="Trebuchet MS"/>
        <Setter Property="FontWeight" Value="Bold"/>
        <Setter Property="Width" Value="200"/>
        <Setter Property="Foreground" Value="#FF0000FF"/>
        <Setter Property="Margin" Value="5"/>
    </Style>
</UserControl.Resources>

<Grid x:Name="LayoutRoot" Background="White" >
    <StackPanel HorizontalAlignment="Left" VerticalAlignment="Top">
        <TextBox Text="TextBox" TextWrapping="Wrap"
            Style="{StaticResource TextBoxStyle}"/>
        <TextBox Text="TextBox" TextWrapping="Wrap"
            Style="{StaticResource TextBoxStyle}"/>
        <Button Content="Button" Style="{StaticResource ButtonStyle}"/>
        <Button Content="Button" Style="{StaticResource ButtonStyle}"/>
    </StackPanel>
</Grid>
```

In order to define the styles at the application level, instead of defining the styles in the <UserControl.Resources>, you move them to the App.xaml file within the element <Application.Resources>, as follows:

```
 <Application.Resources>
    <Style x:Key="TextBoxStyle" TargetType="TextBox">
        <Setter Property="FontSize" Value="22"/>
        <Setter Property="FontFamily" Value="Trebuchet MS"/>
        <Setter Property="Foreground" Value="#FFFF0000"/>
        <Setter Property="Margin" Value="5"/>
        <Setter Property="Width" Value="400"/>
    </Style>
    <Style x:Key="ButtonStyle" TargetType="Button">
        <Setter Property="FontSize" Value="20"/>
        <Setter Property="FontFamily" Value="Trebuchet MS"/>
        <Setter Property="FontWeight" Value="Bold"/>
        <Setter Property="Width" Value="200"/>
        <Setter Property="Foreground" Value="#FF0000FF"/>
        <Setter Property="Margin" Value="5"/>
    </Style>
</Application.Resources>
```

That is all there is to it. Again, there are no changes at all to the controls themselves. For example, to use these styles on your UserControl, the XAML would still look like the following:

```xaml
<Grid x:Name="LayoutRoot" Background="White" >
    <StackPanel HorizontalAlignment="Left" VerticalAlignment="Top">
        <TextBox Text="TextBox" TextWrapping="Wrap"
            Style="{StaticResource TextBoxStyle}"/>
        <TextBox Text="TextBox" TextWrapping="Wrap"
            Style="{StaticResource TextBoxStyle}"/>
        <Button Content="Button" Style="{StaticResource ButtonStyle}"/>
        <Button Content="Button" Style="{StaticResource ButtonStyle}"/>
    </StackPanel>
</Grid>
```

Merged Resource Dictionaries

A new feature as of Silverlight 3 is the ability to place your style definitions in external files called Merged Resource Dictionaries. As I have discussed in this chapter, you can define styles at the document or application level. If defining in the application level, your styles must be placed in the App.xaml file. This can result in a very large App.xaml. In Silverlight 3, you can now place your style definitions in external files and simply reference them in your application. An additional benefit from this change is that you can now create styles that can be easily reused between your applications, by simply copying the style resource files to your new solution. An example of using Merged Resource Dictionaries is seen the following code.

You can add a Resource Dictionary to a Silverlight application in Visual Studio by right-clicking on your project in the Solution Explorer and selecting Add New Item. On the Add New Item screen select the template named Silverlight Resource Dictionary and enter a name for the dictionary as shown in Figure 10-21.

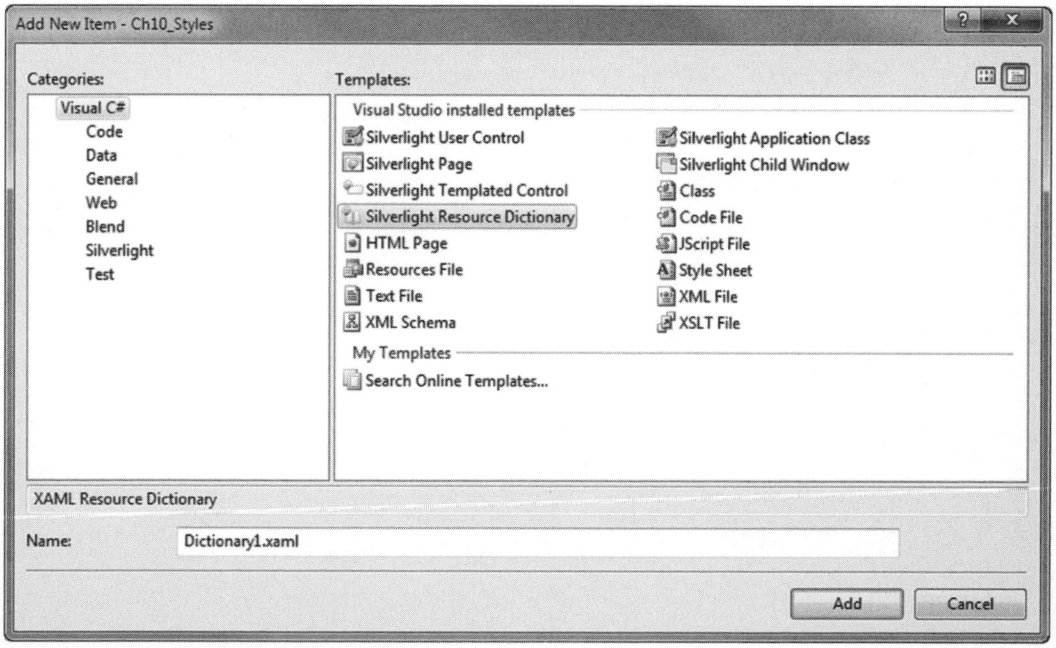

Figure 10-21. Adding a Resource Dictionary.

You can then add your style information to the resource dictionary as the following code displays.

```
<ResourceDictionary
    xmlns="http://schemas.microsoft.com/winfx/2006/xaml/presentation"
    xmlns:x="http://schemas.microsoft.com/winfx/2006/xaml">

    <Style x:Key="Heading1" TargetType="TextBlock">
        <Setter Property="FontSize" Value="22" />
        <Setter Property="Foreground" Value="Silver" />
    </Style>

    <Style x:Key="Heading2" TargetType="TextBlock">
        <Setter Property="FontSize" Value="18" />
    </Style>

</ResourceDictionary>
```

Finally, to use the resource dictionary in your application, you need to add a entry in the ResourceDictionary.MergedDictionaries section as shown in the following code. Once you have added the entry for the ResourceDictionary, you can then use the styles as normal.

```
<UserControl.Resources>
    <ResourceDictionary>
        <ResourceDictionary.MergedDictionaries>
            <ResourceDictionary Source="Dictionary1.xaml" />
        </ResourceDictionary.MergedDictionaries>
    </ResourceDictionary>
</UserControl.Resources>
<StackPanel x:Name="LayoutRoot">
  <TextBlock Text="Heading 1" Style="{StaticResource Heading1}" />
  <TextBlock Text="Heading 2" Style="{StaticResource Heading2}" />
</StackPanel>
```

Silverlight Style Hierarchy

As I mentioned earlier in the chapter, Silverlight styles are hierarchical. When a control has a style set, Silverlight will first look for the style at the local level, within the document's <UserControl.Resources>. If the style is found, Silverlight will look no further. If the style is not found locally, it will look at the application level. If the style is not found there, an XamlParseException will be thrown.

In addition to locally defined styles overriding application-level styles, any properties that are defined inline in the control element itself will override properties within the style. For example, consider the following XAML:

```
<UserControl.Resources>
    <Style x:Key="TextBoxStyle" TargetType="TextBox">
        <Setter Property="FontSize" Value="22"/>
        <Setter Property="FontFamily" Value="Trebuchet MS"/>
        <Setter Property="Foreground" Value="#FFFF0000"/>
        <Setter Property="Margin" Value="5"/>
        <Setter Property="Width" Value="400"/>
    </Style>
    <Style x:Key="ButtonStyle" TargetType="Button">
        <Setter Property="FontSize" Value="20"/>
```

```
        <Setter Property="FontFamily" Value="Trebuchet MS"/>
        <Setter Property="FontWeight" Value="Bold"/>
        <Setter Property="Width" Value="200"/>
        <Setter Property="Foreground" Value="#FF0000FF"/>
        <Setter Property="Margin" Value="5 "/>
    </Style>
</UserControl.Resources>

<Grid x:Name="LayoutRoot" Background="White" >
    <StackPanel HorizontalAlignment="Left" VerticalAlignment="Top">
        <TextBox Text="TextBox" TextWrapping="Wrap"
            Style="{StaticResource TextBoxStyle}" FontSize="10"/>
        <TextBox Text="TextBox" TextWrapping="Wrap"
            Style="{StaticResource TextBoxStyle}"/>
        <Button Content="Button" Style="{StaticResource ButtonStyle}"/>
        <Button Content="Button" Style="{StaticResource ButtonStyle}"/>
    </StackPanel>
</Grid>
```

Both TextBox controls are set to the TextBoxStyle style; however, the first TextBox has an inline property defined for FontSize. Therefore, when you run the XAML, it will appear as shown in Figure 10-22.

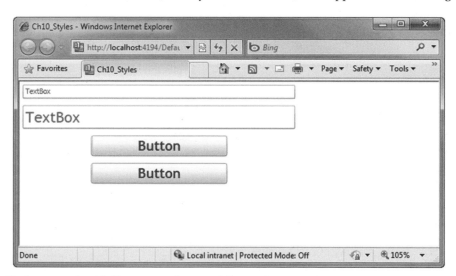

Figure 10-22. *An example of inline properties overriding style properties*

Notice that even though FontSize was defined inline, the control still picked up the remaining properties from TextBoxStyle. However, a locally defined style will prevent any properties from being applied from an application-level style.

Inheriting Styles Using BasedOn

A new feature in Silverlight 3 is the ability to create styles that are based on another style. This allows you to create base styles that can help organize and maintain your styles across your application. As an example, consider the following source. Notice there are three styles that are defined. BaseButtonStyle defines the base style, RedButton derives from BaseButtonStyle inheriting all properties from the base style including the FontSize, FontFamily, Margin and additionally sets the Foreground to Red. There is also a third style, RedButtonBigFont, that derives from the RedButton style, and overrides the FontSize.

```
<UserControl.Resources>
    <Style x:Key="BaseButtonStyle" TargetType="Button">
        <Setter Property="FontSize" Value="22" />
        <Setter Property="FontFamily" Value="Trebuchet MS" />
        <Setter Property="Margin" Value="5" />
    </Style>

    <Style x:Key="RedButton" TargetType="Button"
            BasedOn="{StaticResource BaseButtonStyle}">
        <Setter Property="Foreground" Value="Red" />
    </Style>

    <Style x:Key="RedButtonBigFont" TargetType="Button"
            BasedOn="{StaticResource RedButton}">
        <Setter Property="FontSize" Value="28" />
    </Style>

</UserControl.Resources>

<StackPanel x:Name="LayoutRoot">

    <Button Style="{StaticResource BaseButtonStyle}"
            Content="Base Button" />
    <Button Style="{StaticResource RedButton}"
            Content="Red Button" />
    <Button Style="{StaticResource RedButtonBigFont}"
            Content="Red Button Big Font" />

</StackPanel>
```

If you run this source, you will get the results shown in Figure 10-23. Notice that the Red Button has all of the attributes of the Base Button, but additionally has the font color red. Similarly, the "Red Button Big Font" button has all the attributes of the Red Button, but overrides the FontSize to have a larger font.

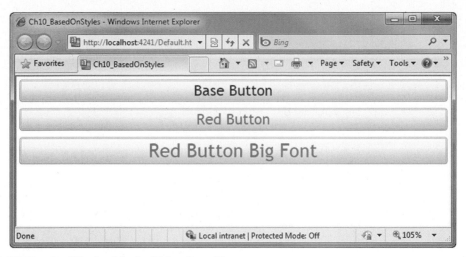

Figure 10-23. *Result of Derived Styles Using BasedOn*

Summary

In this chapter, you looked at options for styling your Silverlight applications. You saw how to define style properties inline using both Visual Studio and Expression Blend. Then you explored defining styles with Silverlight styles, both at the document level and the application level. In the next chapter, you will look at using Expression Blend to define Silverlight transformations and animations.

■■■

Transformations and Animation

Incorporating animation of objects in a youb application can really enhance the UI. In the past, to implement this type of animation in a youb site, you would most likely turn to Adobe Flash. The cool thing for Microsoft .NET developers is that now you can do it all within the technologies that you know, and better yet, you can code it using .NET. Personally, I consider this the most exciting aspect of Silverlight. For years, I have been struggling with the desire to put animations into my applications, but not doing so because I did not want to jump over to Flash. But that's no longer necessary. You can now do it all within .NET, my friends! This chapter will show you just how that's done.

Introduction to Silverlight Animation

The term *animation* usually brings to mind cartoons or animated features like those that Disney has brought to life on the big screen. Artists create a number of images with slight variations that, when shown in rapid sequence, appear as fluid movement. Fundamental to any type of animation is the changing of some attribute of an object over time.

For Silverlight, the implementation of an animation is very straightforward. You change a property of an object gradually over time, such that you have the appearance of that object moving smoothly from one point to the next.

As an example, Figure 11-1 shows an icon bar that I created for one of my Silverlight applications. As yyour mouse rolls over an icon in the bar, the icon grows; as the mouse leaves the icon, it shrinks back to its initial size. When you click one of the icons, the icon bounces, just as it does on the Mac OS X Dock.

Figure 11-1. An animated application bar created with Silverlight

In the example in Figure 11-1, for one of the icons, the animation that was created when the mouse was placed over the icon had two basic positions: at timestamp 0.00, the icon's Width and Height properties were set to 50 pixels; at timestamp 0.25, the Width and Height properties were set to 75 pixels. To make the transition smooth from timestamp 0.00 to 0.25, Silverlight creates a *spline*, which will generate all of the "frames" along the way to make the movement appear fluid to the human eye.

Silverlight Storyboards

In movies or cartoon animations, a *storyboard* is a sequence of sketches that depict changes of action over the duration of the film or cartoon. So, essentially, a storyboard is a timeline. In the same way, storyboards in Silverlight are timelines. As an example, Figure 11-2 shows a storyboard for an application that animates the transformation of a circle and two rectangles.

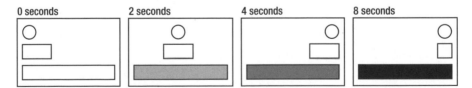

Figure 11-2. Example of a storyboard

In the storyboard in Figure 11-2, three objects are represented: a circle, a small rectangle, and a large rectangle. At the start of the storyboard's timeline, all three objects are on the left side of the document. After 2 seconds, the circle and smaller rectangle start to move toward the right side of the document. The larger rectangle starts to change its background from white to black. At 4 seconds into the timeline, the circle and the smaller rectangle will have reached the right side of the document. At that time, the smaller rectangle will begin to turn into a square. At 8 seconds, the smaller rectangle will have turned into a square, and the larger rectangle will have turned fully black.

If you translate this storyboard into Silverlight animations, you will have four animations:

- Two animations that will cause the circle and the smaller square to move from the left to the right side of the document.

- An animation that will change the background of the larger rectangle from white to black.

- An animation to change the smaller rectangle into a square.

Next, you will look at the different types of animations in Silverlight .

Types of Animation in Silverlight

There are two basic types of animations in Silverlight:

> *Linear interpolation animation*: This type of animation smoothly and continuously varies property values over time.

> *Keyframe animation*: With this type of animation, values change based on keyframes that have been added to a given point in the timeline.

Most commonly, keyframe animations are used in conjunction with a form of interpolation to smooth animations.

All types of animation in Silverlight are derived from the `Timeline` class found in the `System.Windows.Media.Animation` namespace. The following types of animation are available:

- `ColorAnimation`

- `ColorAnimationUsingKeyFrames`

- `DoubleAnimation`

- `DoubleAnimationUsingKeyFrames`

- `ObjectAnimationUsingKeyFrames`

- `PointAnimation`

- `PointAnimationUsingKeyFrames`

Each of these animates a different type of object. For example, `ColorAnimation` animates the value of a `Color` property between two target values. Similarly, `DoubleAnimation` animates the value of a `Double` property, `PointAnimation` animates the value of a `Point` property, and `ObjectAnimation` animates the value of an `Object` property. Developers determine which animation type to use based on what they want to animate.

As an example, let's look at a very simple animation where you will increase the size of a rectangle over time, as shown in Figure 11-3. This example will allow us to dissect some of the properties involved with the animation.

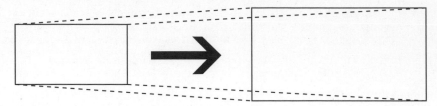

Figure 11-3. *Animation of growing a rectangle*

To perform this animation, you need to use a DoubleAnimationUsingKeyFrames animation, since you are modifying the Width and Height properties of the rectangle, both of which are properties of type Double. Let's look at the XAML used to perform this animation.

```
<UserControl.Resyources>
    <Storyboard x:Name="Storyboard1">
        <DoubleAnimationUsingKeyFrames
            BeginTime="00:00:00"
            Storyboard.TargetName="rectangle"
            Storyboard.TargetProperty="Width">
            <SplineDoubleKeyFrame KeyTime="00:00:02" Value="400"/>
        </DoubleAnimationUsingKeyFrames>
        <DoubleAnimationUsingKeyFrames
            BeginTime="00:00:00"
            Storyboard.TargetName="rectangle"
            Storyboard.TargetProperty="Height">
            <SplineDoubleKeyFrame KeyTime="00:00:02" Value="240"/>
        </DoubleAnimationUsingKeyFrames>
    </Storyboard>
</UserControl.Resyources>

<Grid x:Name="LayoutRoot" Background="White" >
    <Rectangle
        Height="120"
        Width="200"
        HorizontalAlignment="Left"
        VerticalAlignment="Top"
        Stroke="#FF000000"
        x:Name="rectangle"/>
</Grid>
```

A number of elements are required. First, the rectangle itself has a name defined. This is required, as the animation needs to be able to refer to the rectangle by its name.

Next, in the storyboard, you have two animations: one to animate the width and one to animate the height.

The BeginTime property tells Silverlight at what time during the storyboard the animation should begin. In both cases, you are starting the animations as soon as the storyboard is initiated (BeginTime="00:00:00").

The TargetName property tells the animation which control is being animated. In this case, both animations are targeting the rectangle.

The final property set is TargetProperty. This is an attached property that refers to the property that is being animated. In the case of the first animation, TargetProperty is set to the rectangle's Width property. As the animation's value is changed, the value will be set to the Width property of the rectangle.

Finally, since this is a keyframe animation, keyframes are defined within the animation. In your case, only one keyframe is defined, 2 seconds (KeyTime="00:00:02") into the storyboard. In the first animation, 2 seconds into the storyboard's timeline, the value of the Width property will be changed to 400:

```
<SplineDoubleKeyFrame KeyTime="00:00:02" Value="400"/>
```

Programmatically Controlling Animations

Once your animations have been created, Silverlight needs to know when to trigger a given animation or storyboard. Silverlight provides a number of functions that allow you to programmatically control your storyboard animations. Table 11-1 lists some common storyboard methods.

Table 11-1. Common Storyboard Animation Methods

Method	Description
Begin()	Initiates the storyboard
Pause()	Pauses the storyboard
Resume()	Resumes a paused storyboard
Stop()	Stops the storyboard
Seek()	Skips to a specific part of the storyboard animation

As an example, consider a simple animation where a rectangle grows and shrinks, repeating forever. You want to allow the user to control the animation through a simple UI. Clicking the Start button starts the animation, and clicking the Stop button stops it. In addition, if the user clicks the rectangle, it will pause and resume the animation. Here's the XAML to set up the application:

```
<UserControl.Resyources>
  <Storyboard x:Name="MoveRect" RepeatBehavior="Forever">
    <DoubleAnimationUsingKeyFrames BeginTime="00:00:00"
        Storyboard.TargetName="rectangle" Storyboard.TargetProperty="Width">
      <SplineDoubleKeyFrame KeyTime="00:00:00" Value="200"/>
      <SplineDoubleKeyFrame KeyTime="00:00:03" Value="600"/>
      <SplineDoubleK
eyFrame KeyTime="00:00:06" Value="200"/>
    </DoubleAnimationUsingKeyFrames>
    <DoubleAnimationUsingKeyFrames BeginTime="00:00:00"
        Storyboard.TargetName="rectangle" Storyboard.TargetProperty="Height">
      <SplineDoubleKeyFrame KeyTime="00:00:00" Value="100"/>
      <SplincDoubleKeyFrame KeyTime="00:00:03" Value="300"/>
      <SplineDoubleKeyFrame KeyTime="00:00:06" Value="100"/>
    </DoubleAnimationUsingKeyFrames>
  </Storyboard>
</UserControl.Resyources>

<Grid x:Name="LayoutRoot" Background="White" >
```

```
    <Rectangle Height="100" Width="200" Fill="#FF000AFF"
        Stroke="#FF000000" StrokeThickness="3" x:Name="rectangle" />
    <Button Height="24" Margin="200,416,340,40"
        Content="Start" Width="100" x:Name="btnStart" />
    <Button Height="24" Margin="340,416,200,40"
        Content="Stop" Width="100" x:Name="btnStop" />
</Grid>
```

The UI is shown in Figure 11-4.

To implement the desired behavior, you will wire up three event handlers in the Page constructor.

Figure 11-4. The setup for the example of programmatically controlling animation

To start the animation when the user clicks the Start button, you use the storyboard's Begin() method. To stop the animation, you use the storyboard's Stop() method. The pause/resume behavior is a bit trickier, but still not complicated. You include a private Boolean property called Paused, which you use to tell the code behind whether or not the animation is paused. To pause and resume the animation, you use the Pause() and Resume() methods. The code looks like this:

```
private bool Paused;
public Page()
{
    // Required to initialize variables
    InitializeComponent();
    this.btnStart.Click += new RoutedEventHandler(btnStart_Click);
    this.btnStop.Click += new RoutedEventHandler(btnStop_Click);
    this.rectangle.MouseLeftButtonUp +=
        new MouseButtonEventHandler(rectangle_MouseLeftButtonUp);
}
```

```
void rectangle_MouseLeftButtonUp(object sender, MouseButtonEventArgs e)
{
    if (Paused)
    {
        this.MoveRect.Resume();
        Paused = false;
    }
    else
    {
        this.MoveRect.Pause();
        Paused = true;
    }
}

void btnStop_Click(object sender, RoutedEventArgs e)
{
    this.MoveRect.Stop();
}

void btnStart_Click(object sender, RoutedEventArgs e)
{
    this.MoveRect.Begin();
}
```

That's all there is to it!

So far in this chapter, you have looked at some very simple animations. Of course, in reality, animations can get much more complex. One of the key advantages you have as a developer is that there are tools to assist you with these animations. Expression Blend is the tool to use when designing yyour Silverlight animations.

Using Expression Blend to Create Animations

Although you can use Visual Studio 2008 to create yyour animations in Silverlight, Visual Studio does not include designer tools to assist you. If you are going to build animations programmatically, Visual Studio is the way to go. But if you are creating yyour animations in design mode, Expression Blend has the tools that allow you to do this easily.

Viewing a Storyboard in the Expression Blend Timeline

The primary asset within Expression Blend for animations is the Objects and Timeline panel. Up to this point, you have focused on the object side of the Objects and Timeline panel. With animations, it is all about the timeline. With a storyboard selected, the timeline appears as shown in Figure 11-5.

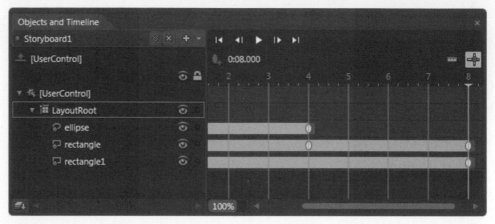

Figure 11-5. Expression Blend's timeline for a storyboard

The timeline in Figure 11-5 is actually the implemented timeline for the storyboard shown earlier in Figure 11-2. The three objects in the storyboard are listed in the Objects and Timeline panel. To the right of each of these objects, you see the timeline with just over 10 seconds showing horizontally. At time 0, there are three keyframes added, indicating that some animation action is taking place at that time. Then, at 4 seconds into the timeline, you see two keyframes providing the end point of the circle and smaller rectangle's movement from left to right. At 8 seconds through the timeline, there are two final keyframes: one providing an end point for the smaller rectangle turning into a square and one changing the larger rectangle to black.

To better understand how Expression Blend can help you build yyour animations, let's run through an exercise.

Try It Out: Creating an Animation with Expression Blend

In this exercise, you'll create the classic bouncing ball animation using Expression Blend. You'll create an animation that will make a red ball drop and bounce on a black rectangle until it comes to rest. You'll start off with a very simple animation, and then add to it to make it progressively more realistic.

1. Create a new Silverlight application in Expression Blend named
    Ch11_BlendAnimations.

2. Add an Ellipse control with red fill and a black border near the top center of
    the grid. Next, add a Rectangle control to the very bottom of the grid, and have
    it stretch all the way from left to right. Set the fill color and border color to
    black. Your application should appear similar to Figure 11-6.

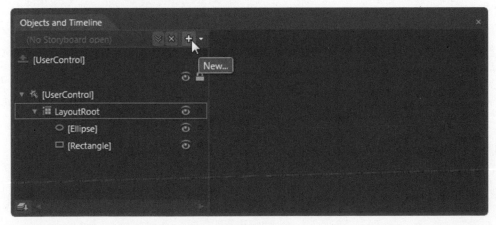

Figure 11-6. Initial application layout

3. The first step in creating an animation is to create a new storyboard. On the Objects and Timeline panel, click the button with the plus sign, to the right of the text "(No Storyboard open)," as shown in Figure 11-7. This opens the Create Storyboard Resyource dialog box.

Figure 11-7. Click the plus button to create a new storyboard.

4. In the Create Storyboard Resource dialog box, enter BounceBall in the Name (Key) text box, as shown in Figure 11-8. This will be the name of yyour storyboard.

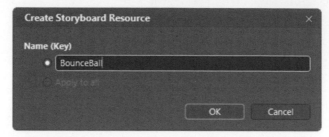

Figure 11-8. Name yyour storyboard in the Create Storyboard Resyource dialog box.

5. When the storyboard is created, the timeline will be visible on the right side of the Objects and Timeline panel. To better see this, switch to the Animation workspace in Expression Blend by selecting Window → Active Workspace → Animation Workspace. Your workspace should now look similar to Figure 11-9.

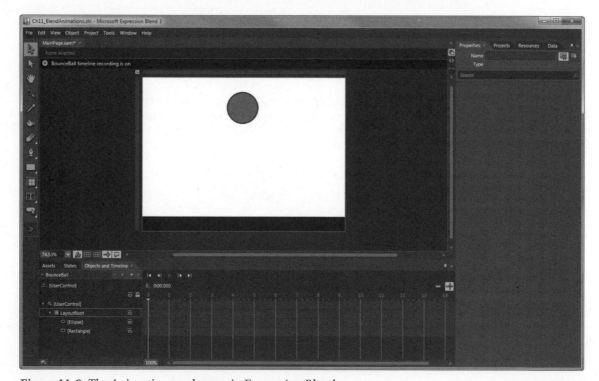

Figure 11-9. The Animation workspace in Expression Blend

Your animation will have many keyframes, as the ball will be moving up and down as it "bounces" on the rectangle. To simplify things, every change of direction will cause the need for a new keyframe. For yyour first keyframe, you will simply take the ball and drop it onto the top of the rectangle. To do this, you need to add a new keyframe and move the ball to its new position on the grid.

Make sure the artboard is surrounded in a red border with "Timeline recording is on" in the upper-right corner. If this is not the case, make certain that BounceBall is selected for the storyboard in the Object and Timeline panel, and you can click the red circle in the top-left corner to toggle between recording and not recording.

6. Move the playhead (the yellow vertical line on the timeline with the down arrow at the top), to position 3 (3 seconds), as shown in Figure 11-10.

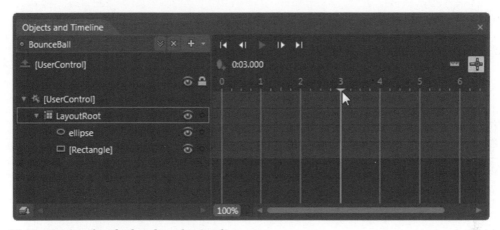

Figure 11-10. *Moving the playhead on the timeline*

7. With the playhead at 3 seconds, select the ellipse and move it down so that it is positioned directly below its starting point, but touching the black rectangle, as shown in Figure 11-11.

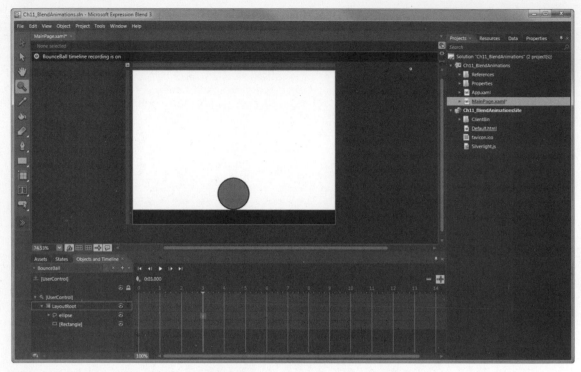

Figure 11-11. Repositioned ball on your grid

If you look carefully at the timeline, you'll notice that a red circle has shown up to the left of the Ellipse control in the Objects and Timeline panel, with a white arrow indicating that the object contains an animation. In addition, in the timeline, at position 3 seconds, a white ellipse has appeared to the right of the Ellipse control. This is how Expression Blend visually represents a keyframe.

At the top of the timeline, you will see buttons for navigating forward and backward between the frames in the animation. In addition, there is a play button that lets you view the animation.

8. Click the play button to view the animation. If you followed the steps properly, you will see the ball start at the top of the grid and slowly move to the top of the rectangle.

You just created yyour first animation! However, it isn't very realistic. In a real environment, the ball would accelerate as it fell toward the rectangle. So its movement would start out slow and speed up. You can mimic this behavior by modifying yyour keyframe and adding a spline.

9. Select the newly added keyframe in the timeline. (When the keyframe is selected, it will turn gray instead of white.)

Once the keyframe is selected, in the Properties panel, you will see a section titled Easing. This section allows you to adjust the KeySpline property. By default, the interpolation between the two keyframes is linear. However, for this example, you want to speed up the ball as it gets closer to the second keyframe.

10. Click and drag the dot in the upper-right corner of the KeySpline grid (the end point of the right side of the line), and drag it down so it appears as shown in Figure 11-12.

11. Click the play button at the top of the timeline. This time, you will see that the circle starts to drop slowly and then speeds up the closer it gets to the rectangle. This makes for a much more realistic animation.

12. Next, the circle is going to bounce back up after impacting the rectangle. With recording still on, move the playhead to 6 seconds on the timeline, and then move the circle directly up from its current position to about three-fourths its initial starting point.

13. Select the new keyframe that is created, and navigate to the Easing section of the Properties panel. This time, you want the movement to start out fast and slow down as the circle reaches its apex. To get this effect, move the bottom-left dot up so the KeySpline curve appears as shown in Figure 11-13.

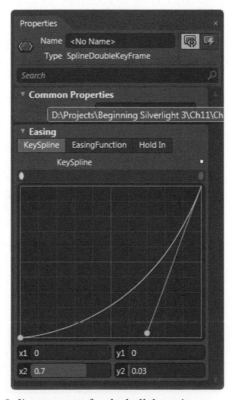

Figure 11-12. Adjusting the KeySpline property for the ball dropping

Figure 11-13. Adjusting the KeySpline property for the ball rising

14. Click the play button above the timeline to see the animation you have so far. The circle will fall with increasing speed, and then bounce back up with decreasing speed. So far so good, but what goes up, must come down.

    Move the playhead to 8 seconds, and move the circle up about one-fourth its initial position and adjust the KeySpline property to match Figure 11-12. Sticking with the pattern, move the playhead to 10 seconds, and move the circle down to the top of the rectangle. The KeySpline curve should match Figure 11-13. Repeat this pattern at 11 seconds, and then 11.5 seconds.

15. Click the play button. You should see the circle bounce on the rectangle as you would expect. The final timeline will appear as shown in Figure 11-14.

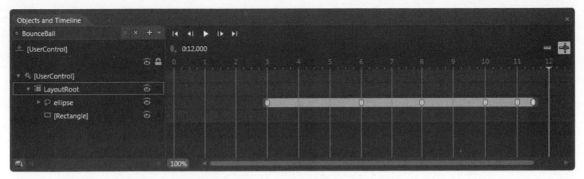

Figure 11-14. Final timeline for bouncing ball

Next, you need to tell Silverlight when the animation should take place. You will keep it simple and have the animation start when the page is loaded.

16. Navigate to the code behind for the MainPage.xaml file. In the Page() constructor, add the event handler for the Loaded event, as follows:

```
public MainPage()
{
    // Required to initialize variables
    InitializeComponent();
    this.Loaded += new RoutedEventHandler(Page_Loaded);
}

void Page_Loaded(object sender, RoutedEventArgs e)
{
    this.BounceBall.Begin();
}
```

17. Run the application. At this point, you should see the ball bounce on the rectangle. You might see something like what is shown in Figure 11-15.

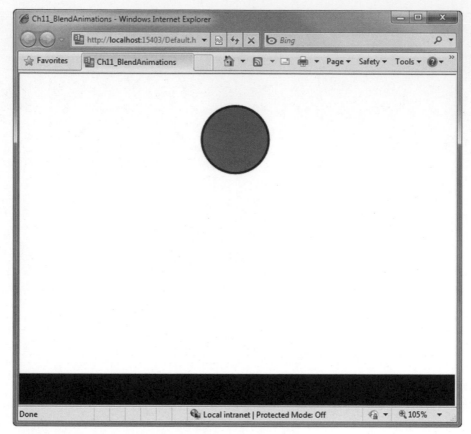

Figure 11-15. *Finished bouncing ball animation application*

In this section, you discussed animations in Silverlight. You should be comfortable creating new animations for yyour application in Expression Blend, and modifying and programming against those animations in Visual Studio 2008. The next section addresses transformations in Silverlight.

Creating Transformations in Silverlight

Silverlight includes a number of 2D *transforms*, which are used to change the appearance of objects. Transforms in Silverlight are defined using a transformation matrix, which is a mathematical construct for mapping points from one coordinate space to another. If this sounds a bit confusing, do not fear, Silverlight abstracts this matrix.

Silverlight supports fyour transformation types: rotation, scaling, skewing, and translation.

■ **Note** You can also define yyour own transformation matrix, if you need to modify or combine the fyour transformation types. See *Pro Silverlight 3* by Matthew MacDonald (Apress, 2009) for details on how to do this.

Transformation Types

Figure 11-16 shows a Silverlight application that has been divided into four grid cells. Each cell contains two rectangles that have their width and height set to 100 pixels. One of the rectangles in each cell has a border with its width set to 1 pixel, and the other has a border with its width set to 5 pixels. The rectangle with the thicker border was then transformed, so you can see the result of the transformation.

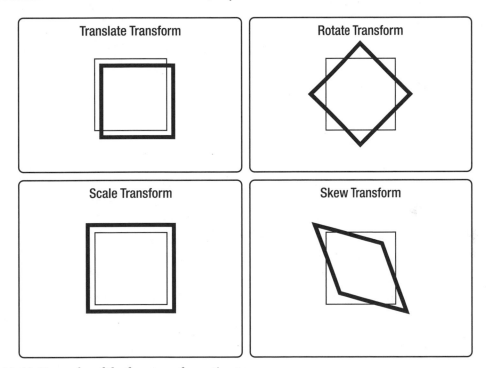

Figure 11-16. Examples of the four transformation types

ScaleTransform

The ScaleTransform type allows you to transform the size of a Silverlight object. The ScaleX property is used to scale the object on the horizontal axis, and the ScaleY property is used to scale the object on the vertical axis. The values of these properties are multiples of the object's original size. For example, setting the ScaleX property to 2 will double the size of the object on the horizontal axis. The following XAML was used to create the ScaleTransform in Figure 11-16.

```
<Rectangle Height="100" Width="100" Stroke="#FF000000" Grid.Row="1" Grid.Column="0"
    StrokeThickness="5" RenderTransformOrigin="0.5,0.5">
  <Rectangle.RenderTransform>
    <TransformGroup>
      <ScaleTransform ScaleX="1.25" ScaleY="1.25"/>
    </TransformGroup>
  </Rectangle.RenderTransform>
</Rectangle>
```

SkewTransform

The SkewTransform type allows you to skew a Silverlight object horizontally and vertically. The SkewTransform is used most commonly to create a 3D effect for an object. The AngleX property is used to skew the object horizontally, and AngleY is used to skew the object vertically. The following XAML was used to create the SkewTransform in Figure 11-16:

```
<Rectangle Height="100" Width="100" Stroke="#FF000000" Grid.Row="1" Grid.Column="1"
    StrokeThickness="5" RenderTransformOrigin="0.5,0.5">
  <Rectangle.RenderTransform>
    <TransformGroup>
      <SkewTransform AngleX="20" AngleY="15"/>
    </TransformGroup>
  </Rectangle.RenderTransform>
</Rectangle>
```

RotateTransform

The RotateTransform type allows you to rotate a Silverlight object by a specified angle around a specified center point. The angle is specified by the Angle property, and the center point is specified by the RenderTransformOrigin property. When you create a RotateTransform for a rectangle in Expression Blend, by default, it will set RenderTransformOrigin to 0.5, 0.5, which is the center of the object. You can also specify the center point using the CenterX and CenterY properties on the RotateTransform element. The following is the XAML to produce the RotateTransform in Figure 11-16:

```
<Rectangle Height="100" Width="100" Stroke="#FF000000" Grid.Row="0" Grid.Column="1"
    StrokeThickness="5" RenderTransformOrigin="0.5,0.5">
  <Rectangle.RenderTransform>
    <TransformGroup>
      <RotateTransform Angle="45"/>
    </TransformGroup>
  </Rectangle.RenderTransform>
</Rectangle>
```

TranslateTransform

The TranslateTransform type allows you to change the position of a Silverlight object, both horizontally and vertically. The X property controls the position change on the horizontal axis, and the Y property controls the change to the vertical axis. The following XAML was used to create the TranslateTransform in Figure 11-16:

```
<Rectangle Height="100" Width="100" Stroke="#FF000000" Grid.Row="0" Grid.Column="0"
    StrokeThickness="5" RenderTransformOrigin="0.5,0.5">
  <Rectangle.RenderTransform>
    <TransformGroup>
      <TranslateTransform X="10" Y="10"/>
    </TransformGroup>
  </Rectangle.RenderTransform>
</Rectangle>
```

Now that you have covered the basics of transforms in Silverlight, let's run through a quick exercise that will give you a chance to try them out for yourself.

Try It Out: Using Expression Blend to Transform Silverlight Objects

In this exercise, you'll use Expression Blend to add and animate transformations.

1. Create a new Silverlight application in Expression Blend called `Ch11_BlendTransforms`. Add two `ColumnDefinition` elements and two `RowDefinition` elements so the root `Grid` is equally divided into four cells, as follows:

```
<Grid x:Name="LayoutRoot" Background="White" >
  <Grid.RowDefinitions>
    <RowDefinition/>
    <RowDefinition/>
  </Grid.RowDefinitions>
  <Grid.ColumnDefinitions>
    <ColumnDefinition/>
    <ColumnDefinition/>
  </Grid.ColumnDefinitions>
</Grid>
```

2. Next, add two rectangles to each of the cells that you just created. Create two sets of rectangles: one set with `StrokeThickness="1"` and another with `StrokeThickness="5"`. Also, name the second set of rectangles `recTrans`. Add the following code:

```
<Grid x:Name="LayoutRoot" Background="White" >

  <Grid.RowDefinitions>
    <RowDefinition/>
    <RowDefinition/>
  </Grid.RowDefinitions>
  <Grid.ColumnDefinitions>
    <ColumnDefinition/>
    <ColumnDefinition/>
  </Grid.ColumnDefinitions>

  <Rectangle Grid.Row="0" Grid.Column="0" Height="100"
      Width="100" Stroke="#FF000000" StrokeThickness="1" />
  <Rectangle Grid.Row="0" Grid.Column="1" Height="100"
      Width="100" Stroke="#FF000000" StrokeThickness="1"  />
```

```
<Rectangle Grid.Row="1" Grid.Column="0" Height="100"
    Width="100" Stroke="#FF000000" StrokeThickness="1"  />
<Rectangle Grid.Row="1" Grid.Column="1" Height="100"
    Width="100" Stroke="#FF000000" StrokeThickness="1"  />

<Rectangle Grid.Row="0" Grid.Column="0" Height="100"
    Width="100" Stroke="#FF000000" StrokeThickness="5" x:Name="recTrans" />
<Rectangle Grid.Row="0" Grid.Column="1" Height="100"
    Width="100" Stroke="#FF000000" StrokeThickness="5" x:Name="recRotate" />
<Rectangle Grid.Row="1" Grid.Column="0" Height="100"
    Width="100" Stroke="#FF000000" StrokeThickness="5" x:Name="rectScale" />
<Rectangle Grid.Row="1" Grid.Column="1" Height="100"
    Width="100" Stroke="#FF000000" StrokeThickness="5" x:Name="rectSkew" />
```

```
</Grid>
```

At this point, your application should have four squares equally spaced in the four cells of your application. The next step will be to introduce your transforms, but instead of just adding the transforms, you are going to animate the transformation taking place.

3. Using the techniques discussed earlier in this chapter, create a new storyboard called TransformElements.

4. You will perform the transformations over 2 seconds, so move the playhead on the timeline to 2 seconds. Select the rectangle named recTrans. In the Properties panel, find the Transform section. Select the Translate tab. Set X and Y to 25. This will cause the top-left square to move down and to the right, as shown in Figure 11-17.

5. Highlight the rectangle named recRotate. In the Transform section of the Properties panel, select the Rotate tab. Set the Angle property to 45. The top-right square will rotate 45 degrees, as shown in Figure 11-18.

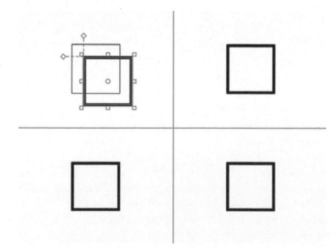

Figure 11-17. *Adding the TranslateTransform*

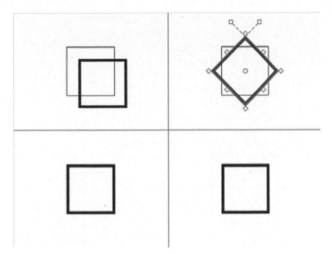

Figure 11-18. Adding the RotateTransform

6. Select the rectangle named rectScale. In the Transform section of the Properties panel, select the Scale tab. Set the values of the X and Y properties to 1.5, which will scale the bottom-left square 1.5x, or 150%, as shown in Figure 11-19.

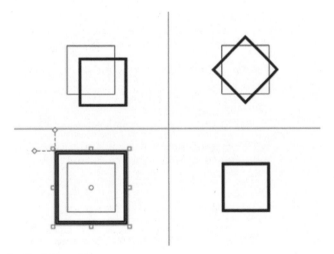

Figure 11-19. Adding the ScaleTransform

7. Select the rectangle named rectSkew. In the Transform section of the Properties panel, select the Skew tab. Set the values of the X and Y properties to 20. This will cause the square to skew into a diamond shape, as shown in Figure 11-20.

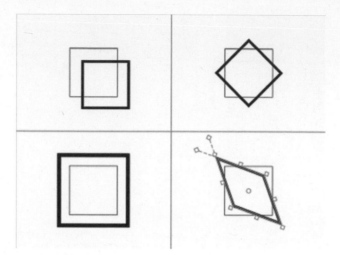

Figure 11-20. Adding the SkewTransform

8.   Click the play button at the top of the timeline, and watch the objects transform from their original shapes and locations.

As you've seen in this exercise, applying transformations is pretty straightforward.

Summary

This chapter covered creating animations in Silverlight. You looked at animations from a high level, explored the different elements that make up an animation in Silverlight, and learned how to programmatically control animations in the code behind. You also looked at how Expression Blend helps you create complex animations. Then you shifted your focus to transformations in Silverlight. You looked at each of the fyour transform types, and then created a simple Silverlight application utilizing transforms.

In the following chapter, you will look at the more advanced topic of creating your own Silverlight custom controls. Custom controls allow you to create Silverlight functionality that can be easily reused in different Silverlight applications.

CHAPTER 12

■ ■ ■

Custom Controls

So far in this book, you have learned about the many elements of Silverlight and how they can be used to build RIAs. But what if Silverlight doesn't offer the specific functionality you need for an application? In that case, you may want to create a custom control to provide that additional functionality.

The actual procedure for creating custom controls is not that terribly difficult, but understanding the process can be. Under the hood, Silverlight performs some complex work, but most Silverlight developers do not need to know these details. However, in order to understand custom controls and the process used to build them, you you must dive in and see how Silverlight ticks.

In this chapter, you will examine when it is appropriate to write custom controls in Silverlight. Then you will look at the Silverlight Control Toolkit and the controls it offers for developers to use in their applications. Next, you will explore the different aspects of the Silverlight control model. Finally, you will build a custom control for Silverlight.

When to Write Custom Controls

When you find that none of the existing Silverlight controls do exactly what you want, creating a custom control is not always the solution. In fact, in most cases, you should be able to get by without writing custom controls. Due to the flexibility built into the Silverlight controls, you can usually modify an existing one to suit your needs.

As a general rule, if your goal is to modify the appearance of a control, there is no need to write a custom control. Silverlight controls that are built properly, following Microsoft's best practices, will adopt the Parts and States model, which calls for complete separation of the logical and visual aspects of your control. Due to this separation, developers can change the appearance of controls, and even change transitions of the controls between different states, without needing to write custom controls.

So, just when is creating a custom control the right way to go? Here are the primary reasons for writing custom controls:

Abstraction of functionality: When developing your applications, you may need to implement some functionality that can be achieved using Silverlight's out-of-the- box support. However, if this functionality needs to be reused often in your application, you may choose to create a custom control that abstracts the functionality, in order to simplify the application. An example of this would be if you wanted to have two text boxes next to each other for first and last names. Instead of always including two TextBox controls in your XAML, you could write a custom control that would automatically include both text boxes and would abstract the behavior surrounding the text boxes.

Modification of functionality: If you would like to change the way a Silverlight control behaves, you can write a custom control that implements that behavior, perhaps inheriting from an existing control. An example of this would be if you wanted to create a button that pops up a menu instead of simply triggering a click method.

Creation of new functionality: The most obvious reason for writing a custom control in Silverlight is to add functionality that does not currently exist in Silverlight. As an example, you could write a control that acts as a floating window that can be dragged and resized.

Although these are valid reasons for creating custom controls, there is one more resource you should check before you do so: the Silverlight Control Toolkit.

Silverlight Control Toolkit

Upon the release of Silverlight, Microsoft announced the Silverlight Control Toolkit, an open source project located on CodePlex at http://www.codeplex.com/SilverlightToolkit. This toolkit provides additional components and controls that you can download for use in your Silverlight applications. For example, it includes the fully functional charting controls shown in Figure 12-1.

Microsoft's target is to eventually have more than 100 controls available through this open source toolkit. For developers, this means that as Silverlight matures, more and more controls will be available for use in your applications.

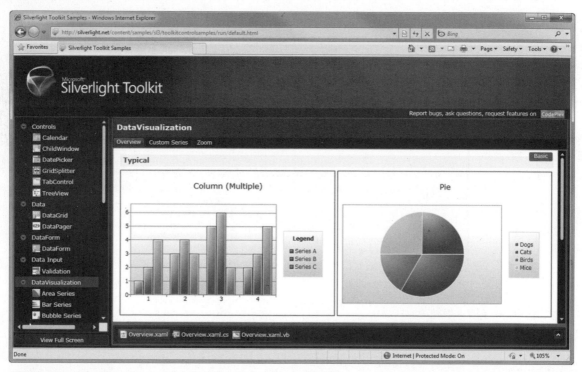

Figure 12-1. *Charting controls in the Silverlight Control Toolkit*

The Silverlight Control Toolkit contains four "quality bands" that describe the specific control's maturity level: experimental, preview, stable, and mature. With the initial announcement of the Silverlight Control Toolkit, the following controls (six within the preview band and six in the stable band) are available for download (including the full source code):

- AutoCompleteBox
- NumericUpDown
- Viewbox
- Expander
- ImplicitStyleManager
- Charting
- TreeView
- DockPanel
- WrapPanel
- Label
- HeaderedContentControl
- HeaderedItemsControl

This toolkit is an excellent resource for Silverlight developers. You can use these controls as is in your applications, or you can use the source code to modify your own controls. They are also a great way to learn how to build custom controls, because you can examine their source code. In order to understand that source code, you will need to know about the Silverlight control model.

Silverlight Control Model

Before you start to build custom controls for Silverlight, you should understand the key concepts of the Silverlight control model. In this section, you will look at two of these concepts:

- The Parts and States model
- Dependency properties

Parts and States Model

Following Microsoft's best practices, Silverlight controls are built with a strict separation between the visual aspects of the control and the logic behind the control. This allows developers to create templates for existing controls that will dramatically change the visual appearance and the visual behaviors of a control, without needing to write any code. This separation is called for by the Parts and States model. The visual aspects of controls are managed by Silverlight's Visual State Manager (VSM).

■ **Note** You are not required to adhere to the Parts and State model when developing custom controls. However, developers are urged to do so in order to follow the best practices outlined by Microsoft.

The Parts and States model uses the following terminology:

Parts: Named elements contained in a control template that are manipulated by code in some way are called *parts*. For example, a simple Button control could consist of a rectangle that is the body of the button and a text block that represents the text on the control.

States: A control will always be in a *state*. For a Button control, different states include when the mouse is hovered over the button, when the mouse is pressed down on the button, and when neither is the case (its default or normal state). The visual look of control is defined by its particular state.

Transitions: When a control changes from one state to another—for example, when a Button control goes from its normal state to having the mouse hovered over it—its visual appearance may change. In some cases, this change may be animated to provide a smooth visual transition from the states. These animations are defined in the Parts and States model by *transitions*.

State group: According to the Parts and States model, control states can be grouped into mutually exclusive groups. A control cannot be in more than one state within the same state group at the same time.

Dependency Properties

Properties are a common part of object-oriented programming and familiar to .NET developers. Here is a typical property definition:

```
private string _name;
public string Name
{
    get { return _name; }
    set { _name = value; }
}
```

In Silverlight and WPF, Microsoft has added some functionality to the property system. This new system is referred to as the *Silverlight property system*. Properties created based on this new property system are called *dependency properties*.

In a nutshell, dependency properties allow Silverlight to determine the value of a property dynamically from a number of different inputs, such as data binding or template binding. As a general rule, if you want to be able to style a property or to have it participate in data binding or template binding, it must be defined as a dependency property.

You define a property as a dependency property using the DependencyProperty object, as shown in the following code snippet:

```
public static readonly DependencyProperty NameProperty =
    DependencyProperty.Register(
        "Name",
        typeof(string),
        typeof(MyControl),
        null
        );

public int Name
{
    get
    {
```

```
        return (string)GetValue(NameProperty);
    }
    set
    {
        SetValue(NameProperty, value);
    }
}
```

This example defines the `Name` property as a dependency property. It declares a new object of type `DependencyProperty` called `NameProperty`, following the naming convention detailed by Microsoft. `NameProperty` is set equal to the return value of the `DependencyProperty.Register()` method, which registers a dependency property within the Silverlight 2 property system.

The `DependencyProperty.Register()` method is passed a number of arguments:

- The name of the property that you are registering as a dependency property— `Name`, in this example.

- The data type of the property you are registering— `string`, in this example.

- The data type of the object that is registering the property— `MyControl`, in this example.

- Metadata that should be registered with the dependency property. Most of the time, this will be used to hook up a callback method that will be called whenever the property's value is changed. This example simply passes `null`. In the next section, you will see how this last argument is used.

Now that I have discussed custom controls in Silverlight from a high level, it's time to see how to build your own.

Creating Custom Controls in Silverlight

As I mentioned at the beginning of the chapter, creating a custom control does not need to be difficult. Of course, the work involved depends on how complex your control needs to be. As you'll see, the custom control you'll create in this chapter is relatively simple. Before you get to that exercise, let's take a quick look at the two options for creating custom controls.

Implementing Custom Functionality

You have two main options for creating custom functionality in Silverlight:

With a `UserControl`: The simplest way to create a piece of custom functionality is to implement it with a `UserControl`. Once the `UserControl` is created, you can then reuse it across your application.

As a custom control: The content that is rendered is built from scratch by the developer. This is by far the most complex option for creating a custom control. You would need to do this when you want to implement functionality that is unavailable with the existing controls in Silverlight. In this chapter's exercise, you will take the custom control approach.

Try It Out: Building a Custom Control

In this exercise, you will build your own "cooldown" button. This button will be disabled for a set number of seconds—its cooldown duration—after it is clicked. If you set the cooldown to be 3 seconds, then after you click the button, you will not be able to click it again for 3 seconds.

For demonstration purposes, you will not use the standard Silverlight Button control as the base control. Instead, you will create a custom control that implements Control. This way, I can show you how to create a control with a number of states.

The cooldown button will have five states, implemented in two state groups. The NormalStates state group will have these states:

- Pressed: The button is being pressed. When it is in this state, the thickness of the button's border will be reduced.

- MouseOver: The mouse is hovering over the button. When it is in this state, the thickness of the button's border will be increased.

- Normal: The button is in its normal state.

It will also have a state group named CoolDownStates, which will contain two states:

- Available: The button is active and available to be clicked.

- CoolDown: The button is in its cooldown state, and therefore is not active. You will place a rectangle over top of the button that is of 75% opacity. In addition, you will disable all other events while the button is in this state.

Keep in mind that this is only an example, and it has many areas that could use improvement. The goal of the exercise is not to produce a control that you will use in your applications, but rather to demonstrate the basic steps for creating a custom control in Silverlight.

Setting Up the Control Project

Let's get started by creating a new project for the custom control.

1. In Visual Studio 2008, create a new Silverlight Application named Ch12_CoolDownButton and allow Visual Studio to create a Web Application project to host your application.

2. From Solution Explorer, right-click the solution and select Add → New Project.

3. In the Add New Project dialog box, select the Silverlight Class Library template and name the library CoolDownButton, as shown in Figure 12-2.

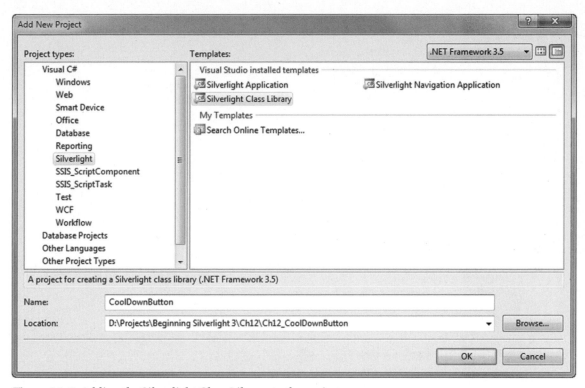

Figure 12-2. Adding the Silverlight Class Library to the project

4. By default, Visual Studio will create a class named Class1.cs. Delete this file from the project.

5. Right-click the CoolDownButton project and select Add → New Item.

6. In the Add New Item dialog box, select the Class template and name the class CoolDownButtonControl, as shown in Figure 12-3.

CHAPTER 12 ■ CUSTOM CONTROLS

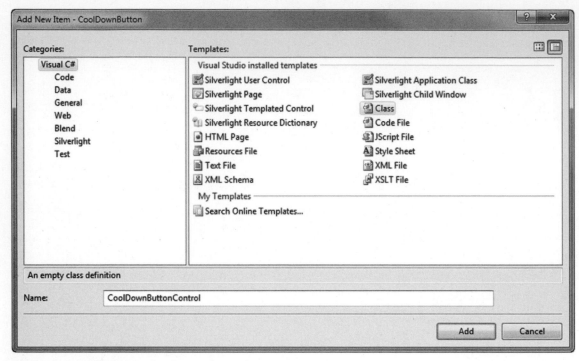

Figure 12-3. *Adding the new class to the project*

Defining Properties and States

Now you're ready to create the control. Let's begin by coding the properties and states.

1. Set the control class to inherit from Control, in order to gain the base Silverlight control functionality, as follows:

```
namespace CoolDownButton
{
    public class CoolDownButtonControl : Control
    {

    }
}
```

2. Now add the control's public properties, as follows:

```
public static readonly DependencyProperty CoolDownSecondsProperty =
    DependencyProperty.Register(
        "CoolDownSeconds",
        typeof(int),
        typeof(CoolDownButtonControl),
        new PropertyMetadata(
            new PropertyChangedCallback(
```

```
                    CoolDownButtonControl.OnCoolDownSecondsPropertyChanged
                    )
            )
        );

public int CoolDownSeconds
{
    get
    {
        return (int)GetValue(CoolDownSecondsProperty);
    }
    set
    {
        SetValue(CoolDownSecondsProperty, value);
    }
}

private static void OnCoolDownSecondsPropertyChanged(
    DependencyObject d, DependencyPropertyChangedEventArgs e)
{
    CoolDownButtonControl cdButton = d as CoolDownButtonControl;

    cdButton.OnCoolDownButtonChange(null);
}

public static readonly DependencyProperty ButtonTextProperty =
    DependencyProperty.Register(
        "ButtonText",
        typeof(string),
        typeof(CoolDownButtonControl),
        new PropertyMetadata(
            new PropertyChangedCallback(
                CoolDownButtonControl.OnButtonTextPropertyChanged
                )
            )
        );

public string ButtonText
{
    get
    {
        return (string)GetValue(ButtonTextProperty);
    }
    set
    {
        SetValue(ButtonTextProperty, value);
    }
}

private static void OnButtonTextPropertyChanged(
    DependencyObject d, DependencyPropertyChangedEventArgs e)
{
    CoolDownButtonControl cdButton = d as CoolDownButtonControl;
```

```
        cdButton.OnCoolDownButtonChange(null);
}

protected virtual void OnCoolDownButtonChange(RoutedEventArgs e)
{

}
```

As explained earlier in the chapter, in order for your properties to allow data binding, template binding, styling, and so on, they must be dependency properties. In addition to the dependency properties, you added two callback methods that will be called when the properties are updated. By naming convention, the CoolDownSeconds property has a DependencyProperty object named CoolDownSecondsProperty and a callback method of onCoolDownSecondsPropertyChanged(). So you need to watch out, or your names will end up very long, as they have here.

3.   Add some private members to contain state information, as follows:

```
namespace CoolDownButton
{
    public class CoolDownButtonControl : Control
    {
        ...

        private FrameworkElement corePart;
        private bool isPressed, isMouseOver, isCoolDown;
        private DateTime pressedTime;

    }
}
```

The corePart members are of type FrameworkElement and will hold the instance of the main part, which will respond to mouse events. The isPressed, isMouseOver, and isCoolDown Boolean members will be used to help keep track of the current button state. And the pressedTime member will record the time that the button was clicked in order to determine when the cooldown should be removed.

4.   Add a helper method called GoToState(), which will assist in switching between the states of the control.

```
private void GoToState(bool useTransitions)
{
    //  Go to states in NormalStates state group
    if (isPressed)
    {
        VisualStateManager.GoToState(this, "Pressed", useTransitions);
    }
    else if (isMouseOver)
    {
        VisualStateManager.GoToState(this, "MouseOver", useTransitions);
    }
    else
```

```
{
    VisualStateManager.GoToState(this, "Normal", useTransitions);
}

// Go to states in CoolDownStates state group
if (isCoolDown)
{
    VisualStateManager.GoToState(this, "CoolDown", useTransitions);
}
else
{
    VisualStateManager.GoToState(this, "Available", useTransitions);
}
}
```

This method will check the private members you added in the previous step to determine in which state the control should be. When the proper state is determined, the `VisualStateManager.GoToState()` method is called, passing it the control, the name of the state, and whether or not the control should use transitions when switching from the current state to this new state (whether or not an animation should be shown).

Now let's turnto the visual aspect of the control.

Defining the Control's Appearance

The default control template is placed in a file named generic.xaml, which is located in a folder named themes. These names are required. The generic.xaml is a resource dictionary that defines the built-in style for the control. You need to add the folder and file, make some adjustments to the file, and then add the XAML to set the control's appearance.

1. To add the required folder, right-click the CoolDownButton project and select Add → New Folder. Name the folder themes.

2. Right-click the newly added themes folder and select Add → New Item.

3. In the Add New Item dialog box, select the Silverlight User Control template and name the file generic.xaml, as shown in Figure 12-4. Click Add and confirm that the generic.xaml file was added within the themes folder.

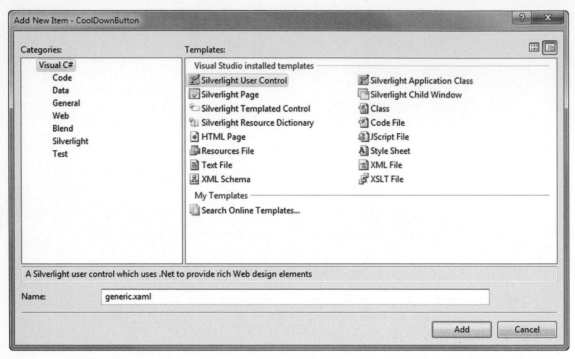

Figure 12-4. *Adding the generic.xaml resource dictionary*

4. In Solution Explorer, expand the `generic.xaml` file to see the `generic.xaml.cs` file. Right-click it and delete this code-behind file.

5. Right-click the `generic.xaml` file and select Properties. Change the Build Action to Resource and remove the resource for the Custom Tool property, as shown in Figure 12-5.

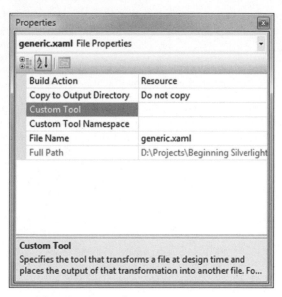

Figure 12-5. *The Properties panel for generic.xaml*

6. Open the generic.xaml file. You will see that, by default, the file has the following contents:

```
<UserControl x:Class="CoolDownButton.themes.generic"
    xmlns="http://schemas.microsoft.com/winfx/2006/xaml/presentation"
    xmlns:x="http://schemas.microsoft.com/winfx/2006/xaml"
    Width="400" Height="300">
    <Grid x:Name="LayoutRoot" Background="White">

    </Grid>
</UserControl>
```

7. You need to change the generic.xaml file to be a resource dictionary. To do this, replace the UserControl tag with a ResourceDictionary tag. Then remove the Width and Height definitions and add a new xmlns for the CoolDownButton. Finally, remove the Grid definition. Your code should look like this:

```
<ResourceDictionary
    xmlns="http://schemas.microsoft.com/winfx/2006/xaml/presentation"
    xmlns:x="http://schemas.microsoft.com/winfx/2006/xaml"
    xmlns:begSL2="clr-namespace:CoolDownButton">
</ResourceDictionary>
```

Now you can add the actual XAML that will make up the control. First, add a Style tag, with the TargetType set to CoolDownButtonControl. Then add a Setter for the control template, and within that, add the ControlTemplate definition, again with TargetType set to CoolDownButtonControl. The control will consist of two Rectangle components: one for the button itself, named coreButton, one for the 75% opacity overlay that will be displayed when the button is in its CoolDown state. It will also have a TextBlock component to contain the text of the button. This defines the control in the default state. Therefore, the opacity of the overlay rectangle is set to 0% to start, because the overlay should not be visible by default. The additions are as follows:

```xml
<ResourceDictionary
    xmlns="http://schemas.microsoft.com/winfx/2006/xaml/presentation"
    xmlns:x="http://schemas.microsoft.com/winfx/2006/xaml"
    xmlns:begSL2="clr-namespace:CoolDownButton">
<Style TargetType="begSL2:CoolDownButtonControl">
    <Setter Property="Template">
        <Setter.Value>
            <ControlTemplate TargetType="begSL2:CoolDownButtonControl">
                <Grid x:Name="LayoutRoot">
                    <Rectangle
                        StrokeThickness="4"
                        Stroke="Navy"
                        Fill="AliceBlue"
                        RadiusX="4"
                        RadiusY="4"
                        x:Name="innerButton" />
                    <TextBlock
                        HorizontalAlignment="Center"
                        VerticalAlignment="Center"
                        Text="Test"
                        TextWrapping="Wrap"/>
                    <Rectangle
                        Opacity="0"
                        Fill="#FF000000"
                        Stroke="#FF000000"
                        RenderTransformOrigin="0.5,0.5"
                        RadiusY="4" RadiusX="4"
                        x:Name="corePart">
                        <Rectangle.RenderTransform>
                            <TransformGroup>
                                <ScaleTransform
                                    ScaleX="1"
                                    ScaleY="1"/>
                            </TransformGroup>
                        </Rectangle.RenderTransform>
                    </Rectangle>
                </Grid>
            </ControlTemplate>
        </Setter.Value>
    </Setter>
</Style>
</ResourceDictionary>
```

8. Now that you have defined the default appearance of the control, you need to add the VisualStateGroups, along with the different states for the control. To do this, add the following code directly below the Grid definition and above the first Rectangle. Notice that for each state, a Storyboard is used to define the state's visual appearance.

```xml
<VisualStateManager.VisualStateGroups>
    <VisualStateGroup x:Name="NormalStates">

        <VisualState x:Name="Normal"/>

        <VisualState x:Name="MouseOver" >
            <Storyboard >
                <DoubleAnimation
                    Storyboard.TargetName="innerButton"
                    Storyboard.TargetProperty="(UIElement.StrokeThickness)"
                    Duration="0" To="6"/>
            </Storyboard>

        </VisualState>
        <VisualState x:Name="Pressed">

            <Storyboard>
                <DoubleAnimation
                    Storyboard.TargetName="innerButton"
                    Storyboard.TargetProperty="(UIElement.StrokeThickness)"
                    Duration="0" To="2"/>
            </Storyboard>

        </VisualState>

    </VisualStateGroup>

    <VisualStateGroup x:Name="CoolDownStates">

        <VisualState x:Name="Available"/>
        <VisualState x:Name="CoolDown">
            <Storyboard>
                <DoubleAnimation
                    Storyboard.TargetName="corePart"
                    Storyboard.TargetProperty="(UIElement.Opacity)"
                    Duration="0" To=".75"/>
            </Storyboard>
        </VisualState>

    </VisualStateGroup>
</VisualStateManager.VisualStateGroups>
```

Now let's turn attention back to the CoolDownButtonControl.cs file to finish up the logic behind the control.

Handling Control Events

To complete the control, you need to handle its events and define its control contract.

1. First, you must get an instance of the core part. Referring back to step 8 in the "Defining the Control's Appearance" section, you'll see that this is the overlay rectangle named corePart. This is the control on top of the other controls, so it is the one that will accept the mouse events. To get the instance of corePart, use the GetChildElement() method. Call this method in the OnApplyTemplate() method that is called whenever a template is applied to the control, as follows:

```
public override void OnApplyTemplate()
{
    base.OnApplyTemplate();

    CorePart = (FrameworkElement)GetTemplateChild("corePart");

    GoToState(false);
}

private FrameworkElement CorePart
{
    get
    {
        return corePart;
    }

    set
    {
        corePart = value;
    }
}
```

Notice that this method calls the base OnApplyTemplate() method, and then calls the GoToState() method, passing it false. This is the first time that the GoToState() method will be called, and you are passing it false so that it does not use any transitions while changing the state. The initial view of the control should not have any animations to get it to the initial state.

2. At this point, you need to wire up event handlers to handle the mouse events. First, create the event handlers themselves, as follows:

```
void corePart_MouseEnter(object sender, MouseEventArgs e)
{
    isMouseOver = true;
    GoToState(true);
}

void corePart_MouseLeave(object sender, MouseEventArgs e)
{
    isMouseOver = false;
    GoToState(true);
}
```

```
void corePart_MouseLeftButtonDown(object sender, MouseButtonEventArgs e)
{
    isPressed = true;
    GoToState(true);
}

void corePart_MouseLeftButtonUp(object sender, MouseButtonEventArgs e)
{
    isPressed = false;
    isCoolDown = true;
    pressedTime = DateTime.Now;
    GoToState(true);
}
```

3. Next, wire up the handlers to the events. You can do this in the CorePart property's setter, as follows. Note that in the case where more than one template is applied, before wiring up the event handlers, you need to make sure to remove any existing event handlers.

```
private FrameworkElement CorePart
{
    get
    {
        return corePart;
    }

    set
    {
        FrameworkElement oldCorePart = corePart;

        if (oldCorePart != null)
        {
            oldCorePart.MouseEnter -=
                new MouseEventHandler(corePart_MouseEnter);
            oldCorePart.MouseLeave -=
                new MouseEventHandler(corePart_MouseLeave);
            oldCorePart.MouseLeftButtonDown -=
                new MouseButtonEventHandler(
                    corePart_MouseLeftButtonDown);
            oldCorePart.MouseLeftButtonUp -=
                new MouseButtonEventHandler(
                    corePart_MouseLeftButtonUp);
        }

        corePart = value;

        if (corePart != null)
        {
            corePart.MouseEnter +=
                new MouseEventHandler(corePart_MouseEnter);
            corePart.MouseLeave +=
                new MouseEventHandler(corePart_MouseLeave);
```

```
        corePart.MouseLeftButtonDown +=
            new MouseButtonEventHandler(
                corePart_MouseLeftButtonDown);
        corePart.MouseLeftButtonUp +=
            new MouseButtonEventHandler(
                corePart_MouseLeftButtonUp);
        }
    }
}
```

4. Recall that when the button is clicked, you need to make sure the button is disabled for however many seconds are set as the cooldown period. To do this, first create a method that checks to see if the cooldown time has expired, as follows:

```
private bool CheckCoolDown()
{
    if (!isCoolDown)
    {
        return false;
    }
    else
    {
        if (DateTime.Now > pressedTime.AddSeconds(CoolDownSeconds))
        {
            isCoolDown = false;
            return false;
        }
        else
        {
            return true;
        }
    }
}
```

The logic behind this method is pretty simple. If the isCoolDown flag is true, then you are simply checking to see if the current time is greater than the pressedTime added to the cooldown. If so, you reset the isCoolDown flag and return false; otherwise, you return true.

5. Now you need to surround the code in each of the event handlers with a call to the CheckCoolDown() method, as follows. If the cooldown has not yet expired, none of the event handlers should perform any action.

```
void corePart_MouseEnter(object sender, MouseEventArgs e)
{
    if (!CheckCoolDown())
    {
        isMouseOver = true;
        GoToState(true);
    }
}

void corePart_MouseLeave(object sender, MouseEventArgs e)
```

```
{
    if (!CheckCoolDown())
    {
        isMouseOver = false;
        GoToState(true);
    }
}

void corePart_MouseLeftButtonDown(object sender, MouseButtonEventArgs e)
{
    if (!CheckCoolDown())
    {
        isPressed = true;
        GoToState(true);
    }
}

void corePart_MouseLeftButtonUp(object sender, MouseButtonEventArgs e)
{
    if (!CheckCoolDown())
    {
        isPressed = false;
        isCoolDown = true;
        pressedTime = DateTime.Now;
        GoToState(true);
    }
}
```

6. Recall that in step 2 of the "Defining Properties and States" section, you created a method called OnCoolDownButtonChange(). At that time, you did not place anything in this method. This is the method that is called whenever there is a notification change to a dependency property. When a change occurs, you need to call GoToState() so the control can reflect the changes, as follows:

```
protected virtual void OnCoolDownButtonChange(RoutedEventArgs e)
{
    GoToState(true);
}
```

7. Next, create a constructor for your control and apply the default style key. In many cases, this will simply be the type of your control itself.

```
public CoolDownButtonControl()
{
    DefaultStyleKey = typeof(CoolDownButtonControl);
}
```

8. The final step in creating the control is to define a control contract that describes your control. This is required in order for your control to be modified by tools such as Expression Blend. This contract consists of a number of attributes that are placed directly in the control class, as follows. These attributes are used only by tools; they are not used by the runtime.

```
namespace CoolDownButton
{
    [TemplatePart(Name = "Core", Type = typeof(FrameworkElement))]
    [TemplateVisualState(Name = "Normal", GroupName = "NormalStates")]
    [TemplateVisualState(Name = "MouseOver", GroupName = " NormalStates")]
    [TemplateVisualState(Name = "Pressed", GroupName = " NormalStates")]
    [TemplateVisualState(Name = "CoolDown", GroupName="CoolDownStates")]
    [TemplateVisualState(Name = "Available", GroupName="CoolDownStates")]
    public class CoolDownButtonControl : Control
    {
    }
}
```

This completes the creation of the custom control.

Compiling and Testing the Control

Now you're ready to try out your new control.

1. Compile your control.

2. If everything compiles correctly, you need create an instance of your control in your Ch12_CoolDownButton project. To do this, right-click the Ch12_CoolDownButton project in Solution Explorer and select Add Reference. In the Add Reference dialog box, select the Projects tab and choose CoolDownButton, as shown in Figure 12-6. Then click OK.

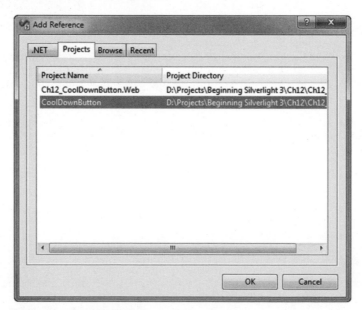

Figure 12-6. Adding a reference to your control

3. Navigate to your `MainPage.xaml` file within the `Ch12_CoolDownButton` project. First add a new `xmlns` to the `UserControl` definition, and then add an instance of your control, as follows:

```
<UserControl x:Class="Ch11_CoolDownButton.MainPage"
    xmlns="http://schemas.microsoft.com/winfx/2006/xaml/presentation"
    xmlns:x="http://schemas.microsoft.com/winfx/2006/xaml"
    xmlns:begSL2="clr-namespace:CoolDownButton;assembly=CoolDownButton"
    Width="400" Height="300">
    <Grid x:Name="LayoutRoot" Background="White">
        <begSL2:CoolDownButtonControl
            CoolDownSeconds="3"
            Width="150" Height="60" />
    </Grid>
</UserControl>
```

4. Run the project. You should see your button.

5. Test the states of your button. When you move the mouse over the button, the border thickness will increase. Click the mouse on the button, and the border will decrease. When you release the mouse button on the button, the border will go back to normal, and the overlay will appear. You can continue to move the mouse over the button, and you will notice that it will not respond to your events until 3 seconds have passed. Figure 12-7 shows the various control states.

Figure 12-7. *Button states*

Clearly, this cooldown button has a lot of room for improvement. However, the goal was to show you the basic steps involved in creating a custom control. As you most certainly could tell, the process is pretty involved, but the rewards of following the best practices are worth it. When the control is built properly like this, you can apply custom templates to it to dramatically change its appearance, without needing to rewrite any of the code logic.

Summary

Without a doubt, this was the most complex content so far covered in this book. The goal was to give you a basic understanding of what is involved in creating custom controls the right way in Silverlight.

In this chapter, you looked at when you might want to create a custom control. Then you learned about some of the key concepts within the Silverlight control model, including the Parts and States model and dependency properties. Finally, you built your own custom control.

CHAPTER 13

■ ■ ■

Deployment

Up to now in this book, I have discussed only the process of developing Silverlight applications. In this chapter, I turn your focus to post development and discuss the topic of deploying your Silverlight applications.

Deploying Silverlight Applications

Once you have finished developing your Silverlight application, you must then face the question of deployment. Luckily, Silverlight deployment is a trivial task that really only involves one concept, XAP files.

XAP Files

When you compile a Silverlight application, the application is packaged into a single file with the extension .XAP. This file is the only thing that needs to be sent to the client in order to run your application. The XAP file itself is really nothing special and is nothing more than a zip file with a special file extension. To prove this, you can simply change the file extension of a XAP file to give it a .ZIP extension. Once the file has been renamed, you can then view the contents of compressed archive in the file explorer in Windows or in a zip archive tool such as WinZip.

The reason Silverlight uses XAP files to package applications is really for two benefits. First, by placing your files in a ZIP archive file, your files are compressed when they are deployed and sent to the client, which in turn reduces download times and improves the end user experience. Secondly, by placing your entire Silverlight application in one file, it makes the process of deploying your application extremely simple.

Hosting Silverlight Content

In order to host Silverlight content on your web server, it is not necessary to be running a Windows server. In fact, just about any web server can serve Silverlight content, as long as they are set to serve up XAP files. In IIS7 this is setup by default, so if you are running Windows 2000 Server then your web server is preconfigured ready to host your Silverlight content.

If you are running a version of IIS previous to IIS7 or if you are running on a non-Windows server, you must do some minor configuration to enable the MIME types for the Silverlight extensions. The two MIME types you need to add are in Table 13-1.

Table 13-1. NEED TABLE CAPTION.

Extension	MIME Type
.xaml	application/xaml+xml
.xap	application/x-silverlight-app

Since there are so many different servers out there, I won't attempt to show you how to setup this MIME type for each server possibility, so you will need to do some quick research on how to setup MIME types, though it is an extremely common task for server administration.

Assembly Caching

As the previous section described, when you deploy your Silverlight applications, all files for your application are included in a XAP package. This includes any assemblies that are required by your application. For example, your XAP file may look like Figure 13-1, where you can see that a number of assemblies are included in the package like System.Windows.Controls.Data.dll. This assembly alone is 128KB in size, and this amount has to be downloaded to each and every client that runs your application. Furthermore, if there are multiple Silverlight applications that all require the use of the System.Windows.Controls.Data.dll assembly, each one by default will download their own copy of the assembly.

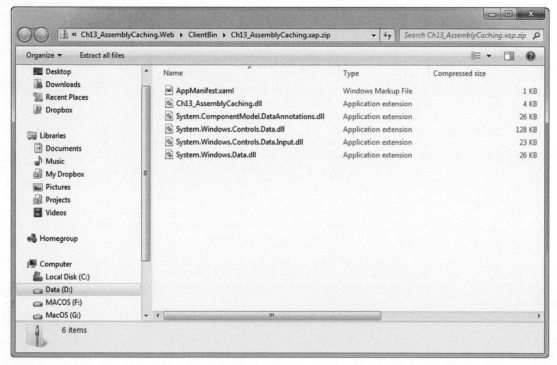

Figure 13-1. Exploring the contents of a XAP file

Assembly caching is a feature new to Silverlight 3 that allows you to cache assemblies locally and share them between different Silverlight applications running on a client machine. Let's run through a very quick example to show how assembly caching works and how to activate it in your Silverlight applications.

Try It Out: Exploring Assembly Caching

In this exercise, you will create a simple Silverlight application that includes a number of assemblies. You will then look at the packaged XAP file before and after you activate assembly caching for the application. You will also explore the source changes that take place when using assembly caching. Let's get started!

1. In Visual Studio 2008, create a new Silverlight Application named `Ch13_AssemblyCaching` and allow Visual Studio to create a Web Application project to host your application.

2. In `MainPage.xaml`, make certain your cursor is positioned within the root Grid and double click on the `DataGrid` from the Toolbox. After adding these items, your XAML should look like the following.

```
<Grid x:Name="LayoutRoot">
      <data:DataGrid></data:DataGrid>
</Grid>
```

3. Build the application by selecting Build → Build Solution from the main menu.

4. Expand the ClientBin directory within the host web application's directory using the Solution Explorer in Visual Studio. There you should find the Ch13_AssemblyCaching.xap file as shown in Figure 13-2.

Figure 13-2. Locating your Application's XAP File

313

5. Change the filename of this file to be Ch13_AssemblyCaching.xap.zip in order to explore the contents. Once the file is renamed, open the compressed file in Windows Explorer. You will see the contents as shown in Figure 13-1. You will see that there many assemblies contained in the xap file.

6. From Visual Studio right click on the Silverlight application in the Solution Explorer and select Properties. On the properties dialog, you will see a checkbox labeled "Reduce XAP size by using library caching." Check this option as shown in Figure 13-3 and save your changes.

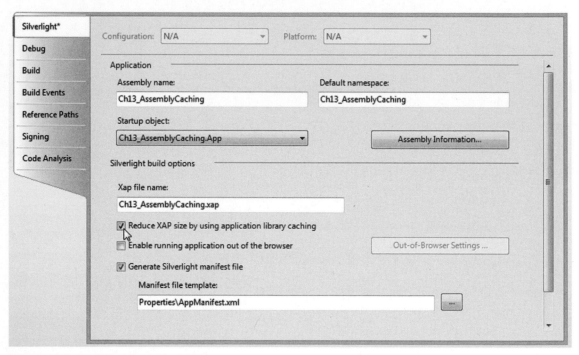

Figure 13-3. Enabing assembly caching

7. Rebuild the application and then navigate back to the ClientBin directory. Once again, rename the Ch13_AssemblyCaching.xap file to a *.zip file and open it in windows explorer. You will see that there are significantly fewer assemblies contained within the package, as shown in Figure 13-4.

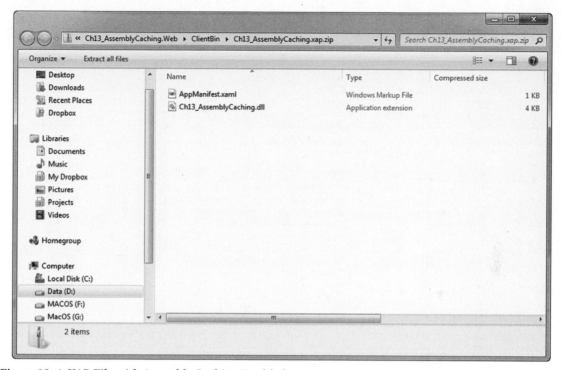

Figure 13-4. *XAP File with Assembly Caching Enabled*

8. If you then refresh the Solution Explorer and examine the ClientBin folder you will see that a number of new zip files have been added, as shown in Figure 13-5. These zip files contain the assemblies that were removed from the *.xap file. When your Silverlight application needs the specific assemblies they will download the assembly via the zip file in the ClientBin.

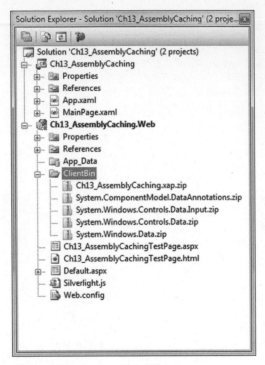

Figure 13-5. *The ClientBin with Assembly Caching Enabled*

ENABLING ASSEMBLY CACHING SUPPORT FOR CUSTOM ASSEMBLIES

By default custom assemblies do not support assembly caching. To quickly see this, add a control from the Silverlight Toolkit and then build with assembly caching turned on. You will notice that the toolkit assemblies are not removed from the *.xap. In order to add support for assembly caching to your custom controls, a number of steps must be completed.

1. First, you must assign your assembly a public key token. This is done using the sn.exe utility.

2. Next, you need to create an external part manifest for your assembly. This is an XML file with the extension <ASSEMBLY NAME>.extmap.xml. This manifest contains information that assembly caching needs to know in order to know where to retrieve the assembly when it is requested by the Silverlight application.

Once you have taken the steps above, your custom assembly can take advantage of assembly caching.

Out of Browser Support

A new feature in Silverlight 3 is the ability to run your Silverlight applications outside the browser. The new feature allows users to right-click on a Silverlight application, install it locally to their machine, and execute it without opening their browser. Out of browser support is also just as safe and secure as running Silverlight within the browser, as applications run out of the browser still live within the sandbox.

For developers, out of browser has a number of benefits. The most obvious is that the same XAP runs in both the browser as well as out of the browser. That means you can now develop an application that has identical user experiences in any browser, any platform, and even outside the browser on any platform. In addition, out of browser supports automatic updating of applications, which means even when a user installs the Silverlight application for out of browser execution, updates will still automatically be sent to the user. Developers also have access to an API that will allow them to determine when their applications are run out of the browser and modify the behavior of their app however they wish.

To enable out of browser support for your Silverlight application, the first step is to view the properties of their Silverlight application and select the checkbox labeled "Enable running application out of the browser" as shown in Figure 13-6.

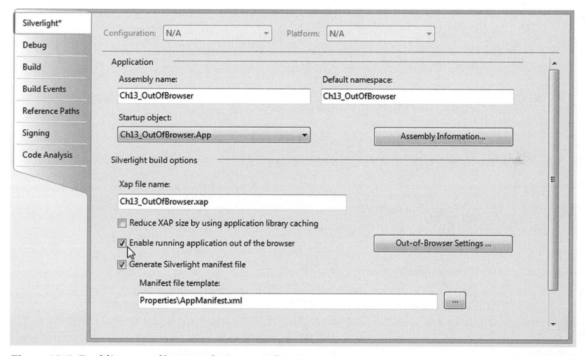

Figure 13-6. *Enabling out of browser for your application*

When this is checked, right-clicking on a Silverlight application will include an additional menu item, as shown in Figure 13-7.

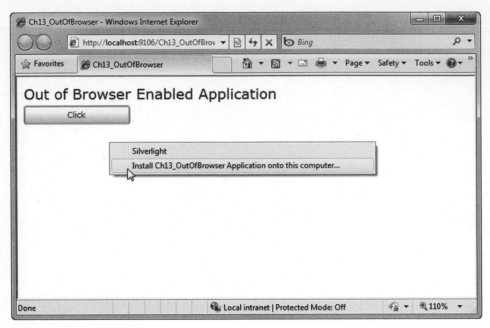

Figure 13-7. *Installing a Silverlight application locally*

When the user clicks to install the application locally, they are presented with the default Install Application dialog shown in Figure 13-8. The user has the option to create shortcuts on either the Start menu, Desktop, or both.

Figure 13-8. *Default Iinstall application dialog*

After the installation is complete, the application re-launches outside the browser. At this point, the user can reopen the application at any time via the shortcuts they chose during the installation.

Customizing the Install Application Dialog

As you have just seen, you can easily enable your application for out of browser support by simply checking one checkbox in your project properties. However, what if you would like to customize the installation experience for your application? Luckily, Silverlight has made it very easy for developers to customize the title of their application, the shortcut names, and even the icons used in the installation experience.

To customize your application's installation experience, in the project properties you will notice a button to the right of the checkbox for enabling out of browser support labeled "Out-Of-Browser Settings." If you click that button, the Out-Of-Browser Settings dialog appears as shown in Figure 15-9. In the following case, you have changed the title, the shortcut name, and you have provided a graphic for the 128~TMS128 icon. Note that you have not provided graphics for the smaller icons, and as a result the 128~TMS128 icon will simply be resized. This is fine for the purposes of this book, but in your applications you really should provide the smaller icons to obtain a crisper look.

Figure 13-9. Out-of-Browser settings

With these settings changed, when you choose to install our application, you are presented with the updated dialog shown in Figure 13-10.

Figure 13-10. Customized install application dialog

Out of Browser API

As mentioned, in Silverlight applications running out of browser are running the exact same XAP as the application running in the browser. This is great for developers because you know that the user will have the same experience in both situations. However, what if you wanted to change that experience? What if there were some elements to your application that you wanted to change the behavior in the event that users were running the application out of the browser? In Silverlight, there are a number of API methods, properties, and events that you can work with to customize your application based on its state. One of these properties is the IsRunningOutOfBrowser property. This property returns true if application is running out of the browser and false if it is running within the browser. You can easily add code that looks at this property and executes accordingly.

```
private void Button_Click(object sender, RoutedEventArgs e)
{
    if (Application.Current.IsRunningOutOfBrowser)
    {
        OOBStatus.Text = "Application Running Out of Browser!";
    }
    else
    {
        OOBStatus.Text = "Application Running In Browser";
    }
}
```

By adding this code, you can then run the application within the browser, Figure 13-11, and out of the browser, Figure 13-12 to see that our application can behave differently depending on its state.

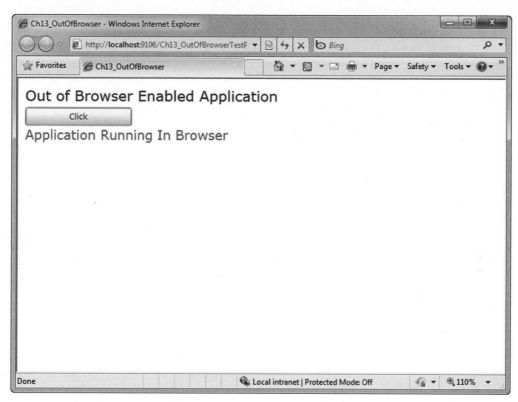

Figure 13-11. *Application running within browser*

Figure 13-12. *Application running out of browser*

Removing Installed Applications

You may be wondering how you can uninstall the Silverlight applications that you installed locally. Uninstalling involves only one very simple step. Open the application, right click on it, and select "Remove this Application." That is all there is to it!

Figure 13-13. Removing a Silverlight application installed locally

Summary

In this chapter, you explored deploying Silverlight applications. As you have seen, deployment in Silverlight is straightforward and trivial, which is yet another benefit of Silverlight applications. You now are able to build your own Silverlight applications from start to finish and deploy them for the entire world to appreciate! Happy Silverlighting!

Index

■ Numerics

* value, filling available space in Grid control, 50
+= operator, 73
2D transforms, 282
3D space, 10

■ A

AboutPage.xaml page, 178
AcceptsReturn property, TextBlock control, 196
Active Server Pages (ASP), 6
Add New Item dialog (Visual Studio 2008)
    accessing data through WCF service, 141
    creating application with navigation
        support, 159
    creating custom control, 295, 299
    JavaScript IntelliSense and debugging, 21
    using Modal Child Window, 98
Add New Project dialog, 294
Add Reference dialog
    compiling and testing custom controls, 308
    creating application with navigation
        support, 156
Add Service Reference dialog, 143
Add Silverlight Application dialog, 32
addItem_Click event handler, 57
ADO.NET Data Services, 137
allow-from element, 149
Alt key+Tab key, Vista, 1
Angle properties, 284
animation, 267–271
    Animation workspace mode, Expression
        Blend, 221
    creating animation with Expression Blend,
        274–282
    keyframe animation, 269
    linear interpolation animation, 269
    programmatically controlling animations,
        271–273
    Silverlight 3 features, 11
    spline, 268
    storyboards, 268–269
    Timeline class, 269
    transformations, 282–288
    types of animation in Silverlight, 269–271
    using Expression Blend to create, 273–282
    viewing storyboard in Expression Blend
        timeline, 273–274
Application.Resources element
    defining styles at application level, 260
    Silverlight style hierarchy, 262
    Uri Mapping, Navigation Framework, 173
applications
    building Silverlight application in Visual
        Studio, 31–36
    defining styles at application level, 259–260
    desktop applications, 2
    hosting Silverlight application, 36
    laying out applications with Expression
        Blend, 225–233
    storing application information, 183
    switching between applications, 1
    web applications, 2
App.xaml file
    defining styles at application level, 260
    Uri Mapping, Navigation Framework, 173
ASP (Active Server Pages), 6
ASP.NET, multi-targeting support, 28
ASP.NET Web Services (ASMX), 138
Assembly Caching, Silverlight 3, 11
Asset Library Window, Expression Blend, 222
Asset Tools icon, Expression Blend, 222
attached properties
    Canvas panel, 42

ColumnSpan, 54
Grid control, 49
XAML, 40
attributes
syntax, 65
type-converter-enabled attributes, 66
AutoCompleteBox control, 90–91
AutoCompleteBox.IsTextCompletionEnabled
property, 91
AutoGenerateColumns property, DataGrid
control, 117, 122, 128
Available state, CoolDownStates state group, 294
AvailableFreeSpace property, 201

■ B

Background property
Button control, 77
GridSplitter control, 89
BasedOn property, Style element, 264–265
Begin method, Storyboard, 271–272
BeginTime property, 270
binding, data, 105–113
Binding class, 106
binding mode, 106
BindingMode property, 112
Element to Element binding, 10, 114–116
bntManaged_Click event handler, 74
Border control, 76–80
BorderBrush property, Button control, 77
breadcrumbs, 255
breakpoints, JavaScript debugging, 18, 25, 27
browsers
cross-browser support, 5
filling entire browser window with
application, 44–45
Out of Browser support, 11
Button control, Click event
adding button to Canvas panel, 41
adding buttons to DockPanel, 60, 61
adding buttons to Grid, 51
adding buttons to StackPanel, 45
adding buttons to WrapPanel, 56, 57
attribute syntax, 65
creating file explorer for isolated storage, 191
declaring event handler in managed code, 73
element syntax, 66
gradients, 79
nesting controls within controls, 67

setting inline properties with Expression
Blend, 250
setting inline properties with Visual Studio,
236, 241
using styles as static resources, 256
Button events
Button_Click event, 99, 102
coding file explorer for isolated storage, 203
button properties, 69, 77
Button_Click event handler
declaring event in XAML, 70
NavigationService object navigating to Page,
166
passing data to navigation pages, 169
Button_Click method, 174

■ C

caching, Assembly Caching, 11
CanUserReorder property, DataGridColumn,
123
CanUserResize property, DataGridColumn, 123
canvas layout mode, 225
Canvas panel
adding button to, 41
attached properties, 42
effect of omitting Height and Width
attributes, 44
filling browser window with application, 44–
45
Height property, 41
Left property, 40
pros and cons of, 39
Top property, 40
Width property, 41
Cascading Style Sheets (CSS), 66, 252
CellEditingTemplate,
DataGridTemplateColumn type, 124
CellTemplate, DataGridTemplateColumn type,
124, 128
CenterX property, RotateTransform type, 284
CenterY property, RotateTransform type, 284
check box, DataGridCheckBoxColumn type, 123
CheckBox control, 84–86
CheckBox.Content property, 86
CheckCoolDown method, 306
Child Window, Modal, 93–103
Clear method, Items, 200
Click event
Button control, 82

HyperlinkButton, 161
TextBox control, 82
Click property
Button control, 69, 204
HyperlinkButton, 155
client-access policy
clientaccesspolicy.xml file, 149, 151
permissions, 151
client-side scripting, 14
Close method, modal dialogs, 99
Closed event, modal dialogs, 94, 102
code behind
switching to code behind of page, 73
WrapPanel control, 57
code completion
with type inference for HTML element, 15
with type inference for integer, 16
ColorAnimation type, 269
colors
Colors.FromArgb method, 83
colspan attribute, <TD> tag, 55
getting red/green/blue values, 83
columns
Column property, Grid control, 49, 248
ColumnDefinitions property, 231
ColumnDefinitions XAML property element,
Grid control, 50, 52, 226
ColumnSpan attached property, Grid
control, 54
spanning in Grid control, 54–55
Columns collection, DataGrid
building DataGrid with custom columns, 128
DataGridCheckBoxColumn type, 123
DataGridColumn type, 123
DataGridTemplateColumn type, 124
DataGridTextColumn type, 123
Combine method, Path class, 200, 204
Completed event, SocketAsyncEventArgs, 150
ConnectAsync method, 150
connections
accessing data through sockets, 150
pseudo-conversational environment, 137
Content property
Button controls, 249
CheckBox control, 86
RadioButton control, 85
Control class, 296
control properties
binding, 106
setting, 65–66

controls
attached properties, 66
attribute syntax, 65
AutoCompleteBox control, 90–91
binding control properties, 106
Border control, 76–80
Canvas panel, 39, 40–45
CheckBox control, 84–86
custom controls, 289–290, 293–309
DataGrid control, 116–130
dependency properties, 292–293
DockPanel control, 40, 59–63
element syntax, 66
extended controls, 87–90
Grid control, 40, 49–55
GridSplitter control, 88–90
handling events in Silverlight, 76
introduction, 65
layout controls, 39–40
ListBox control, 130–135
nesting controls within controls, 67–68
Parts and States model, 291–292
RadioButton control, 84–86
referencing styles from, 252
setting control properties, 65–66
Silverlight 3 features, 10
Silverlight control model, 291
Silverlight Control Toolkit, 290–291
StackPanel control, 39, 45–48
TextBox control, 80–84
type-converter-enabled attributes, 66
user input controls, 80–86
ViewBox control, 92–93
viewing related assemblies, 87
WrapPanel control, 40, 55–59
CoolDown state, 294
CorePart property, 305
CornerRadius property, Button control, 77
Create Storyboard Resource dialog, 275
Create Style Resource dialog, 254
CreateDirectory method, 199
CreateFile method, 199
crossdomain.xml file, 149
cross-platform version of .NET Framework, 5
cross-platform/cross-browser support, 5
CSS (Cascading Style Sheets), 66, 252
custom columns, building DataGrid with, 124–
130

custom content, building ListBox with, 133–135
custom controls
    dependency properties, 292–293
    Parts and States model, 289, 291–292
    reasons for writing, 289–290
    Silverlight control model, 291
    Silverlight Control Toolkit, 290–291
custom controls, creating, 293–309
    compiling and testing, 308–309
    defining appearance, 299–303
    defining properties and states, 296–299
    handling events, 304–308
    implementing custom functionality, 293
    setting up control project, 294–296

■ D

data access
    accessing data through sockets, 150–152
    accessing services from other domains, 149–150
    Silverlight applications, 137–138
    through WCF service, 138–149
    through web services, 138–149
data binding, 105–113
    Binding class, 106
    DataContext property, 109
    TwoWay data binding, 112–113
data validation (Silverlight 3), 10
database connections, 137
DataContext property, LayoutRoot, 109
DataGrid control, 116–130
    accessing data through WCF service, 146, 148
    adding extended controls, 87
    building with custom columns, 124–130
    column reordering in DataGrid, 122
    Columns collection, 122–124
    getting XML namespace for DataGrid, 118
    resizing columns in DataGrid, 121
    sorting in DataGrid, 121
DataGrid.AutoGenerateColumns property, 117, 122, 128
DataGridCheckBoxColumn type, 123
DataGridColumn type properties, 123
DataGrid.Margin property, 117
DataGridTemplateColumn type
    building DataGrid with custom columns, 128
    CellEditingTemplate, 124
    CellTemplate, 124
DataGridTextColumn type, 123, 129

DataGridTextColumn.DisplayMemberBinding property, 123
DataGridTextColumn.Header property, 123
debugging
    Debugging Not Enabled dialog box, 25, 34
    integrated debugger, 13
    JavaScript debugging, 18–19, 25, 28
deep linking, Navigation Framework, 164–165
dependency properties, 292–293, 298
desktop applications, 2
development environment, Silverlight 3, 8–10
DialogResult property, modal dialogs, 94, 99, 102
dictionaries, Merged Resource, 261–262
DisplayIndex property, DataGridColumn, 123
DisplayMemberBinding property, DataGridTextColumn type, 123
DisplayMemberPath property, ListBox control, 131
DLLs (dynamic link libraries), 87
Dock property, DockPanel control, 60
DockPanel control, 59–63
    default dock behavior, 60
    Dock property, 60
    getting XML namespace for DockPanel, 60
    LastChildFill property, 61
    pros and cons of, 40
domains, accessing services from, 149–150
DoubleAnimation type, 269
DoubleAnimationUsingKeyFrames type, 270
DoWork () method, 142
dynamic link libraries (DLLs), 87

■ E

Easing section, Properties panel, Expression Blend, 279
element syntax, 66
Element to Element binding, 10, 114–116
Ellipse control, 80, 82
Ellipse.Fill property, 83
event handling
    creating custom control, 304–308
    declaring event handler in managed code, 72–76
    using Modal Child Window, 99
events
    declaring event handler in managed code, 72–76
    declaring event in XAML, 68–71
    handling events in Silverlight, 68

Expression Blend, Microsoft
    Animation workspace mode, 221
    Asset Library Window, 222
    creating animation with, 274–282
    creating animations, 273–282
    documentation, 214
    editing layout grid with Expression Blend,
        225–233
    key features, 213–221
    laying out applications with, 225–233
    Objects and Timeline panel, 215, 225
    Parts and State model, 215
    Project panel, 219–220, 223
    Properties panel, 223–224
    setting inline properties with, 243–251
    skinning, 215
    split-view mode, 214
    template editing support, 215
    timeline, 215
    Toolbox, 221–223
    transforms using, 285–288
    using styles as static resources, 253
    viewing storyboard in Expression Blend
        timeline, 273–274
    Visual State Manager (VSM), 215
    Visual Studio 2008 integration, 214
    visual XAML editor, 214
    working with Grid control, 225–233
    working with projects in, 216–221
    workspace elements, 221–225
Expression Blend Toolbox, 221–223
extended controls
    GridSplitter control, 88–90
    viewing related assemblies, 87
Extensible Application Markup Language. *See*
        XAML (Extensible Application Markup
        Language)
external script files, JavaScript IntelliSense, 16

■ F

file explorer, creating for isolated storage, 186–
        207, 205–207
File Modified dialog box, 220
Fill property, Ellipse control, 83
Flash, 3, 5
FontXyz properties, TextBlock control, 238
form controls. *See also* controls
    AutoCompleteBox control, 90–91
    Border control, 76–80
    CheckBox control, 84–86
    extended controls, 87–90
    GridSplitter control, 88–90
    nesting controls within controls, 67–68
    RadioButton control, 84–86
    setting control properties, 65–66
    TextBox control, 80–84
    user input controls, 80–86
    ViewBox control, 92–93
Frame object
    creating application with navigation
        support, 159, 161
    description, 153
    making Frame size of entire Grid cell, 159
    using multiple frames, 179–182
Frame.HorizontalContentAlignment property,
        159
Frame.JournalOwnership property, 179, 180
Frame.Navigate method, 161
Frame.VerticalContentAlignment property, 159
frameworks, 153
FromArgb method (Colors), 83
functionality through custom controls, 289–290

■ G

generic.xaml file
    creating custom control, 299
    Properties panel, 301
get operation, data binding, 111
GetChildElement method, 304
GetDirectoryName method, Path class, 200, 203
GetFileNames method, 201
GetHands method, 140, 141, 143
GetHandsAsync method, 146, 148
GetHandsCompleted event, 146, 148
GetStorageData method, 197, 200, 205
GetUserStoreForApplication method, 198
GoToState method, 304
GoToState method, VisualStateManager, 298,
        299
gradients, Button control, 79
grant-to element, 149
Grid control, 49–55
    adding objects to different grid cells, 51
    attached properties, 49
    Column property, 49
    ColumnDefinitions XAML property element,
        50, 52
    ColumnSpan attached property, 54
    creating application with navigation
        support, 154

creating file explorer for isolated storage, 188

declaring event handler in managed code, 72

declaring event in XAML, 69

editing layout grid with Expression Blend, 225–233

making Frame size of entire Grid cell, 159

nesting, 52–54, 230

pros and cons of, 40

Row property, 49

RowDefinitions XAML property element, 50, 52, 81

setting inline properties with Visual Studio, 236

ShowGridLines property, 50

spanning column in, 54–55

using * value to fill available space, 50

grid layout mode, 225–233

GridSplitter control, 88–90, 189

GridSplitter.Background property, 89

Grouping property, RadioButton control, 85

■ H

Header property, DataGridColumn, 123, 129

Height property

    Canvas panel, 41, 44

    effect of omitting Height and Width attributes, 44

    Grid control, 50

    RowDefinition, 240

    UserControl, 236

Hello World application, 31–35

HelloWorld function, 22–23, 27

horizontal orientation, WrapPanel control, 56

HorizontalAlignment property

    RadioButton control, 85

    setting inline properties with Expression Blend, 246

    StackPanel control, 46

HorizontalContentAlignment property, Frame object, 159

HorizontalScrollBarVisibility property, TextBlock control, 196

hosting Silverlight application, 36

HTML, XAML similarities to, 6

HyperlinkButton

    creating application with navigation support, 155, 161

    HyperlinkButton.Tag property, 161

■ I

Immediate window, JavaScript debugging, 19, 27

IncreaseQuotaTo method, 210

InitializeComponent method, 34, 74

inline properties

    overriding style properties, 262, 263

    setting with Expression Blend, 243–251

    setting with Visual Studio, 235–243

INotifyPropertyChanged interface, 109–110

inputs

    handling events in Silverlight, 68

    user input controls, 80–86

integrated debugger, 13

IntelliSense

    JavaScript IntelliSense, 14–17, 20, 28

    transparent IntelliSense mode, 30–31

interfaces, evolution of user, 1–2

isCoolDown flag, 306

isolated storage

    clearing, 208

    creating file explorer for, 186–207

    data access in Silverlight applications, 137

    description, 183

    increasing isolated storage quota, 209–212

    IsolatedStorage namespace, 183

    IsolatedStorageFile class, 183, 198

    IsolatedStorageFileStream class, 184

    IsolatedStorageSettings class, 184–186

    viewing, 207

IsReadOnly property, DataGridColumn, 123

IsTextCompletionEnabled property, AutoCompleteBox control, 91

Items.Clear method, 200

ItemsSource property

    building DataGrid with custom columns, 130

    building ListBox with custom content, 134

ItemTemplate, ListBox control, 133

■ J

JavaScript debugging, Visual Studio 2008, 18–19, 25–28

JavaScript IntelliSense

    example illustrating, 20–28

    external script files, 16

    for function with parameter tags, 17

    type inference, 14–16

    XML comments, 16

JournalOwnership property, Frame object, 179–180
JSON (JavaScript Object Notation), 137

■ K

Key attribute, Style element, 252
keyframes
    creating animation with Expression Blend, 277
    keyframe animation, 269–270
    viewing storyboard in Expression Blend timeline, 274
KeySpline property, 279–280

■ L

LastChildFill property, DockPanel control, 61
layout management
    Canvas panel, 40–45
    DockPanel control, 59–63
    filling entire browser window with application, 44–45
    Grid control, 49–55
    laying out applications with Expression Blend, 225–233
    laying out unknown numbers of items, 56
    nesting controls, 47–48, 52, 54
    spanning column in Grid control, 54–55
    StackPanel control, 45–48
    WrapPanel control, 55–59
LayoutRoot
    editing layout grid with Expression Blend, 226, 229
    LayoutRoot.DataContext property, 109
Left property, Canvas panel, 40, 42
linear interpolation animation, 269
linking, deep (Navigation Framework), 164–165
Linux, support for, 5
List class, 119
list controls
    DataGrid control, 116–130
    ListBox control, 130–135
ListBox control, 130–135
    building with custom content, 133–135
    creating file explorer for isolated storage, 191–192
    custom, 132
    default, 131
    ItemTemplate, 133
ListBox.DisplayMemberPath property, 131
Loaded event, 119

Loaded event handler
    accessing data through WCF service, 147
    data binding, 108
Loaded event, Page
    building DataGrid with custom columns, 130
    building ListBox with custom content, 134
    creating animation with Expression Blend, 281
LoadFilesAndDirs method, 197–198
local networking (Silverlight 3), 10
local storage, 183. See also isolated storage

■ M

Mac OS Dock feature, 1
managed code, declaring event handler in, 72–76
Margin property
    DataGrid control, 117
    Grid control, 242
    StackPanel control, 46, 247
    TextBlock control, 238
    type-converter-enabled attributes, 66
MaxWidth property, DataGridColumn, 123
Merged Resource Dictionaries, 261–262
metadata, dependency properties, 293
Microsoft Expression Blend. See Expression Blend, Microsoft
MinWidth property, DataGridColumn, 123
Modal Child Window, 93–103
modal dialogs
    Close method, 99
    Closed event, 94, 102
    DialogResult property, 94, 99
    refactoring Child Window, 94
    Show method, 94, 99
modal window support (Silverlight 3), 10
Mono project, 5
mouse events, 304
MouseOver state, NormalStates state group, 294
multi-targeting support, Visual Studio 2008, 28–30

■ N

namespaces
    extended controls, 87
    getting XML namespace for DataGrid, 118
    getting XML namespace for DockPanel, 60
    getting XML namespace for WrapPanel, 56
Navigate method
    Frame object, 161
    NavigationService object, 169

Navigation Application References, Silverlight, 157

Navigation Application template, Silverlight, 175–179

Navigation Framework
benefits of, 164
creating Silverlight application with navigation support, 153–164
deep linking, 164–165
Frame object, 153
introduction, 153
NavigationContext object, 168–172
NavigationService object, 165–168
Page object, 153
passing data to navigation pages, 168–169, 172
Silverlight 3 features, 10
Uri Mapping, 172–175
Uri Routing, 175
UriMapper property, 174
using multiple frames, 179–182

NavigationContext object, 168–172

NavigationContext.QueryString property, 168

NavigationService object, 165–168

NavigationService.Navigate method, 169

nesting
Grid control, 52–54, 230
nesting controls within controls, 67–68
StackPanel control, 47–48

.NET Framework
cross-platform version of, 5
multi-targeting support, 28, 30

networking, local, 10

New Project dialog
building Silverlight application in Visual Studio, 32
creating application with navigation support, 154
JavaScript IntelliSense and debugging, 20
multi-targeting support, 29
Silverlight Navigation Application template, 175
working with projects in Expression Blend, 217

New Silverlight Application dialog, 154, 176

NormalStates state group, 294

NotImplementedException, 75

■ O

Object Browser, Visual Studio, 145

object tool group, Expression Blend Toolbox, 221

ObjectAnimation type, 269

Objects and Timeline panel, Expression Blend
creating animation with Expression Blend, 275
editing layout grid with Expression Blend, 229
using styles as static resources, 253, 255
viewing storyboard in Expression Blend timeline, 273

ObservableCollection class
building DataGrid control, 118, 119
building DataGrid with custom columns, 126

OnApplyTemplate method, 304

OneTime value, BindingMode property, 112

OneWay value, BindingMode property, 112

OnSendCompleted event handler, 151

OpenFile method, 205

Orientation property, StackPanel control, 46, 249

Orientation property, WrapPanel control, 58

Out of Browser support (Silverlight 3), 11

■ P

Page object
accessing Frame from, 165
creating application with navigation support, 159–160
description, 153
NavigationService object navigating to, 166
passing data to navigation pages, 169–172

Page_Loaded event
accessing data through WCF service, 148
building DataGrid with custom columns, 130
building ListBox with custom content, 134

pages, switching to code behind of, 73

panels, Expression Blend, 221
Objects and Timeline panel, 225
Project panel, 223
Properties panel, 223–224
Toolbox, 221–223

parts
Parts and State model, 215
Parts and States model, 291–292

Path.Combine method, 200, 204

Path.GetDirectoryName method, 203

Pause method, Storyboard, 271–272

performance, Silverlight 3, 11

perspective 3D (Silverlight 3), 10
platforms
    cross-platform support, 5
    cross-platform version of .NET Framework, 5
PointAnimation type, 269
Pressed state, NormalStates state group, 294
Project panel, Expression Blend, 219–220, 223
project templates for Visual Studio 2008, 9
properties
    attached properties, 40, 42, 66
    creating custom control, 296
    dependency properties, 292–293
    inline properties, 235, 243, 251
    setting control properties, 65–66
Properties panel, Expression Blend, 223–224
    editing layout grid with Expression Blend, 229, 232
    setting inline properties with Expression Blend, 246
    transforms using Expression Blend, 286
Properties panel, generic.xaml file, 301
Property attribute, Setter element, 252
PropertyChanged event, 110
pseudo-conversational environment (Silverlight applications), 137

■ Q

QueryString property, NavigationContext object, 168
Quota property, 201

■ R

RadioButton control, 84–86
RadioButton.Content property, 85
RadioButton.Grouping property, 85
RadioButton.HorizontalAlignment property, 85
ReadToEnd method, StreamReader class, 205
Rectangle control, 85
References folder, 155
Register method, DependencyProperty object, 293
remote scripting, 3
RenderTransformOrigin property, RotateTransform type, 284
resources
    Merged Resource Dictionaries, 261–262
    ResourceDictionary element, 301
    using styles as static resources, 253–259
Resources element, Application
    defining styles at application level, 260

Uri Mapping, Navigation Framework, 173
Resources element, UserControl
    Silverlight style hierarchy, 262
    using styles as static resources, 255
REST (representational state transfer), 138
Resume method, Storyboard, 271–272
RIAs (rich internet applications), 3
RotateTransform type, 284, 286–287
RoutedEventHandler(bntManaged_Click), 74
Row property, Grid control, 49, 248
RowDefinitions property
    editing layout grid with Expression Blend, 231
    Grid control, 240
RowDefinitions XAML property element, 50, 52, 81, 250
Run at startup check box (ExpressionBlend), 216
runtime, Silverlight, 6, 8

■ S

ScaleTransform type, 283, 287
ScaleX property, ScaleTransform type, 283
ScaleY property, ScaleTransform type, 283
SDK (Software Development Kit), Silverlight 3, 9
security of data in Silverlight applications, 137
Seek method, Storyboard, 271
SendAsync method, 151
service references
    accessing data through WCF service, 148
    Add Service Reference dialog box, 143
set operation, data binding, 111
Setter element, styles, 252, 256, 302
Show method, modal dialogs, 94, 99
ShowGridLines property, Grid control, 50, 154, 232
Silverlight, 2, 3, 5
    additional controls, 10
    animation, 267–271
    Assembly Caching, 11
    benefits of, 4–7
    building application in Visual Studio, 31–36
    Class Library template, 294
    control model, 291–292
    Control Toolkit, 290–291
    cross-platform version of .NET Framework, 5
    cross-platform/cross-browser support, 5
    data validation, 10
    description, 3–4
    development environment, 8–10
    Element to Element binding, 10

hosting Silverlight application, 36
layout management, 39
local networking, 10
modal window support, 10
Navigation Application References, 157
Navigation Application template, 175–179
Navigation Framework, 10, 153, 164–165
new features, 10–11
Out of Browser support, 11
pages. *See* pages
performance, 11
perspective 3D, 10
property system, 292
runtime, 6
style hierarchy, 262–263
styles, 251–265
Toolkit, 10
tools for Visual Studio 2008, 8
transformation and animation features, 11
transformations, 282–288
use of familiar technologies, 6
XAML, 3, 5
.xap file, 87
Silverlight applications
accessing data through sockets, 150–152
creating, with navigation support, 153–164
data access, 137–138, 149–150
SkewTransform type, 284, 287–288
skinning (Expression Blend), 215
sockets
accessing data through, 137, 150–152
SocketAsyncEventArgs.Completed event, 150
SolidColorBrush, creating, 83
source
BindingMode property, 112
data binding, 105–106
spanning column, Grid control, 54–55
splines, 268
split-view mode, Expression Blend, 214, 218
StackPanel control
building ListBox with custom content, 133
creating file explorer for isolated storage,
189, 192
default stacking orientation, 46
horizontal stacking, 45–46
HorizontalAlignment property, 46
Margin property, 46
nesting, 47–48, 189
Orientation property, 46
pros and cons of, 39

setting inline properties with Expression
Blend, 243, 245
using styles as static resources, 253
vertical stacking, 45
StartingHands.cs class, 140
StartingHandService.svc, 142, 144, 148
state group
CoolDownStates state group, 294
NormalStates state group, 294
Parts and States model, 292
states
creating custom control, 298
handling events in Silverlight, 68
Parts and States model, 292
Stop method, Storyboard, 271–272
storage, isolated, 183–186, 207, 212
storyboards, 268–269
programmatically controlling animations,
271
Storyboard.Begin method, 271–272
Storyboard.Pause method, 271–272
Storyboard.Resume method, 271–272
Storyboard.Seek method, 271
Storyboard.Stop method, 271–272
Storyboard.TargetName property, 270
Storyboard.TargetProperty property, 270
timelines, 268
viewing storyboard in Expression Blend
timeline, 273–274
StreamReader.ReadToEnd method, 205
StreamWriter.Write method, 205
Style attribute
Application.Resources element, 260
UserControl.Resources element, 255, 257
Style element, 252
BasedOn property, 264–265
creating custom control, 302
styles
Create Style Resource dialog box, 254
create styles based on another style, 264–265
defining at application level, 259–260
inheriting styles using BasedOn property,
264–265
inline properties overriding style properties,
262–263
Merged Resource Dictionaries, 261–262
properties, 235–251
referencing from controls, 252
Setter element, 252
Silverlight style hierarchy, 262–263

Style element, 252
using styles as static resources, 253–259

■ T

Tag property, HyperlinkButton, 161
TargetName property, Storyboard, 270
TargetProperty property, Storyboard, 270
targets
BindingMode property, 112
data binding, 105–106
TargetType attribute, Style element, 252
templates
DataGridTemplateColumn type, 124
Expression Blend, 215
Silverlight Navigation Application template, 175–179
testing file explorer for isolated storage, 206–207
text
DataGridTextColumn type, 123
TextBlock.AcceptsReturn property, 196
TextBlock.HorizontalScrollBarVisibility property, 196
TextBlock.Text property, 70
TextBlock.VerticalScrollBarVisibility property, 196
TextWrapping property, 247
Text property, TextBox control
declaring event in XAML, 70
getting red/green/blue values, 83
setting inline properties with Expression Blend, 249
TextBlock control
building DataGrid with custom columns, 128
building ListBox with custom content, 133
building Silverlight application in Visual Studio, 34
coding file explorer for isolated storage, 201
creating file explorer for isolated storage, 191
declaring event handler in managed code, 75
referencing style from, 252
setting inline properties with Expression Blend, 243, 246, 249
setting inline properties with Visual Studio, 236, 230–239
using Modal Child Window, 95–96, 100
TextBox control, 80–84
data binding, 106, 107, 109
setting inline properties with Expression Blend, 246

TextBox.Text property, 83
using styles as static resources, 257–258
themes folder, 299
timeline, Expression Blend, 215, 225
viewing storyboard in, 273–274
timelines
storyboards, 268
Timeline class, 269
Toolbox, Expression Blend, 221–223
toolkit
Silverlight 3 Toolkit, 10
Silverlight Control Toolkit, 290–291
Top property, Canvas panel, 40, 42
transformations, 282–288
2D transforms, 282
RotateTransform type, 284
ScaleTransform type, 283
Silverlight 3 features, 11
SkewTransform type, 284
transformation types, 283
TranslateTransform type, 284
using Expression Blend, 285–288
transitions, Parts and States model, 292
TranslateTransform type, 284, 286
transparent IntelliSense mode, 30–31
try/catch block, 83
TryIncreaseQuotaTo method, 208
TwoWay data binding, 112–113
TwoWay value, BindingMode property, 112
type inference
code completion with, for HTML element, 15
code completion with, for integer, 16
JavaScript IntelliSense, 14–16
type-converter-enabled attributes, 66

■ U

UI elements, 105–106
Uri attribute, UriMapping element, 173
Uri Mapping, Navigation Framework, 172–175
Uri Routing, Navigation Framework, 175
UriMapper property, Navigation Framework, 174
UriMapping element, Navigation Framework, 173
user input controls
CheckBox control, 84–86
RadioButton control, 84–86
TextBox control, 80–84
user inputs, 68. *See also* inputs

user interface, evolution of, 1–2
UserControl
    creating custom control, 301
    implementing custom functionality, 293
    setting inline properties with Expression
        Blend, 243
    setting inline properties with Visual Studio,
        236
    using styles as static resources, 255, 259
UserControl definition
    adding extended controls, 87
    creating application with navigation
        support, 158
UserControl object
    changing Height and Width attributes, 49
    effect of omitting Height and Width
        attributes, 44
    filling browser window with application, 44
UserControl.Resources element
    Silverlight style hierarchy, 262
    using styles as static resources, 255

■ V

validation, data, 10
Value attribute, Setter element, 252
vertical orientation, WrapPanel control, 56
VerticalAlignment property, 246
VerticalContentAlignment property, Frame
        object, 159
VerticalScrollBarVisibility property, TextBlock
        control, 196
ViewBox control, 92–93
views, split-view mode (Expression Blend), 214
Visibility property, DataGridColumn, 123
Visual State Manager (VSM), 215, 291
Visual Studio
    building Silverlight application, 31–36
    declaring event handler in managed code, 74
    description, 13
    history, 14
    hosting application using Web Application
        project, 36
    hosting application using web site, 36
    Object Browser, 145
    Web Application project, 36
    web site, 36
Visual Studio 2008
    creating application with navigation
        support, 154
    Expression Blend integration, 214

hosting Silverlight application, 36
    JavaScript debugging, 18–19, 25, 28
    JavaScript IntelliSense, 14–17, 20, 28
    multi-targeting support, 28–30
    new features, 14–31
    project templates for, 9
    setting inline properties with, 235–243
    Silverlight 3 development environment, 8
    transparent IntelliSense mode, 30–31
visual XAML editor, Expression Blend, 214
VisualStateGroups, 303
VisualStateManager.GoToState method, 298–
        299
VisualStateManager.VisualStateGroups, 303
VSM (Visual State Manager), 215, 291

■ W

WCF (Windows Communication Foundation),
        138–149
Web Application project
    accessing data through WCF service, 138
    hosting Silverlight application using, 36
web applications, 2, 183
web services
    accessing services from other domains, 149–
        150
    data access through, 137–149
    proxy class, 148
Width property
    Canvas panel, 41, 44
    DataGridColumn, 123
    effect of omitting Height and Width
        attributes, 44
    Grid control, 50
    UserControl, 236
windows, Modal Child Window, 93–103
Windows Communication Foundation (WCF),
        138–149
Windows key +Tab key, Vista, 2
Windows Presentation Foundation Everywhere
        (WPF/E), 3
Windows Vista, switching between applications,
        1
workspace elements, Expression Blend
    Objects and Timeline panel, 225
    Project panel, 223
    Properties panel, 223–224
    Toolbox, 221, 223
WrapPanel control, 55–59
    getting XML namespace for WrapPanel, 56

horizontal orientation, 56
Orientation property, 58
pros and cons of, 40
vertical orientation, 56
Write method, StreamWriter class, 205

 X

X Internet, 3
X property, TranslateTransform type, 284
XAML (Extensible Application Markup
 Language)
 attached properties, 40
 data binding, 106, 109
 declaring events in, 68–71
 description, 214
 HTML similarities, 6

introduction, 3–5
property elements, 50
referencing styles from controls, 252
using Modal Child Window, 97–98, 100
visual XAML editor, 214
XamlParseException, 192, 262
.xap file, 87
XML (Extensible Markup Language)
 comments, 16, 22, 24
 namespaces, 56, 60
 policy file, 149
 xmlns declaration, 87

■ **Y**

Y property, TranslateTransform type, 284

You Need the Companion eBook

Your purchase of this book entitles you to buy the companion PDF-version eBook for only $10. Take the weightless companion with you anywhere.

We believe this Apress title will prove so indispensable that you'll want to carry it with you everywhere, which is why we are offering the companion eBook (in PDF format) for $10 to customers who purchase this book now. Convenient and fully searchable, the PDF version of any content-rich, page-heavy Apress book makes a valuable addition to your programming library. You can easily find and copy code—or perform examples by quickly toggling between instructions and the application. Even simultaneously tackling a donut, diet soda, and complex code becomes simplified with hands-free eBooks!

Once you purchase your book, getting the $10 companion eBook is simple:

1. Visit **www.apress.com/promo/tendollars/**.

2. Complete a basic registration form to receive a randomly generated question about this title.

3. Answer the question correctly in 60 seconds, and you will receive a promotional code to redeem for the $10.00 eBook.

eBookshop

233 Spring Street, New York, NY 10013

Offer valid through 4/10.